CHURCH HISTORIANS

including papers on

EUSEBIUS · OROSIUS · ST. BEDE THE VENERABLE
ORDERICUS VITALIS · LAS CASAS · BARONIUS
BOLLANDUS · MURATORI · MOEHLER
LINGARD · HERGENROETHER · JANSSEN
DENIFLE · LUDWIG VON PASTOR

WITH FOREWORD AND INDEX BY
PETER GUILDAY, Ph.D.

NEW YORK
P. J. KENEDY & SONS
Publishers to the Holy Apostolic See
1926

Nihil Obstat:

ARTHUR J. SCANLAN, S.T.D.

Censor Librorum

Imprimatur:

✠ PATRICK CARDINAL HAYES

Archbishop, New York

New York, June 24, 1926

FOREWORD

FOUNDED at Cleveland on December thirtieth, 1919, the American Catholic Historical Association has as its object the promotion of study and research in the domain of ecclesiastical history.

Annual meetings of the Association have been held at Washington, D.C. (1920), St. Louis (1921), New Haven (1922), Columbus (1923), Philadelphia (1924), and Ann Arbor (1925). Over eighty papers on special topics in the general field of Church History have been read at these meetings, and many of these carefully prepared essays have been published in the official organ of the Association, the *Catholic Historical Review.*

The success of the new historical movement thus inaugurated among American Catholic scholars warranted a further development in the plans of the Association: namely, that of presenting at each annual meeting the result of the past year's study on a composite subject. Accordingly, the programme of the Ann Arbor meeting (December twenty-ninth to thirty-first, 1925) was so arranged that the papers formed a series of critical biographies of eminent Catholic historians from Eusebius in the fourth century to Ludwig von Pastor, who is still living.

Fourteen of these papers make up the contents of

the present volume, to which the title *Church Historians* has been given.

Any attempt to compress the vast scope of ecclesiastical historiography into the compass of one volume would be a rash undertaking. In his *Historiographia Ecclesiastica* which the late Bishop Stang compiled in 1897 for his students at Louvain, five hundred and fifteen Church historians are listed, beginning with the Evangelists and ending with the illustrious Jungmann, who had passed away in 1895, after laying the foundations of sound critical historical scholarship in the great Belgian University.

Since the time at the disposal of the annual meeting is necessarily limited, it was impossible to burden the programme of 1925 with a series of papers representative of all the various phases of ecclesiastical historiography. Hence, a choice had to be made; not, indeed, a narrowed choice, but one that might fairly display the history of history-writing in the Church during the past twenty centuries. It is the intention of the Association to return from time to time to this fascinating subject and to present at future meetings other groups of critical biographies of Church historians.

We may congratulate those who have contributed to this initial symposium; for, as the years pass, it will be followed by other volumes containing the most recent scholarship in a science that has the loyal defense of historical truth as its chief aim and purpose.

It is no reproach to Catholic scholarship in the

United States that neither Gooch in his *History and Historians of the Nineteenth Century* (1922) nor Fueter in his *Geschichte den neuern Historiographie* (1914) has listed a single American name among those who have forwarded the general study of Catholic Church history. The organized hierarchical life of the Church in the United States is not yet a century and a half old. The numerical growth alone of the Church — from 25,000 in 1785 to almost twenty millions at the present day — reveals the untold demands made upon its bishops, priests, religious Orders and Sisterhoods for the constant and watchful spiritual care of such a vast body of the faithful. The development of the Church in America has of necessity been almost exclusively in its external side. It has marched side-by-side with the growth of the nation; and all individual energies to a greater or less degree have been drawn upon to assist in this growth. Even now with thoroughly organized dioceses and parishes, and with an increased centralization in Catholic education and social welfare work, years must pass before that freedom from the multitude of missionary duties which still crowd the lives of our priests and bishops can be assured to those whose talents and training fit them for the absorbing themes of higher learning.

Meanwhile, the American Catholic Historical Association is meeting an outstanding problem in the defense of the Faith by bringing together in one group the Catholic students, teachers, and writers of Church history, upon whom the Church depends for legitimate protection against the continuance of erroneous historical teaching.

The Association is indebted to the fourteen writers whose scholarly essays comprise this first volume of its publications. To them and to the publishers, Messrs. Kenedy and Sons, of New York City, and to their capable staff of assistants, the Association expresses its gratitude and appreciation.

PETER GUILDAY

Catholic University of America
February 18, 1926

CONTENTS

CHURCH HISTORIANS

EUSEBIUS (c. 260 — c. 340)

Roy J. Deferrari, Ph.D., Professor of Latin
Catholic University of America

1. Life

THE year of the Edict of Milan, which divides the first from the second epoch of church history, does like service for the life and for the literary medium of the Church's first historian. It is 313 that by the growing assent of scholars marks off chronologically the Alexandrian from the Byzantine period of Greek literature, and it is 313 that cleaves into uneven but appropriate parts the career of Eusebius Pamphili. In training and in literary taste Eusebius belongs to the earlier time. Officially and in literary productivity he belongs to the later. It was shortly after 313 that Eusebius became a bishop, as it was for the most part after 313 that his works were actually composed. Of events contemporary with these later years Eusebius recorded much that is valued, but it is for what he tells of the earlier time — of the days before the Peace of the Church — that he looms so large in the history of history and of literature. Through him — through him almost alone — are preserved to us the feeble memories of an age that died with himself. It is this aspect of Eusebius that receives emphasis in this paper.

Of the facts of his life we know but little. Neither the place nor the year of his birth are known. The best conjecture makes Palestine his native land and assigns to the period 260–264 the date of his birth. Palestine in Caesarea may have been his native city. All the known associations of his youth, at any rate, and the chief activities of his maturity are linked with her. He was certainly not born a Jew, but that he was born a Christian we do not know. His parents, whether pagan or Christian, were not of high rank.

At Caesarea in Eusebius' youth lived the learned priest Pamphilus. A native of Phoenicia and at one time a student of Alexandria, he had been ordained to the priesthood by Bishop Agapius of Caesarea, and had there established a school and library where the Bible was studied, and the scholarly tradition of Origen preserved. To this school came Eusebius as pupil, and in this library, which seems to have been unrivalled in Christian circles, he laid the foundation of his future work. A common enthusiasm drew master and pupil together. They became most intimate friends, co-workers in the acquisition of books and in the acquisition of the knowledge that these books contained, united and inspired in both these enterprises by the deepest reverence for Origen. These were the formative years and these the master influences of Eusebius as we know him, and the memory of both Origen and Pamphilus stands out large in his works — Origen in the encyclopaedic sweep of Eusebius'

scholarly interests and Pamphilus in the very name
which his grateful pupil assumed — Εὐσέβιος ὁ
Παμφίλου.

This time of peaceful industry was at length affected by the conflict of the world outside. Paganism was making its last stand against the Church;
and, in the violence of the struggle, the most
unwarlike of Christian scholars could not remain
undisturbed. Maximinus' persecution stretched from
303 to 310, and in this time of the Church's transition from the old order to the new, the earliest of
her historians was frequently absent from Caesarea.
Details of his movements have not come down to
us. Stories creditable and discreditable to him and
equally without foundation flourished in the poverty of real evidence. We do know of his presence
in Tyre and in the Thebais during this time, for
he describes as an eye-witness and with deep emo-
tion the martyrdoms that the persecution visited
on these unhappy districts. We also know that
Pamphilus was in prison from November 307 until
February 310, and that Eusebius, despite the peril
to himself, visited his master and co-worker in
prison.[1]

There is no conclusive evidence that Eusebius
himself shared in this imprisonment or that he
escaped martyrdom by some unworthy concession
such as offering sacrifice to pagan divinities. Some-

---

[1] It is to this period that the first five books of the *Apology
for Origen* were written by both in common. After Pamphilus
had suffered martyrdom in 310, Eusebius added the sixth book
to the *Apology*, and wrote the biography of Pamphilus.

time during this period Eusebius visited Egypt, apparently after the martyrdom of Pamphilus in the latest and fiercest days of the persecution. If Eusebius suffered imprisonment at any time, it was after his visit to Egypt, and in that event the general amnesty in the spring of 310 would have effected his own release.

Some years later, between 313 and 315, Eusebius succeeded Agapius as bishop of Caesarea, and thus inevitably became involved in another struggle — this time a theological one. In the Arian controversy Eusebius strove to keep to the middle of the road. He wrote several letters favorable to Arius; through his offices the religious creed of Arius was declared orthodox at a synod of Caesarea. On the other hand he asked Arius to be obedient to his bishop and opponent in the controversy, Alexander of Alexandria, and to seek readmission into the Alexandrian church. In a synod held at Antioch toward the end of 324, under the influence of Alexander, the creed of Arius was condemned, and Eusebius, on his refusal to subscribe, was excommunicated. In the next year at Nicea he was reinstated, however, and subscribed to the creed formulated by that Council, though unrepresentative in this of the baptismal creed of his people. In the story of the struggle that followed the Council, the name of Eusebius occasionally appears. He had a hand in the removal of the bishop Eustathius from Antioch (probably in 330) and in the excommunication of Athanasius of Alexandria ten years after Nicaea. Against Mar-

subdivisions, for that matter, is not a satisfactory
scheme, since some of Eusebius' works have an
equally clear title to inclusion under several heads;
but it serves to suggest something of that astounding range of labours that beyond historiography
touch every corner of theology up to his time cul-
ᵗ ⁻ᵗed.

⸴ *Pamphilus*.
᷍f Ancient Martyrdoms, also lost.
rs of Palestine.

istory.
istantine.

the emperor to prepare fifty
Bible for use in the churches of
ple.
anons.
mphilus and Eusebius in editing the

ᵤe Interpretation of the ethnological
ın the Hebrew Scriptures; (b) Chorog-
ɣ of Ancient Judea with the Inheritances
ıe Ten Tribes; (c) A plan of Jerusalem
the Temple; (d) On the Names of Places
ın the Holy Scriptures; only the last is extant.
ɪ. On the nomenclature of the Book of the Prophets.
ɀ. Commentary on the Psalms, missing in part.
3. Commentary on Isaiah.
14-19. Commentaries on other books of Holy Scripture, of some of which we may have extracts.

cellus of Ancyra, deposed in 336, he wrote two polemics.

At Nicaea apparently began that friendship between Eusebius and Constantine which endured, it seems, until the emperor's death. On the twentieth and thirtieth anniversaries of Constantine's assuming the purple, Eusebius was the orator of the da and when Constantine died in 337, E a panegyric in his memory: *On th Blessed Emperor Constantine* (Εἰς μακαρίου Κονσταντίνου βασιλέως after, certainly not later than 340, was dead.[2]

2. LITERARY ACT

For our purposes the work as follows: A. *Historical;* B. *E getic;* D. *Doctrinal;* E. *Letters,* precise grouping the foregoing o

[2] According to a Syrian Martyrology, he May. The appearance of his name in any i of the taint of Arianism, is a very remarkabl bius' name has had a place in several. In the *Hieronymianum* for XI Kal. Jul. we read: In C dociae depositio sancti Eusebii. The word " Capp gests that the person indicated here is Eusebius, th of St. Basil the Great. However, the fame of Palest bius overshadowed his Cappadocian namesake, and finally padociae " disappeared from the Latin calendars. Where no tinct reference is made to another, the historian Eusebius doubtless understood in the old Latin martyrologies. Thus some Gallican service books the historian is commemorated a saint. For many centuries he held his place even in the *Mar tyrologium Romanum.* When this Martyrology was revised under Pope Gregory XIII, his name was struck out and replaced by that of Eusebius of Samosata.

usebius wrote
e Life of the
τὸν βίον τοῦ
). A short time
Eusebius himself

IVITY

of Eusebius divide
egetical; C. *Apolo-*
F. *Homilies.* For
any assembly of

died on the 30th of
artyrology, in spite
 fact. Yet Euse-
Martyrologium
iesarea Cappa-
adociae " sug-
 predecessor
nian Euse-
" Cap-
dis-
is
in
us

tiva

20. Commentary on St. Luke, extracts alone preserved.
21. Commentary on I Corinthians. Not extant.
22. Commentary on Hebrews. A possible single fragment alone preserved.
23. On the Discrepancies of the Gospel. An epitome and some extracts from the original are preserved.
24. General Elementary Introduction.

C. *Apologetic.*

25. Against Hierocles.
26. Against Porphyry. Not extant.
27. The *Praeparatio Evangelica.*
28. The *Demonstratio Evangelica.* Of the twenty books, the last ten, with the exception of a fragment of book XV, are lost.
29. The *Praeparatio Ecclesiastica.* Lost.
30. The *Demonstratio Ecclesiastica.* Lost.
31. Two Books of Objection and Defense. Lost.
32. The *Theophania* or Divine Manifestation. Except for a few fragments of the original, extant only in a Syriac version.
33. On the Numerous Progeny of the Ancients. Not extant.

D. *Dogmatic.*

34. The Apology for Origen. Only first book extant.
35. Against Marcellus, Bishop of Ancyra. Authenticity doubted.
36. On the Theology of the Church. Authenticity doubted.
37. On the Paschal Festival. Long fragment survives.
38. A treatise against the Manichaeans. Existence only implied by Epiphanius (*Haer.*, LXVI, 21).

E. *Letters*.

39. To Alexander of Alexandria.
40. To Euphrasion, or Euphration.
41. To the Empress Constantia.
42. To the Church of Caesarea, after the Council of Nicaea.

F. *Homilies*.

43. At the Dedication of the Church in Tyre.
44. At the Vicennalia of Constantine. Not extant.
45. On the Sepulchre of the Saviour. Not extant.
46. At the Tricennalia of Constantine.
47. In praise of the Martyrs.
48. On the Failure of Rain. Lost.

The mere recital of the above list of works is an impressive index to the industry of their author. That so much has perished occasions no surprise, of course, to one familiar with the posthumous fortunes of other ancient authors. That so much of Eusebius remains is a tribute to the good sense of the centuries that followed his death. His own style — even apart from the copious and often bald excerpts that he quotes — is monotonous and dull. He knew the rules of rhetoric and could apply them correctly, but never with that power and freshness which was to bring distinction to the Greek literature of the later fourth century. And then, too, in the growing and sensitive orthodoxy of the ages that followed Nicaea and Constantinople, suggestions of Origen and of Arius were not titles to literary immortality. Yet Eusebius was tolerated, and his remains have thus come down to us almost, as it were, despite themselves, largely because of their altogether unique service to history as the witness to the Ante-Nicene church.

3. HISTORICAL WORKS

At present we are chiefly concerned with the historical writings of Eusebius. Eusebius probably wrote his *Chronicle* before the persecution of 303. Its full title is *Chronological Tables to Which is Prefixed an Epitome of Universal History Drawn from Various Sources* (Χρονικοὶ κανόνες καὶ ἐπιτομὴ παντοδαπῆς ἱστορίας Ἑλλήνων τε καὶ βαρβάρων), as he himself tells us in the beginning of his *Eclogae Propheticae*. An introduction, now designated as the first book, contains short summaries of the history of the Chaldeans, based on Alexander Polyhistor, Abydenus, and Josephus; of the Assyrians, drawn from Abydenus, Castor, Diodorus, and Cephalaion; of the Hebrews, taken from the Old Testament, Josephus, and Clement of Alexandria; of the Egyptians, based on Diodorus, Manethus, and Porphyrius; of the Greeks, taken from Castor, Porphyrius, and Diodorus; and of the Romans, drawn from Dionysius of Halicarnassus, Diodorus, and Castor. The more important part of the work is the second book, with its chronological tables (Χρονικοὶ κανόνες) and its epitome of universal history (ἐπιτομὴ παντοδαπῆς ἱστορίας).

In his *Praeparatio Evangelica*, X, 9, Eusebius accounts for the interest that Christians felt in the study of comparative chronology. In substance he says that, if heathen opponents contrasted the antiquity of their rites with the newness of the Christian religion, the Christian apologists could reply by proving that the most celebrated legislators and philosophers, whom they thought the font of their religious ideas, flourished later than the Hebrew legislator and the other prophets who had foretold the coming of Christ, and who had taught a religion of which the Christian was the legitimate continuance. And so Eusebius argues in this section of the *Praeparatio Evangelica,* quoting largely from preceding writers who had proved the greater antiquity of the Jews, namely, Josephus, Tatian, Clement of Alexandria, and especially Africanus. Africanus had already discovered synchronisms between sacred and profane history, and had published the chronological work which Eusebius used as a model and to a great extent for the materials of his own *Chronicle.*

How Eusebius arranged the details of the strictly chronological part of his work can not be ascertained, since the translations, which are alone preserved, are not made from the original but from a revision which came out shortly after the death of Eusebius. In the chronological tables, the years of Abraham are numbered with years of the reigns of kings, and sometimes those of other periods are combined with them synchronously in parallel columns. With these columns, varying in number through the centuries until we have only the years of the emperors parallel with the Olympiads and the years of Abraham, are incorporated important dates taken from Jewish and profane history.

As we have said above, Eusebius is dependent here largely upon Africanus. We are not justified, however, in assuming as Scaliger did that Eusebius copied Africanus slavishly in every place where he did not express himself as in utter disagreement with him. There are convincing indications to show that Eusebius views his material much more critically. He avoids that division into world eras which is connected with the millennium theory, and he does not begin with the creation of the world but with the first year of Abraham (2016/5 B.C.). That Eusebius is fully aware of the difficulties of his task we see at the very beginning of his work. He tells us that we must not expect minute accuracy from such an investigation as he is about to enter upon. He says that our Lord's words, "It is not for you to know the times and the seasons," are applicable not only to the end of the world, but also to the knowledge of all times and seasons. In the case of the Greeks, he presents the difficulties that arise from the comparatively recent beginning of their civilization and quotes the well-known story in Plato's *Timaeus,* that the Greeks were but children. As for the Egyptians and the Chaldaeans, difficulties arise from the fables of which their early history is full. And even Hebrew chronology is not free from difficulties of its own. The solutions for these problems represent what he considers as sound judgment on the part of his forerunners, and sometimes his own

independent consideration. It was much easier for
Eusebius to maintain historical accuracy in the
early periods of his *Chronicle,* where he could follow trustworthy historians, than in the later periods
after these reliable sources had come to an end, and
he had to make a way for himself, as best he could.
In the latter case, Eusebius only excerpted later
authors, and, regardless of the efficiency of this
procedure for the establishment of a chronology,
by his care and good judgment rescued much valuable historical material from destruction.

Eusebius' second great Historical work is the ten
books of *Ecclesiastical History* (Ἐκκλησιαστικὴ
ἱστορία), an expansion of the last part of the
Chronicle. As in the case of the *Chronicle,* the
Ecclesiastical History possesses no continuous historical narrative, but its whole subject matter is
inserted, as it were, into a chronological frame-work.

The popular translation of the title (Ἐκκλησιαστικὴ ἱστορία) as *Church History* must not lead
us to believe that it was Eusebius' purpose to relate the fortunes of the Christian Church from the
time of our Saviour to his own times. To emulate
profane historiography in the grand style could not
enter the mind of a Christian at this period, for
such a procedure would savour too much of the
spirit of the profane, and would not befit a record
of the Church of God. Ἱστορία is used here by
Eusebius in its most general sense, to be compared
in a way with the titles Παντοδαπὴ or Ποικίλη
ἱστορία, and Porphyry's Φιλόσοφος ἱστορία. It

signifies the collection of material handed down, as Eusebius also calls the collected subject matter of the most varied character in the *Praeparatio Evangelica* and *Demonstratio Evangelica* ἰστορία (Cf. *Praep. ev.*, 1, 6, 7). The fact that Eusebius in his *Church History* quotes so many excerpts directly, as he does also in the *Praeparatio Evangelica*, suits this kind of ἰστορία, but not the strict forms of historiography which Sozomenus strives to follow. It is also in keeping with the author's undefined and free interpretation of ἰστορία, when in his proemium he describes the frame work into which he intends to place his material.

The work gives no indication that it was written at the suggestion of anyone else. If Constantine had prompted Eusebius to the task, Eusebius would hardly have passed over this fact in silence, for elsewhere in his writings he seems only too glad to parade the flatteries of his imperial patron. In the preface his own words suggest simply what we have stated above, that it grew out of his previous work, the *Chronicle*. He speaks of it as an expansion of the narrative which he had given in epitome in that work. Thus in the opening words, he sums up its contents as follows, placing the chronological element in the forefront: " The successions of the holy apostles together with the times which have been accomplished from the days of our Saviour to our own age."

After his introduction, Eusebius proposes to take up the following topics:

1. The succession of bishops in the most important sees.

2. Christian teachers and writers.

3. Heretics.

4. The punishments which came upon the Jewish people on account of their execution of Jesus.

5. The persecutions of the Christians.

6. The martyrs and the deliverance wrought by the Saviour in the author's own day.

Eusebius is dependent upon ancient models for the plan of his work. The διαδοχαί of the bishops correspond to the διαδοχαί of the schools of philosophy. Christian teachers and heretics are treated from a literary historical view point, their chronology being fixed, together with a list of their works, according to the manner of Alexandrian scholarship. In a similar spirit are added long verbatim citations by way of documentary evidence. As for events over and above such as have been mentioned above, only the judgment on the Jews, the Christian persecutions, and the final victory of Christianity are treated. All the material is approached from the point of view that the history of the Church is at the same time its vindication, and proves it to be a divine institution.

The *Ecclesiastical History* as we know it today is not in its original form. Many events of importance occurred in such rapid succession after the year 311 that Eusebius was obliged several times to alter and amplify the end of his work. E. Schwartz, partly from indications in the text, and partly from manuscript evidence, has concluded that there were four editions, portions of which he has attempted to reconstruct. In his last edition, Eusebius brought the narrative down to 323, the year in which Constantine became sole Emperor.

The *Ecclesiastical History* is chiefly responsible for perpetuating the name of Eusebius. It was received with enthusiasm on its first appearance. The six or seven ancient manuscripts (ninth to eleventh centuries) show an intercrossing of variants which could hardly have taken place except in a rich and ramified tradition of an early date. The work must have been copied frequently even in the first centuries after its publication. The history of the ancient church, of which we would know very little indeed without this work, lived on in the memory of men as pictured by Eusebius, and almost all later descriptions are closely allied to his, or are even direct imitations. This holds true alike for the Greek East and the West where the translation by Rufinus had a wide circulation.

Eusebius' less important works of historiography may be passed over more briefly.

A collection of the ancient acts of the martyrs (Συναγωγὴ τῶν ἀρχαίων μαρτυρίων) was a preliminary exercise to the writing of the *Ecclesiastical History*. Although this work is now lost, most of its material, at least in an abridged form, was included in the *Ecclesiastical History*.

A work on the martyrs of Palestine (Περὶ τῶν ἐν Παλαιστίνῃ μαρτυρησάντων), which describes the martyrdoms in Palestine during the persecution of Diocletian, has survived in two recensions. The shorter recension is always edited with the *Ecclesiastical History*, and is found in several manuscripts of that work, placed after the eighth or tenth books. The longer recension is preserved in its entirety only in a Syriac translation. Certain portions, however, are extant also in Greek.

Eusebius in his *Martyrs of Palestine* speaks as follows about the lost biography of Pamphilus (Περὶ τοῦ βίου Παμφίλου): "The rest of the triumphs of his virtue, requiring a longer narration, we have already before this given to the world in a separate work in three books, of which his life is the subject." He refers to it again three times in his *Ecclesiastical History* (VI, 32; VII, 32; VIII, 13). St. Jerome likewise refers to it several times (*Ep.* 34; *Op.* i, p. 154 ff.; *Vir. Ill.* 81; c. Rufin. 1, 9), in one case (the last) describing it as containing "tres libros elegantissimos," and giving a short extract from the third book, the only surviving fragment. From the standpoint of literary history, the loss of this biography is particularly serious. We could scarcely apply the term "elegantissimos" to the surviving works of Eusebius, and we have enough respect for St. Jerome's literary taste to believe that he could not have used the superlative without some reason. In this work, Eusebius' main and probably only source was his personal knowledge of Pamphilus. This circumstance together with Eusebius' intense admiration for his friend must have coöperated in causing Eusebius to employ his very best style. Any consideration of outside sources could not have interfered with his development of the theme.

The *Life of Constantine* (Εἰς τὸν βίον τοῦ μακαρίου Κωνσταντίνου βασιλέως) in four books should not strictly be placed among the historical works. It is rather an encomium in panegyrical style, restricted in particular to the pious deeds of the Emperor (τὰ πρὸς τὸν θεοφιλῆ συντείνοντα βίον). The literary character of the work would stand out more clearly if its original draught were still preserved. But as G. Pasquali has shown, the original form of the work was considerably enlarged by additions, above all, through the incorporation of documents. Thus only with such modifications has the work been handed down to us. Regarding the authenticity of the documents contained in this eulogy (e.g. edicts and letters of the Emperor), which were questioned by Crivelucci and others, there can be no doubt. Their genuine character has been ably defended, especially by I. A. Heikel. Eusebius saw in the Emperor Constantine a new Moses, destined by God to lead the people of God from oppression into freedom. He heralds the Emperor as the powerful promoter and protector of the Church. In the spirit of the rhetorical panegyric, Eusebius describes Constantine's acts, giving them a one-sided coloring, and omitting whatever does not fit in with the account as planned. However, we must not forget that Eusebius in this work did not intend to write history, and, moreover, truly

believed the historical significance of the Emperor
to be exactly as he described it. Accordingly we
can not accept in this panegyric that complete condemnation of Eusebius which J. Burckhardt gives
us when he calls him "the most contrary of all
writers of the panegyric," "the first thoroughly un-
truthful historian of antiquity."

As supplements to the encomium on Constantine,
Eusebius wrote three works: A speech of the Emperor to the assembly of the saints (λόχος ὃν ἔγραψε
τῷ τῶν ἀγίων συλλόχῳ), the speech delivered by
Eusebius on the occasion of the thirtieth anniver-
sary of the Emperor's reign (τριακονταετηρικός),
and a discourse (βασιλικός) delivered to the Emperor regarding the dedication of the Church of
the Holy Sepulchre in Jerusalem. Eusebius himself
speaks of these works in his *Vita Constantini*, IV,
32, 46.

The authenticity of the Emperor's speech to the
assembly of the saints is seriously questioned.
Heikel seems to have proved that in its present
form it cannot be a direct translation from the
Latin. On the other hand, an evident dependence
on Lactantius and the employment of verses from
Vergil's fourth eclogue make a Latin source quite
probable, and this source may be the actual, authentic speech of the Emperor himself.

Two other works, the Τριακονταετηρικός and
the βασιλικός, which up to the present have always appeared in the editions as one work, are often
cited as the *Laus Constantini*. P. Wendland was the

first to discover that chapters I to X of the *Laus Constantini* form the speech of *Tricennalia*, and chapters XI to XVIII compose the discourse delivered on the occasion of the dedication of the Church of the Holy Sepulchre.

The oration of the *Tricennalia* was delivered before the Emperor in the palace at Constantinople. It celebrates in powerful, though somewhat bombastic language, Constantine's reign of thirty years and especially his services to the Church. The βασιλικός on the other hand is not an oration at all, but a treatise which aims to defend the Emperor for erecting the magnificent church buildings in Jerusalem by setting forth the divinity of the Logos. An apologetic air prevails throughout. In fact the work consists almost entirely of extracts from his *Theophany,* whose elaborate scientific arguments appear here in concise popular form.

4. EUSEBIUS AS AN HISTORIAN

Eusebius was primarily a scholar, a philologian in the broad sense of the term. His industry and care in the collection and employment of documentary material, and his eminent skill in the disposition of great quantities of subject matter, make him one of the greatest Christian scholars, and make his works the most valuable and far-reaching in their influence upon early Christian literature. Few writers have ever shown as keen an insight in the selection of subjects which would have a lasting interest for later generations. As we noted in the beginning of this paper, Eusebius lived in the period of transition between two great epochs which were separated from each other by such marked differences as appear only at intervals of many centuries. It remained for Eusebius to appreciate the greatness of the crisis. He alone seized the opportunity, and preserved the past in all its phases — history, doctrine, criticism and even topography — for the instruction of later generations. In this lies his chief claim to greatness.

In the presentation of his facts, as a stylist, or as a deep and original thinker, it would be absurd to compare Eusebius with the great masters of classical antiquity. Eusebius probably did not strive to obtain stylistic excellence, although he always shows himself under the influence of rhetoric. His style is often monotonous and tires the reader with its endless periods, and when it attempts to rise to rhetorical pathos, it passes proper bounds and becomes overburdened and bombastic. He was rather the slave than the master of his vast learning. His ideas were lofty and great, but he was unequal to the task of adequately executing them. His isolated thoughts were valuable, but he could not place them together in a proper synthesis. He accumulated material with great diligence, but he was careless and perfunctory in the use of them when accumulated. Thus in aftertime many succeeded him who surpassed him in their style of writing, but stood far below him in scientific sense and learning.

Although his writings are of a wide and varied character, they all have the mark of apologetic literature. In other words, his rôle as an apologist is not confined to his strictly apologetic works. Whatever subjects he may be treating, his thoughts seem to turn instinctively into the same mould. In dealing with the subject of chronology, one of his main objects is to show the superior antiquity of the Hebrew oracles to the wisdom of the Greeks. When he writes ecclesiastical history, the course of events presents to him a vindication of the Divine Word, in whom the faith of Christians centres. If his theme is as worldly as the encomium of a sovereign, he sees in the subject of his panegyric an instrument used by a higher power to fulfil a divine economy. Again, if he enters on so technical a task as dividing the Gospels into sections, his real motive is to supply materials for a harmony, and thus to vindicate the essential unity of the evangelical narratives against those who denied it. His character as an apologist may be traced to two sources: the period and circumstances in which he lived, and his own natural disposition. Living in the great crisis of transition, between the Hellenism of the past and the Christianity of the future, he was forced to witness their contact, both hostile and friendly. His knowledge of the wisdom of the Greeks and the teaching of the Scriptures together with his natural breadth of sympathy and moderation of temper fitted him, far better than anyone else of the time, for the task of treating their conflicts and associations.

In a similar way Eusebius brings the literary-historical point of view to all his works, even the apologetic. The literary-historical point of view is wholly foreign to all other opponents of paganism and heresy. They wish only to enter upon polemical discussion, and if they bring forward chronological facts occasionally these facts only serve the purpose of showing their chronological inferiority. The work of Eusebius emanated from the treasures of the Christian libraries of Caesarea and Oelia, just as profane literary-historical research also stood in closest connection with the works of librarians. Eusebius was the first to grasp clearly the concept of a Christian literature, and to employ with it the ancient methods, fixing the dates of writers and cataloguing their works. He transplanted the tradition of Alexandrian philology to Christian soil.

5. Eusebius' Reputation in Later Years

Eusebius' reputation after his death was varied. In the Greek Church, as long as the Arian controversy was still fresh, the tendency was to depreciate him as an orthodox father. But in proportion as the theological disputes died out, a disposition grew up to clear him of any taint of Arian doctrine. Socrates (*H. E.*, II, 21) goes to great length to prove Eusebius orthodox, quoting passages to substantiate his orthodoxy. Gelasius of Cyzicus is quite enthusiastic in his defense of Eusebius. He calls him "most noble tiller of ecclesiastical husbandry," and "strict

lover of truth," and says that, if there is the faint-
est suggestion of Arianism in Eusebius' writings, it
is due to his simplicity, as Eusebius himself pleaded
in his self-defense. The Second Council of Nicaea, or
more exactly the Iconoclastic controversy, marked
a decided change in this attitude. Since the Iconoclasts quoted Eusebius in support of their views,
the opposite party did their best to disparage him,
for if they could prove conclusively that Eusebius
was an Arian, the claims of the Iconoclasts would
have little foundation. This attitude toward Eusebius found expression in Photius. In fact Eusebius'
reputation never fully recovered from the injury it
suffered by being involved in the Iconoclastic controversy.

In the West, Eusebius had a better fate; St.
Jerome being the only person of prominence to hold
a marked antipathy for him. " The chief of the
Arians," " the standard bearer of the Arian faction," " the most flagrant champion of the impiety
of Arians," are some of the choice phrases hurled
at him by the fiery Jerome. However, the great
service which Eusebius had done for Christian literature prevailed with the Westerners over the attacks of St. Jerome. The two popes, Gelasius and
Pelagius II, successively shielded the reputation of
Eusebius, the one by refusing to place the *Ecclesiastical History* and the *Chronicle* on the Index,
and the other by expressing several noble sentiments
in his defense. The offense of Eusebius, however,
which in the minds of these two popes did require

an apology was his defence of the heretic Origen.
Neither Gelasius nor Pelagius once refers directly to
the charge of Arianism. Another Latin writer, anonymous, of a later period, calls Eusebius "the key
of the Scriptures and the guardian of the New Testament." Finally, the remarkable fact of the appearance of Eusebius' name in martyrologies of
both the East and West, in spite of the suspicions
of heresy which hovered about his name, has already been considered.

BIBLIOGRAPHY

A. BIOGRAPHY

All the works listed in this section contain bibliographies giving full information regarding editions, complete
and partial, as well as translations of the writings of
Eusebius. Editions and translations will, accordingly, not
be included in the present bibliography.

BARDENHEWER, O., *Eusebius von Cäsarea*, in *Geschichte
der altchristlichen Litteratur*. Vol. III, 240–262.
München, 1912.

CHRIST, WILHELM VON, *Eusebius*, in *Griechische Litteratur Geschichte*. München, 1913.

FAULHABER, M., *Die griechischen Apologeten der klass-
ischen Väterzeit: 1. Eusebius von Cäsarea*. Würzburg, 1896.

GUTSCHMID, ALFRED VON, *Aus Vorlesungen über die
Geschichte der römischen Kaiserzeit*. Leipzig, 1894.

GWATKIN, H. M., *Eusebius of Caesarea*, in *Lectures on
ecclesiastical history delivered in Norwich Cathedral*.
London, 1896.

HARNACK, A., *Eusebius*, in *Geschichte der altchristlichen Litteratur*. Vol. II, 242 ff. Leipzig, 1894.

HELY, V., *Eusèbe de Césarée, premier historien de l'Église*. Paris, 1877.

HILLER, E., *Eusebius und Cyrillus*, in *Rhein. Mus. N. F.* 25. Bd. (1870), 253–262.

LIGHTFOOT, J. B., *Eusebius of Caesarea*, in *Dictionary of Christian Biography*, Vol. II, 308–348. (Antiquated in many places.)

PREUSCHEN, E., *Eusebius*, in *Prot. Realencyc.*, Vol. V, 605–618.

SCHWARTZ, E., *Eusebios*, in Pauly-Wissowa *Realencyc.*, Vol. VI, 1370–1439.

STEIN, F. G., *Eusebius, Bischof von Cäsarea*. Würzburg, 1859.

VAN DEN GHEYN, *Eusèbe*, in VIGOUROUX, *Dictionnaire de la Bible*, Vol. II, 2051–2056.

B. GENERAL WORKS ON EUSEBIUS
AND HIS WRITINGS

BIGELMAIR, A., *Zur Theologie des Eusebius von Caesarea*, in *Festschrift für Georg von Hertling*. Kempten, 1914.

CAVALLERA, L., *Le schisme d'Antioche*. Paris, 1905.

CONYBEARE, F. C., *The Oldest Versions of Eusebius' History of the Church*, in the *Academy*, Vol. XLIV (1893), pp. 14 ff.

DHORME, P. *Les sources de le Chronique d'Eusèbe*, in *Revue Biblique*, N. S. Vol. VII (1910), pp. 233 ff.

FRITZE, E., *Beiträge zur sprachlich-stilistischen Würdigung des Eusebios*. Leipzig, 1910.

GÖRRES, F., *Zur Kritik des Eusebius und Lactantius*, in *Philologus*, Vol. XXXVI (1877), pp. 594 ff.

HABMEL, A., *Die Entstehung der Kirchengeschichte des Eusebius von Caesarea untersucht*. Essen, 1896.

HARRIS, J. R., *Euthalius and Eusebius*, in *Hermas in Arcadia and other essays*. Cambridge, 1896.

HEIKEL, I. A., *Kritische Beiträge zu den Constantin-Schriften des Eusebius*. Leipzig, 1911.

KAYE, J., *The Ecclesiastical History of Eusebius*. London, 1888.

LAWLER, H. J., *Eusebiana. Essays on the Ecclesiastical History of Eusebius*. New York, 1912.

LAWLER, H. J., *The Chronology of Eusebius' " Martyrs of Palestine,"* in *Hermathena*, Vol. XXV (1908), pp. 177 ff.

LEO, F., *Die griechisch-römische Biographie nach ihrer literarischen form: De vita Constantini*, pp. 311 ff. Leipzig, 1901.

LICHTENSTEIN, A., *Eusebius von Nikomedien*. Halle, 1903.

ROOS, C., *De Theodoreto Clementis et Eusebii compilatore*. Halis, 1883.

SALMON, G., *Chronicle of Eusebius of Caesarea*, in *Dictionary of Christian Biography*, Vol. II, pp. 348 ff.

SCHÖNE, A., *Die Weltchronik des Eusebius in ihrer Bearbeitung durch Hieronymus*. Berlin, 1900.

SCHULTZE, V., *Quellenuntersuchungen zur Vita Constanti des Eusebius*, in *Zeitschrift für Kirchengeschichte*, Vol. XIV (1894), pp. 503 ff.

SCHWARZ, E., *Die Königslisten des Eratosthenes und Kastor mit Excursen über Interpolationen bei Africanus und Eusebius*. Göttingen, 1895.

SEECK, O., *Die Urkunden der Vita Constantini*, in *Zeitschrift für Kirchengeschichte*, Vol. XVIII, pp. 321 ff.

SENUYS, D., *Les Canons d' Eusèbe, d'Annianos d'Andronicos d'après Elie de Nisibe*, in *Byzantische Zeitschrift*, Vol. XXII (1913), pp. 1 ff.

TRIEBER, C., *Zur Kritik des Eusebius*, in *Hermes*, Vol. XXIX (1894), pp. 124 ff.

TURNER, C. H., *The Early Episcopal Lists*, in *Journal of Theological Studies*, 1900.

VETTER, P., *Ueber die armenische uebersetzung der Kirchengeschichte des Eusebius*, in *Theologische Quartalschrift*, Vol. LXIII (1881), pp. 250 ff.

OROSIUS (c. 380 — c. 420)

WILLIAM M. THOMAS GAMBLE, M.A.
Catholic University of America

THE comparatively little we know about Orosius is enough to sharpen curiosity as to how far he is illuminated and how far overshadowed by the great name with which he is most inseparably associated. He was, clearly, if we judge by his writings, more than an echo of St. Augustine; and while he was far from being anything comparable, say, to what Plato was to Socrates, his relation to his master had more dignity and mental kinship than that which obtained between James Boswell and his hero Samuel Johnson. Orosius was a young priest, perhaps of precocious gifts — for his associates allude to him, however respectfully, as though he were scarcely more than a boy — who came to the great African Doctor to learn such psychological and sociological principles as were consistent with Catholic doctrine, so that he might be the better equipped to fight the Church's battle with heresy.

When he entered the lists of controversy, Orosius showed great keenness and grasp of the issues but (probably through youthful rashness and inexperience) drew upon himself the fire of a hostile and irritated Bishop, and so compromised the success of his polemic. At the suggestion of his master, however, he had already begun work on a piece of apologetic which occupied and still occupies a unique place in the development of the Christian view of the story of human institutions. Orosius, in his survey of the catastrophes of the past, was acting as the mouthpiece for the Patristic interpretation of history, the core of which was to be found in the Old and New Testaments and in Catholic tradition and definitions. Yet the style and the reflections in this as in his other writings, have vivid marks of individuality.

Four years, or five at the most, cover all that is known of the career of Orosius. In that time — between the year 414 (or 413 at the earliest) and the year 417 (or 418 at the latest) — he came into first-hand and interested contact with the most typically significant features that marked the beginning of the transition from the antique to the medieval world.

Orosius was keenly alive to the cosmopolitan aspects of the Empire; a European whose interests carried him to Asia and Africa, he sensed, in an era when the Empire and the Church seemed to be welded more closely than ever together, that quality of universality in the Empire which corresponded to the Catholicity of the Church. This close association of Church and Empire under the Theodosian dynasty, was an exhilarating stimulus to unitary conceptions of life. Keenly as he would feel the ravages of war and invasion, the menace of the

new "tyrants" that were assassinating and succeeding each other, the violence and bigotry of the
Vandals, the young Spaniard seemed to feel lifted
and sustained, on the patriotic side, by the memory
of the greatness of Theodosius. He seems to have
had few, if any misgivings, as had other Latins, as
to the epoch-making creation of the status of the
Foederati, in which Germanic nations could be incorporated into the Empire without subjugation or
assimilation; he seemed to regard the frictions and
the stimulations of the new race-contacts within
the Empire as pulses of new life and growth, not
as disintegrations of the old order. Indeed, Orosius
seems to have been strangely blind, in spite of his
recognition of the vicissitudes and catastrophes of
history, to the "decline and fall" of the civilization under which he lived. He seems to have been
insensible to that mood of foreboding which had
overtaken St. Jerome when the stream of refugees
from Alaric's sack of Rome passed through Palestine.

A man of a new generation, Orosius is seemingly
exhilarated by all the new problems and dangers.
The Priscillianist heresy had goaded him to an insatiable inquiry into the nature and origin of the
soul; he had detected in Origenism that overvalu-
ation of created nature, that a-prioristic bargaining
with the Creator for an apotheosis of the creature,
which prepared him to contend with Pelagius. The
grapple with heresies had been to Orosius the lab-
oratory-work, under his teachers St. Augustine and

St. Jerome, by which he was enabled to survey history as the interaction of free agents whose decisions determined their own destiny and their own attitudes toward the universal plan, yet who at no point could defeat that plan. He was enabled to view the past of mankind as a series of vast kingdoms of culture which on the human side were seen to be determined by human weakness, pride, cupidity, violence, yet in which faith could discern, in dimmer or clearer outline, the triumphs of Omnipotence and Omniscience, ever turning evil into good.

During the four or five years of what we might call his graduate course under St. Augustine and St. Jerome, Orosius, after leaving writings that because of their acute grasp and succinct statement are important sources for the controversies of the time, produced as his masterpiece the first world-history, embodying the fully-developed Patristic doctrine of the sovereignty of God in providence and in grace. And after thus setting forth the rudiments of a philosophy of civilization which shaped the historiography of Christendom for a thousand years at least, Orosius disappears. Perhaps he died an early death; or more presumably, after the adventure of his quest for knowledge, an exciting campaign after error, and a memorable and unique work, the young priest may have disappeared in the blessed and fruitful obscurity of an ordinary cure of souls.

1. LIFE OF OROSIUS

There are two places in the Spanish Peninsula which are connected with the earlier unknown life of Orosius. In the *Seven Books of Histories,* he refers to " nostra Tarracona," which is the " Tarragon " printed on flat flasks of sweet wine, familiar sight among the bottles seen in European grocery windows. The other place is Braga on the coast of Portugal.

The evidence would be quite consistent with a number of hypotheses, such as, for instance, that he was born in Tarragon and exercised his priesthood in Braga. It is fairly certain that it was from the Diocese of Braga that he left for Africa.

In the seventh book of the *Histories,* Orosius seems to be alluding to some personal adventure in which he narrowly escaped capture or violence at the hands of barbarians. The rhetorical form in which this allusion is made, if it is an allusion, leaves it not quite certain whether he is relating an experience or inventing an illustration, but there is a vividness in the passage that suggests biography, in his description of one pursued into the sea, threatened with hurled stones and darts, and almost seized with outstretched hands, until hidden and protected by the unexpected descent of a fog.

Whatever were the circumstances that determined the departure of Orosius to Africa, Orosius took them to be an answer to prayer and to aspiration for spiritual knowledge, and to his desire to be useful to the Church in combatting error. "Through thee, blessed father," he addresses St. Augustine, "through thee, I say, our Lord God by a word healeth those whom by the sword He hath chastised. To thee by God was I sent; owing to thee, I have hope through Him, while I ponder how it has come about that I came hither. I acknowledge why I came, — without choice, without bond, without appointment, I departed from my country, moved by some hidden force, until I was carried to the shore of your land."

St. Augustine, in the letter commendatory which he later sent to St. Jerome with Orosius, associates the violence of the Vandals in Spain with the ravages of the Priscillianist heresy there, when he speaks of doctrines that "much more banefully mangle the souls of the Spaniards than do the barbaric swords their bodies." This parallel not only suggests in connection with other indications, that in some way Orosius may have come in personal contact with Vandal violence, but it also confirms other evidences that the invasions had the effect of intensifying the agitations of the Priscillianist heresy, which had persistently disturbed the peace of the Church in Spain, ever since the condemnation and execution of Priscillian more than thirty years before. A time of disturbance, of invasion and violence would be peculiarly vulnerable to such a savage, ascetic reaction against the responsibilities of civilized life as Priscillianism evidently was, denouncing marriage and the eating of flesh, inculcating a dark and desperate pessimism and joyless fatalism that could easily react into mad license. The persistence of this heresy has induced some to connect it with the similar doctrines of the Albigenses of a much later time; and they were similar in this, that in both instances the heresy was supported or led by persons of rank and wealth.

Not many decades before, Spain had been the most cultured and prosperous part of the Empire. She had given to Latin letters Seneca, Lucan, Martial, Quintilian; to the imperial throne she had sent Trajan, Hadrian, and in more recent times Theodosius the Great himself. Even the lower half of the imperial shield of Theodosius bears a symbolic figure of Spain reclining, and holding the horn of plenty. With the period of the "tyrants" and of the invasions it seems that a cultural decline had set in, due to the insecurity of conditions, and especially to the drain upon the resources of families who formerly supported the arts, and upon whom fell the increasing burden of maintaining the defense and administration of the Empire. It may have been this desperation and uncertainty among those of wealth and title, that rendered them open to the morbid suggestions of gloomy and anti-social heresies. Hatred of the whole imperial system may have smouldered in many a patrician or decurion heart. Certainly something more than the *odium theologicum* entered into the bitterness that culminated in the execution of Priscillian by Maximus.

St. Augustine, in the year 415, writes of Orosius
as a youth. Hence his birth is reckoned as coming
between 380 and 390. Some of the events to which
we have alluded might have occurred in his early
childhood, or would be within the vivid memory of
his elders. In the year 380 occurred the Spanish
Council of Saragossa which condemned Priscillian
ecclesiastically, he later making his ill-starred appeal
to the secular court. In the same year the Emperor
Theodosius the Great published the Edict proclaim-
ing the Faith of St. Peter and his successors as the
official Faith of the Empire, placing heresy under
severe disabilities, and abolishing paganism as a
public cult. In the next year the Goths were made
Foederati of the Empire, and by the treaty were
engaged to defend it and replenish its agricultural
decline. This decade saw, also, the execution of Priscillian. Such were the events Orosius would hear repeatedly discussed during his most impressionable
years.

In the thought of Orosius some trace of the influence of these events may be seen in the habit of
social adaptability to which he evidently schooled
himself, warned by the new racial contacts that
were altering the whole social complexion of the
time, to which adaptability he seems to refer when
he says: "Inter Romanos, ut dixi, Romanus, inter
Christianos, Christianus, inter homines, homo." And
again — "Utor temporarie omni terra quasi patria."
Something of the very real, if not always clearly
conceived toleration that meets us often in the Pa-

tristic period, is discernible in the often-quoted: "Odisse me fateor haeresim, non haereticum."

The persistence of the Priscillianist heresy in Spain awoke in Orosius not merely a zeal to combat the error for the sake of social stability and spiritual truth, but, as we have noted, a desire for better knowledge of the nature and origin of the soul. Two of his fellow-priests in Braga, both named Avitus, had gone, one to Rome, the other to the East, and one of them returned with a translation of Origen, in which they found much that was strange, even though it contradicted the gloomy Priscillianists with a dazzling buoyancy. Creation, to be worthy of the Creator, must be eternal, said the Origenists; and in spite of the seriousness of sin, the world must ultimately be rid of all evil or pain. The pre-existence of the soul also seemed to them to be a necessary corollary of the assumption that all created spirits were originally equal.

When Orosius, by whatever occasion he came to Africa, at length found himself in the presence of the great Doctor, and disclosed his perplexity and his desire for knowledge, St. Augustine requested him to put in writing a memorial of the tenets of the two systems, which could be dealt with more fully and at leisure. In compliance with this request, Orosius wrote his *Commonitorium sive Consultatio de errore Priscillianistorum et Origenistorum*. The analysis is admirable in its clearness and condensation. To this St. Augustine replied in his *Ad Orosium contra Priscillianistas et Origenistas;* but

feeling himself unable to satisfy Orosius in some
of his keen questions as to the origin and nature of
the soul, he directed the young priest to make a
journey to the Holy Land and consult St. Jerome
on this subject. In this connection it is worth noting
that among the didactic dialogues of St. Augustine
is one in which Orosius is made the interlocutor,
and is represented as asking questions as to the
origin of evil and other difficult matters of divinity.
Altogether the language of St. Augustine in using
the name of Orosius seems to reflect impressions of
a mind which could be daring and insistent in its
inquiries, even because of, rather than in spite of,
his readiness to submit to the authority of the
Church; a mind that could candidly admit the difficulties of a problem all the more because of its recognition of human limitation in the attempt of the
intellect to solve it, and hence did not dread to ask
questions that might prove, in the existing state of
knowledge, unanswerable.

The condensed statement of the leading features
of the two opposed theories in the *Consultatio* of
Orosius throws into relief the darkness and barren-
ness of the one heresy, the specious brilliance of
the other: of the first, he cites a Priscillianist interpretation of the Parable of the Sower: " ' He who
goeth forth sowing his seed ' (Matth. xiii, 46) ' was
not a Good Sower; for ' (they assert), ' if he were
good, he would not have been careless; he would
not have tossed the seed on the road, nor among
stones, nor on waste earth.' They would have it

understood that 'this same sower is he that scat-
tereth captive souls in divers bodies as he willeth;
. . . that by cunning, not by the power of God, all
good results are accomplished in this world.' "

After sketching the characteristic tenets of the
Priscillianists, and their denial of Divine providence
and of grace as decisive in earthly affairs, particularly their refusal to admit the union of soul and
body as a matter of Divine appointment — Orosius
tells how the two Avitus, his fellow-priests, left
Braga to find literature that might help in combatting the errors. One went to Rome, the other to Jerusalem, bringing back between them two works in
which they hoped to find material for the purpose;
one, a translation of Origen, the other a work of
Victorinus, which may have been a commentary on
Origen or an interpretation or abstract of his or
some other Alexandrian work. The brief dismissal
of Victorinus as containing little new, and as negligible where he varied from Origen, indicates the existence of a critical sense in Orosius with which he is
not usually credited in most modern references to
him. Certainly the statements of Orosius in this
work have a conciseness and objectivity that at
least suggest the scientific temper. On Origen, Orosius comments discriminately that many grandiose
theories can be expounded from Origen at the start,
which by a more sober and less hasty examination
could be superseded by the truth itself.

That the world should be created out of nothing,
he adds, is Origen's stumbling-block, since the

Origenists argue that it is derogatory to Divine dignity that God should *begin* to do anything; hence the maxim, *Deus enim quaecumque fecit, faciendo non coepit*. Orosius then goes on to refer to Origen's universalism, and to his view of the material creation as serving a purgatorial function for the individual souls born within it, who on account of sins in a preëxistent state were allotted varying conditions of body or estate for the purpose of purgation. He touches on Origen's vast cosmic conception of many worlds needing redemption, and requiring many modes of incarnation, passion and resurrection on the part of the Divine Word. Origen's notion of the Incarnation of a phase to be ultimately transcended, not an eternal union of God with created nature, is not forgotten. In Orosius' special interest in the soul, its nature and origin, we need not go far afield to discern a groping for sound foothold amid conceptions of human nature that made strife and chaos the hopeless element of man's earthly existence, or else surrounded human destiny with vastness and infinities in which any true identity and continuity was bewildered and lost.

Now in the mind of Augustine the destiny of man had taken shape as a coherent story. Birth was not "a sleep and a forgetting," as the Origenists had it; nor was it the senseless loss of a jewel in the mire, as the Priscillianists had it. Birth was the real beginning of a story and a career, and behind birth was not pre-existence, but *heritage*. In this conception of *heritage*, human destiny became coherent.

There were two backgrounds to the soul, its heritage
of impotent estrangement from God, and the slender
thread of its royal inheritance and sonship, which
was the only clue out of the labyrinth of life, leading
to the full heritage of grace. The destiny of the
soul depended on whether it was content with the
futilities of the estranged natural heritage, or
whether it would follow the clue of its " naturally
Christian " instinct to the kingdom of grace. It was
by his fidelity to orthodoxy under St. Augustine's
guidance, that Orosius found his way to a view of
the soul and of society that was fundamental, and
even in a sense genetic and historical, because it was
not rooted in cosmogonies and theosophies, but in
the facts of natural, cultural, and supernatural
heritage.

The first of the two best-known Origenist crises
had died down many years before, leaving, however,
some bitternesses behind. John, Bishop of Jerusalem,
in the nineties of the previous century, had been
resentful against Jerome, partly on personal grounds.
As a champion of Origen at that time, he will not
surprise us as the friend of Pelagius in the contest
with which we are now about to deal. In order,
however, to appreciate the opposing currents of
opinion in the Church at the time, we must give full
weight to the rather strong reaction against the
whole ascetic and monastic ideal which had made
itself felt in more than one way, even as far back as
the virulent coarseness of the campaign conducted
against Priscillian by Ithacius, who accused all of

Priscillianism who practised unusual abstinence. This revulsion against monasticism was not often consciously associated either with Origenism or with Pelagianism, for the former was enthusiastically supported by the Nitrian monks, while Pelagius made much of the disciplinary virtue of asceticism as compensation for his low views on grace. Yet it is significant that on the doctrinal side, Pelagius asserted that natural impulses had in them no taint of sinful quality, thereby removing one of the strongest motives toward the ascetic life. In controverting this error, St. Augustine appealed to the instinct of shame and indignity at the impertinences of the lower nature.

Thus, at the beginning of the fifth century we detect, as an accompaniment of the change in the political and social situation that begins, however faintly, to take on the aspect of the medieval world, a subtle shift also in the centre of controversy in religion: less is said by those who would blunt the full force of the doctrine of the Incarnation, of the two natures of Christ; and more is said in attack upon the principles of sustaining and regulating power in the Church and in the Empire. These attacks stigmatize nature as so vile that nothing can govern, strengthen, nor heal it; or they eulogize nature as endowed with infinite resources that make it self-regulative and self-corrective.

Pelagius and his friend Coelestius left for Carthage in 411, among the refugees that poured into Asia and Africa after the sack of Rome. It does not seem that they remained long there. Perhaps some premonition of the future fate of Catholic Africa prompted the Church there to set its house in order, and to keep the light of its faith trimmed and burning; for with a preternatural clearness of vision, Africa rallied around her great Doctor. Pelagius and his friend found little soil for their doctrines, and very soon departed for Palestine, where they had some reason to hope for a more welcome reception. Well versed in Greek, and familiarized with Greek modes of theological thought by frequent conferences with Rufinus in Rome before his death in 410 (while Rufinus was interpreting the thought of Origen to the Latin mind after the departure of Jerome to Palestine), — Pelagius hoped that he might find the Origenist bishop John of Jerusalem friendly to him, and was not disappointed. It does not seem to be definitely ascertained how long before the arrival of Orosius in Palestine in 415 Pelagius and his friend had been there, or whether they arrived the same year.

It would seem that in any case the movements of Pelagius were being actively followed by priests and bishops who were profoundly convinced of the grave issues growing out of the spread of the new doctrines. Heros, Bishop of Arles, and Lazarus, Bishop of Aix-les-Bains, had resigned their Sees to go to the East and counteract Pelagianism. Avitus, one of the two fellow-priests of Orosius, was also there, with others mentioned by Orosius and St. Augustine in the writings that deal with the pro-

ceedings at Palestine. It is more than possible that
St. Augustine, who had thrown all his energies into
the grapple with Pelagianism as into no other cause,
discerned in the gifts of Orosius the possibility of
help much needed in the East; and no doubt in
sending Orosius to St. Jerome, St. Augustine made
sure that Orosius fully grasped the Pelagian issue,
and that he was personally qualified to present
the matter to St. Jerome. The event justified him
in this confidence, for the reply of St. Jerome to
the letter of introduction marked the restoration of
cordial relations between the two Doctors of the
Church after long years in which silence had followed plain criticism on the one side and cool as-
perity on the other. The affectionate letter of Jerome
to Augustine contains not only explicit commenda-
tion of Orosius, but is itself a proof of the latter's
ability to convince and to reconcile under delicate
circumstances. Jerome, though himself a semi-
Pelagian, was fairly enlisted against the denial of
grace and the minimizing of the ravages of sin; he
wrote against the doctrines; and in the same year,
415, Bishop John of Jerusalem was obliged to call
a council to examine Pelagius.

In this diocesan council Orosius was the principal
accuser. He testified, and Pelagius admitted, that
Pelagius had said to him that " a man could be
without sin and could easily observe the whole com-
mandments of God, if he wished." With his knowledge of Greek, Pelagius was able to explain that of
course the help of God was necessary if a man

should live without sin. This satisfied John, who did not care to go into the distinction which Pelagius later made, between God's help through nature as originally created, and God's help specially given to remedy the ravages of sin in nature. The Latins did not understand Greek well enough to press this important distinction, and moreover had the disadvantage of an incompetent or (as Orosius believed) a malicious interpreter. They fell back on the prestige of St. Augustine, but were only ridiculed for their pains. Pelagius, turning Oriental pride to account, said "Quis mihi Augustinus?" which was followed by John's assertion of his diocesan authority, "Augustinus ego sum!" Fortunately in this synod Pelagianism was not officially countenanced. The serious difficulty of language was recognized, and the whole matter was reserved for papal decision.

In the same year, owing to the efforts of Heros and Lazarus, Bishop Eulogius of Caesarea called a synod at Lydda or Diospolis, which proved to be a worse babel of tongues and which ostensibly favored Pelagius, though in St. Augustine's review of the proceedings he construes the decision as a condemnation of the Pelagian thesis, and an exculpation of Pelagius, on the ground that Pelagius repudiated or explained away his real position, and in view of the fact that the chief accusers of Pelagius, who could have testified to the errors as formerly held, were unable to be present. It seems, however, that on this occasion Pelagius distinctly stated that what he meant by *adjutorium Dei* was nothing more than *gratia creationis,* and it is hard to see how the synod could have failed to feel the full force of this definition, especially as Pelagius could speak Greek.

Thus, failure seemed to attend this aspect of the Eastern pilgrimage. The futile controversy with Bishop John followed. Two consolations remained to Orosius: first, that he had succeeded in arousing to the menace the great scholar and ascetic of Bethlehem, irascible and difficult though he was, and in his old age; second, through the recent discovery of the relics of the Proto-martyr St. Stephen by Lucian, a priest of Kaphor Gamala near Jerusalem, Orosius was enabled to carry a portion of these with him, together with letters from the discoverer and from Avitus the older fellow-priest who was now in Palestine, who translated Lucian's letter, addressed to all Christians and attesting to the facts of the discovery. Associations with St. Jerome were to leave their mark later on the *Histories;* and without doubt he learned from St. Jerome the theory of "creationism" in regard to the origin of the individual soul, which has come to be the favored opinion in the Church.

After a brief stay with his master in Hippo, Orosius embarked for his home; but in the island of Minorca he learned that the Vandals, who had entered Spain in 409, were in possession of Bracara, which was not far from Galicia, where one division of the invaders ultimately settled. Orosius left the relics with the Bishop of Minorca, where they became the occasion of a memorable revival of religious fervor, notable on account of the conversion of a number of Jews. Returning to Africa, he completed the *Seven Books of Histories against the Pagans* which St. Augustine had requested him to undertake, as a historical proof of the thesis of the third book of the *City of God*. We hear of him no more; and are left with quite vivid and definite impression of the ardor, the piety, the venturesomeness, the sensitiveness and the hero-worship of the young Iberian priest, who under his master explored world-history even as his later Peninsular kindred explored the globe itself.

2. WORKS OF OROSIUS

Besides an unedited letter to St. Augustine, the writings of St. Augustine, as far as possible in chronological order, are, first in the year 414, the *Commonitorium sive Consultatio de errore Priscillianistorum et Origenistorum;* next, in the year 415, the *Liber Apologeticus contra Pelagium;* as for the *Septem Libri Historiarum contra Paganos,* that was evidently completed in 417 or 418. Moerner, followed by Teuffel, places the composition of the first part of the *Histories* during the first stay of Orosius with Augustine. Ebert, however, comparing certain sections in one of St. Augustine's letters with statements in the dedication of the *Histories,* concludes that since five, at most, of the books of the *City of God* had been written when Orosius went to Palestine, and since St. Augustine was at work on the eleventh book when Orosius undertook to write the *Histories*, the latter could not have been begun until either the first return to Africa from the East, or the second return from Minorca. There is no disagreement about the general time of the close of the book in 417 or 418, as that is determined by the point at which Orosius ends the contemporary part of the history. If Ebert is right as to the beginning of the *Histories* the date would be 416, or at the end of 415 at the earliest. The *Liber Apologeticus* would be written before leaving Palestine, when the events of the controversy would be still fresh in his mind, in 415.

The plan and framework of the *Seven Books of Histories against the Pagans* is based upon two principal sources: the first is the conception of St. Augustine of the relation of the Divine dispensations of the Jewish and of the Catholic Church, to the equally Divine dispensations overruling the great world-empires with which the Church of the Old and New Testaments had come in contact. The second source is the chronology, contributed by Jerome, by which the periods of the Babylonian and the Roman Empires are represented as corresponding to each other in time. This chronology was originally the *Chronicon* of Eusebius, corrected by St. Jerome. Both these sources are ultimately to be referred to the apocalyptic prophecies of the Old and New Testaments, especially in the Book Daniel, in which four kingdoms are symbolized as succeeding one another. Orosius, under St. Augustine's tutelage, takes Babylon and Rome as the two chief empires affecting the destiny of the Church, and related to each other in some way analogous to the relation between the Churches of the Old and the New dispensations. Macedonia and Carthage are taken as the two intermediate empires which transmit the cultural heritage of Babylon to Rome, and serve as the guardians of Rome in her period of minority. Orosius begins his work with a geographic description of the globe as the theatre of history, in the three divisions which he himself, as pilgrim, inquirer, and contender for the Faith, had touched in his travels.

The division into seven books is in places rather strained in the interest of symbolism, just as the chronology of the Empires suffers some gentle violence for the sake of symmetry. Regularity and correspondence in time-periods was a part of the attempt to exhibit evidence of providential design in history, yet it was not essential to the main argument of the *Histories*. It is necessary to stress the fact that the Patristic historiography makes no pretenses at an explanation of the counsels of God in the course of human events; the thesis is merely to show that calamities had not increased under the " Christian times " and that Christian faith supplied antidotes to temporal evil that pagan sufferers lacked. There is far less tendency to trace events to some supposed design of Providence, than there is among modern positivists the tendency to see the present as the inevitable unfolding of some quite imperfectly understood circumstance in the past. Indeed humility in the presence of Divine wisdom was a far more effective check upon *a priori* views in the Patristic historian, than agnosticism is a restraint upon the cock-sureness of a Wells. Faith in the Divine wisdom, power, and mercy, and acknowledgment of human ill-desert is sufficient usually as the intellectual background of the catalogue of human miseries in the *Histories,* without any attempt to fathom the particular purpose of God in any given event. And the more important generalizations, far from being wholly subjective, were rooted in objective facts and age-long developments in the Mediterranean world which nothing in our own time has been able to explain away. Other civilizations existed apparently unchanged for millenniums in other scarce-known regions of the world, but in them development had reached its limit, and they could await only crystallization or decay. Only around the Mediterranean was civilization dynamic, ever dissolving and transforming itself anew as power shifted from race to race, from east to west. During the Theodosian dynasty the elements of Mediterranean history could be viewed for the first time with a complete perspective, and the eye that first saw this perspective was the eye of Augustine. Perhaps he viewed it not without the distortion of patriotic bias, for Egypt is ignored among the great Empires and Carthage is coupled with Macedonia. Yet the two pivotal centres of the dynamic civilization of antiquity are just where St. Augustine and Orosius placed them, in Mesopotamia and Rome.

And there were some most significant facts that Orosius saw in clearer and more hopeful outline than did either St. Jerome or St. Augustine. St. Jerome, the oldest of the three, the one most steeped in the life and feeling of antiquity, had been shaken and stunned by the humiliation of Rome by Alaric, which to him spelled chaos itself — perhaps the very trump of Judgment would next be heard. In St. Augustine's outlook there is a detached tentativeness which forbids him to be wholly sanguine about the future of society. Yet both St. Augustine and St. Jerome, though dubious about the future, recognize a providential relation between the Empire and the Church, somewhat analogous to St. Joseph's guardianship of the Holy Child. It remained for the youthful Orosius to see the Empire at work as an auxiliary to the Church in adjusting to each other the conflicting races. He assumes, with his teachers, that Rome is the last of the great apocalyptic kingdoms, and that with the fall of Rome must come the world's end. But he seems to see that the Empire is standing the strain of the new times. Troeltsch is hardly wrong in regarding St. Augustine as the "Antique Christian" in spite of the modern note that is struck in the introspective and psychological interest of the *Confessions*. Something in the pages of Orosius makes us aware that the Middle Ages have all but begun; if we analyze this quality, we shall find that one of its elements is the fact that the German is not, as to the older men, a mere barbarian intruder, but an object of vivid human interest. When St. Augustine dwells on the comparative mildness of the Goths in the sack of Rome, it is almost as if he were speaking of a " mild " winter, or of a tornado that had spared a church full of worshippers. Even the idealization of the Germans by Tacitus was not devoid of the sentimental patronage of the safe and superior being toward the " noble savage " whom he is not averse to use as a foil for the tiresome moments of civilization. As for St. Augustine, he does not even deign to speak of the intruders as Goths, much less mention the name of Alaric. He still affects the old classic vagueness about the wild indistinguishable Scythian hordes. But the Vandal penetration of Spain has shocked Orosius into observing that there are barbarians and barbarians; that some are savage destroyers, and others capable of defending and supporting civilization. If the Vandal was a wild beast, the Goth was a human being. Orosius began, doubtless, with a loyal distrust of Stilicho as a watchdog with wolf blood, who was sure to betray the Empire to his Vandal kindred. But he eventually looked to Visigothic leadership in Spain as the only force that could be trusted to counteract disorder. The admiration of Orosius for Athaulf, kinsman of Alaric, colors the whole political outlook of the *Histories*, where contemporary matters are dealt with. Athaulf had been assassinated at Saragossa in

415, the most eventful of those four years of the life of Orosius with which we are acquainted, and the memory of him was a vivid one in the mind of Orosius, as he was busy on his *Histories* the next year. Athaulf, or Adolphus, was a short, forceful man who as the close kinsman of Alaric, held together something of the chief's following after his death, and was eventually recognized as imperial representative in Aquitania and western Spain; he kept, however, in his household a creature called Attalus, whom he and Alaric had set up as Emperor, and whom Athaulf reserved for a favorable occasion to enthrone once more, should he judge that conditions required it. After some oscillation of policy, Athaulf seems to have served loyally under Honorius in Aquitania and Spain. He had captured during the siege of Rome, and later married, Placidia, sister of the Emperor, himself wearing the costume of a Roman dignitary during the nuptials. Orosius puts into his mouth a speech which lights up the principal issue of political and cultural history throughout the whole earlier part of the Middle Ages; which epitomizes the choice that confronted Clovis, Pepin of Heristal, Charlemagne, Rollo the Norman, and Rollo's kinsmen, William the Conqueror and Robert of Sicily. He had once, said Athaulf, hoped to replace the Roman Empire by Gothia, and to make his own name Ataulphus take the place of Augustus; but now he was convinced that only by Roman laws could the world be ruled; and he was resolved now to use Gothic power to support Roman laws. Here, at the very juncture when the power of Rome seemed cracking and crumbling, we perceive that deep sense of the permanence of Rome, of which the *Histories* much more than the *City of God* is the classical embodiment.

The speech of Athaulf seems to reveal the race-pride of the Teuton, who was conscious of possessing a distinct culture of his own, and who found it difficult, even bitter (as later in the case of Theodoric), to adopt the Latin culture. And yet it was just because the Goth, among Germans, was most conscious of a German culture worthy of preservation, that he was the first among Germans to sense its peril at the hands of the destructive Huns that pressed from the North. Other German tribes, it seemed, were content to be vassals to the Hun; but the Goths, facing the choice before them, elected to reënforce, even at the cost of subordination and assimilation, their own system by one of higher type, than to disintegrate it by amalgamation with a lower type. The Hun hegemony must have had its arguments as well as its pressures and compulsions, as may be seen in the account of Priscus, the historian who accompanied an embassage to the court of Attila and discussed civilization there with a runaway or captive Greek. The Goths, in seeking federation under the Empire, had made momentous cultural choice; they had given their voice to the proposition that civilization, slowly and painfully won, is not a thing to be lightly abandoned to follow the restless impulses of tribe or group contagion.

The *Völkerwanderung* had within it no inherent seminal constructive principle, no aspiration to progress in itself; at most, it was the uneasy tossing of a sluggard at dawn, to avoid the pricking of the sunlight. So far was it hopeful, that it was uneasy, and a movement, and therefore an energy, however blind and passive.

It was the heavy drive of this vague, resentful movement southward of the northern nomads, that compelled the frontier tribes of Germans to choose between civilization and a mass-movement of self-conscious barbarism that was gathering human material like an avalanche, preparing to overwhelm the objects of its dull hatred, the Empire and the Church.

It was nothing but the deadly logic of facts that had forced the Goths to decide; and having decided, they bent their energies to defend the Empire with a German heartiness, while with a German stubbornness they held to their own tribal interpretation of Christianity: Arianism. The history of the next four hundred years, until the defeat of the Lombards by Charlemagne, is the story of the Church's contest with the stubbornness of the Goth and the Lombard, willing to accept the Empire and its culture and yet reluctant to accept the Faith of the Empire and its obedience.

Thus, in the contemporary part of his *Histories*, especially in the seventh book, Orosius strikes a historical chord that is seen to vibrate throughout the Middle Ages — the subordination of race-impulse to cultural discipline, and the equally emphatic subordination of cultural interests to the Faith. The modern world has seen the reverse process — first a revolt of cultural interests against Faith, followed hard by a revolt of race-impulses against common culture as well as common Faith.

It is not surprising that the *Histories* of Orosius dominated the historiography of the Medieval period; it not only supplied the framework for a philosophy of history, but it contained some rudimentary inquiries in the direction of the history of institutions. Loyal to the Empire as Orosius is, ne has no illusions as to how empires come into being, as we discern at his first plunge into the beginning of history (as the classical world tended to reckon it) in the conquests of Ninus. By his attempts to subjugate the Scythians, hitherto a peaceful folk, Ninus had only made them bloodthirsty and predatory, so that ever since, invasions from the north were the recurrent nightmare of western Asia. Thus, the foundations of civilization had been laid in blood, booty and enslavement, as Orosius saw them: yet out of the forces of aggression and acquisition, the means of defense, of conservation and of security could be forged. The violence and the luxury and dissipation of Ninus and Semiramis were overruled by the interests of the inheritors of their Empire to keep and cultivate its wealth. Such were the beginnings of Babylon, the civilization between the two rivers. The hand of God so turns man's evil into

good that what had begun in violence and prodigal-
ity could be built up in relative safety, peace and
productiveness. Orosius' view of the nomad beyond
the pale of empire, like that of Herodotus, is not
unsympathetic; the Scythians are the "hardiest of
men, though they be the poorest "; they are, in their
restless ferocity, more sinned against than sinning,
for they must protect themselves against exploita-
tion and slavery. In contemplating the career of
Alexander, Orosius has a vivid sense of the contrast
between history as transmitted among the conquer-
ing race, and that which filters down among the
vanquished folk. The one is a story of triumph,
peace and plenty; the other a story of miseries and
humiliations, kept alive only by pity. Here is a
most pregnant critical hint of universal history,
worthy of the latest sociological school! The task
of relating the calamities of mankind has suddenly
brought the fifth-century scholar into company with
the statistician of occupational diseases and accidents, and of the mortality of infants. Orosius
clearly suggests that history is not merely the story
of wars and of rulers, but the story of the humble,
who are thankful for peace. In dealing with the
period of Rome's expansion and aggression, he
dwells on the significant controversy after the conquest of Scipio, between those who would destroy
Carthage for the sake of Rome's security, and those
who, fearing the moral effects of Rome's security,
would preserve Carthage as Rome's whetstone.
Noting briefly that the Romans decided finally to

sacrifice their whetstone, Carthage, to their desire for safety, the writer seems to check himself
on the verge of a caustic comment, by remarking
in effect that even a whetstone can turn the edge of
a knife if the pressure of the whetting is overdone.

The general plan of the work may be thus briefly
stated: A geographical sketch opens the history,
after the dedication in the beginning. The Mediterranean Sea is called "Mare Nostrum," and Asia,
Africa and Europe are the principal divisions. The
stretches of northeastern Europe and Siberia seem
unreckoned with. There is some detailed knowledge
of the East, as far as Ceylon. The knowledge of
Africa is mainly confined to the Berber and Lybian
coast-lands, Egypt and Abyssinia. There is some
knowledge of the British Isles, but the favorite
ocean-route thither is indicated by the statement
that Ireland is between Spain and Britain. Iceland
is called Thule.

After this sketch, and an outline of the beginnings of history based upon Latin abstract-transla-
tions or compendiums of Herodotus, Ctesias, or
authors that used them, Orosius plunges into Roman history, carrying it as far as the sack of Rome
by the Gauls, which in humiliation and devastation
he stresses as surpassingly more crushing than the
sack of Alaric. The Greek Empire is sketched from
Athens till the defeat of Pyrrhus, and then the
career of Carthage is sketched from its origin to its
destruction. Finally the Roman Empire is resumed
in connection with the coming of Christ and the

history of the Church. The narrative ends with the time of the Visigoth Vallia in 417. The style is sometimes terse to the point of obscurity, sometimes rhetorical and flowing. The influence of Virgil and Cicero have been observed, and of the two teachers of Orosius the style of Jerome seems to have left more trace. Polybius, Livy and Tacitus are used, but mostly at second hand in abstracts by writers like Florus and Eutropius. The Latin version of Trogus by Justin, and Suetonius, are much used. For Jewish and Christian history, besides the sacred sources, Plutarch and Eusebius are his aids. Of the chronological part of the work, mention has already been made.

The zealous orthodoxy of Orosius and his relation with St. Augustine would predispose toward a favorable reception of the work in the Church. In a council of seventy bishops at Rome in 494, Pope Gelasius I alluded to Orosius as " virum eruditissimum " and as having arranged a " most indispensable work against the calumnies of the pagans, woven together with admirable brevity."

The influence of Orosius stimulated the construction of the *Chronicon* of St. Isidore of Seville (560–636) and his *Historia de regibus Gothorum, Wandalorum et Suevorum,* which incorporated much of its material. St. Isidore also continued the *De viris illustribus* begun by St. Jerome and Gennadius. St. Gregory of Tours, too, fits his history of the Franks into the Orosian framework of a universal history. King Alfred's version for his Anglo-Saxon subjects supplemented the geography by accounts from the voyages of Wulstan and Othere about the Baltic regions. In the schools of the Carolingian renaissance, the *Histories* had an important place, and the parent book, the *De Civitate Dei*, was constantly the study of the Emperor himself, who strove to model his realm upon its conceptions.

Otto von Freising, in the Hohenstaufen period, constructs his *Chronicon* wholly on the Augustinian-Orosian framework of world-history, calling the work *De Duabus Civitatibus*. The title, also, of Guibert of Nogent's *Gesta Dei per Francos* is characteristically dominated by the providential conception of history as elaborated by the *Histories* and the *City of God*. Dante makes mention of Orosius seven times in his works.

The " Compendious History of Orosius " came to be the standard textbook for profane history, to such an extent that two hundred manuscripts survive. With the process of time the abbreviated title of the book took the indistinguishable form *Ormesta*, which is generally thought to be a corruption of the abbreviation of *Orosii misericorum mundi historia* to some such form as " Or. mis. m. Hist." Some few have thought the word was a corruption of the word *Orchestra*, meaning the stage of the world's drama, and referring to the geographical sketch with which the history opens.

One of the noblest works based on the Orosian tradition is Bossuet's *Discourse on Universal History*, in which, as Brunetière says, the great Bishop has without any innovation developed a philosophy which, by deductions and applications he had discovered to well-known laws, he has made peculiarly his own.

For the past thirty years, historiography's own account of itself, the " history of history," has been gathering an ever-increasing interest. There is a growing sense of need for synthesis, and a great weariness of those maxims that would keep the mind busy following processes in order to distract it from judging by principles. Just because the Patristic historiography represents synthesis, J. T. Shotwell, in his survey of historiography, gives an important place to Orosius, even while smiling at the mathematical time-schedule on which he arranges the rise and fall of empires. In writing his world-history, Orosius touched important questions in the history of institutions. The philosophy that conceives of successive providential dispensations sees human life under a social category, and advancing from stage to stage. Such philosophy as was implied in Herodotus, in his feelings after a universal history, could hardly render history under a universal concept, very attractive to the pagan mind, and it is not difficult to see why the ancients clung close to the history of the local community, much as they hugged the shores in their navigation. Life, according to Herodotus, was a cycle, carrying the fortunes of man, individually and in the aggregate, up and down, returning upon itself. Human dignity was possible only by a graceful and cool acceptance of an undignified fate, and a Stoic might enjoy a secret consolation in his own moral superiority to a senseless destiny. There were pagans, such as the followers of the Socratic school, who hoped that behind the veil was hidden a beneficent end; but such conceptions were found in poetry rather than in historiography; in the *Aeneid* rather than in Tacitus and Livy. Where the historians generalized, their view was nearer that of the satirist than of the epic poet, and they saw only the vanishing virtue of an elder and better time. But to the Christian Patristic historian the perspective was reversed, and looked forward, not backward. Behind was the Fall, and the slow struggle out of brutalization and enslavement; ahead was emancipation and the mastery of life's materials. The soul found greatness, not only in itself, but in its destiny, in its conscious and loyal coöperation with that destiny. And destiny was not a wheel, revolving drearily, but a developing growth, like a vineyard in which the Husbandman at times varies the cultural treatment at different stages of recovery or growth; like a march, a procession or pilgrimage, an Epic or Drama, with laws of unities and of varieties as well, with an inciting moment, a crescendo of tragic or epic interest, and a climax, with woven and complex rhythms and syncopations throughout, in which design is concealed as well as ultimately vindicated.

Such was the Patristic philosophy of history, and of the cultural story of mankind. All the more significant that, at a time which is stigmatized as a period of decline and decay, when men's minds seemed indeed to have lost their grip upon mundane interests and realities, when the crack of the strain upon ordered life was being heard — Orosius and his teachers should have taught Christendom to think of history in terms of progress. The very crudities and superficialities of the *Histories,* their obvious deficiencies in the spirit of accurate research, their contentment with predigested and second- and third-hand sources, their preoccupation with the forensic and apologetic interest — do not vitiate the essential value and importance of the Orosian contribution to historiography. Just because the gloomy barbarism of Priscillianism had been faced in Spain; just because the coarse anti-ascetic barbarisms of Vigilantius and Jovinian had been met by Jerome in Rome and Palestine; just because the sanguine and wasteful barbarism of Pelagius (a savage creed in spite of the Hellenic knowledge he had and of the Oriental sympathy he met) had been contested with all the concentrated power of St. Augustine's mature years; and just because the Empire was compelled to leave Britain ungarrisoned and Gaul and Spain overrun with Vandals and mushroom tyrants, in order to adjust itself to its internal racial task, and to realize in the West, that the civilization that had undertaken to protect the Church must ultimately find in the Church alone its permanent support — just because of the conjunction of all these elements of solution, crisis, defeat and victory in the early fifth century, Orosius was enabled to sound a clarion that literally echoed for a millennium: Civilization was a work of God utilizing yet overruling the passions of man, and must be protected in order to conserve and develop those human values and virtues of race-inheritance which sin has not destroyed, whether they be in a regenerate or unregenerate state; and the Church, the sphere of regenerate human nature, must be increasingly found to be the only stable support for civilization.

Such was the trumpet, not of optimism but of meliorism, that Orosius sounded throughout the darkness, the dawn and the new darkness of the centuries that followed.

More than a thousand years later, while William Shakespeare was composing one of his greatest tragedies, and was nearing the " climbing sorrow " of its piteous climax, the scene of which was on a lightning-swept heath, where raved a crownless and forsaken old king — it would seem as though in the ears of the poet, while in the imaginative energy of composition, there kept ringing the brave music of a song-fragment — a line whose sense had little to do with the theme, yet whose feeling harmonized with that of the tragedy. This line, which the poet actually put into the mouth of the companions of King Lear, seems to have been a snatch from some old song which kept alive those very exploits of Charlemagne's paladins which Cervantes had not long before taught Europe to laugh at in the tales of Orlando Furioso, even in the Spain of Orosius and his Visigoth heroes. Now this fragment of a ballad refrain was an echo of the many legends of that Frankish hero Roland, who lived four centuries after Orosius and seven centuries before Cervantes and Shakespeare; a hero commemorated all over Germany by curious carved pillars, and whose name sounded in all medieval romance from Castile to the Rhineland.

The haunting quality of this line was felt again, still three centuries after Shakespeare, by another poet, Browning, who wove around it the depiction of a dauntless heart, surrounded by an atmosphere of utter desolation, who, in spite of the dreary doom that awaited him, set his slug-horn to his lips and blew his blast of defiance and of faith:

Childe Rowland to the dark tower came.

Orosius was the " slug-horn " sounded by the Latin Fathers of the Church, just as the ramparted and bastioned gloom of the " dark ages " began to deepen. And if we might counter this line with another, to voice the inner conviction that inspired the first historical interpretation of human progress, we could not do better than to take it from the *Song of Roland* itself, as the minstrels and jongleurs used to sing it, as it was sung at that Battle of Hastings that decided the cultural history of an important nation:

Les paiens ont tort, les chrétiens ont droict!

BIBLIOGRAPHY

A. BIOGRAPHY

The principal sources for the life of Orosius are: for his nativity and early life — his own writings and a letter (mentioned by GAMS, *infra*) of Bishop Braulio of Satagossa to St. Fructuosus of Braga, cited from a Spanish collection of the letters of Braulio by FLOREZ-RISCO, vol. 30, p. 395 of *España Sagrada* (1775); a letter of Avitus, a co-priest of Orosius, mentioned in another connection, may also have a bearing on this; for the pilgrimages to Africa and Palestine — his own writings and those of St. Augustine and St. Jerome in which he is mentioned, or which concern the Oriental phase of the Pelagian controversy. The best text of Orosius' *Consultatio* is that in vol. xviii of *Corp. script. eccl. Lat.*, containing also works of Priscillian comparatively recently discovered, and edited by SCHEPPS; of his *Liber Apologeticus* and the *Histories*, the ZANGEMEISTER text in vol. v, *Ibid.* (Vienna, 1882). The letters of St. Augustine and St. Jerome that are most germane are in Migne, *Patrologia latina*, xxxiii, 720, 748, 752; xliv, 343; *ibid., St. Augustinus*, vol. 2, *caput* xliii. For the homeward journey, its interruption at Minorca, and matters relative to the relics of St. Stephen: The letter of the priest Avitus to Palchomius, Bishop of Braga (Migne, P. L., *S. Augustinus*, vol. 7, p. 805); the letter of Bishop Severus of Minorca (P. L., 41, pp. 821 ff.); the sequel of Orosius' sojourn there, is treated as legendary by Ramon Ruiz AMADO in *Cath. Encyc.*, vol. x, p. 332. Antonio ROIG, a native scholar, defended its authenticity in 1787. For reflections of fifth-century estimates or impressions of Orosius: The notice of Orosius in the continuation of St. Jerome's *De viribus illustribus* by Gennadius of Marseilles; also the praise of the learning and acumen of Orosius by Pope Gelasius in his catalogue of approved and condemned writings published to the synod of Rome, 494 (*Ep.*, xlii. See J. F. X. Murphy, *Cath. Ençyc.*, iv., art. *Gelasius;* Havercamp, p. xxviii; Bosworth, *infra*, p. 288).

Among secondary sources and discussions on the life of Orosius: Dalmasses y Roz (*Dissertacion historica por la Patria de Paulo Orosio etc.* Barcelona, 1702) represents extreme opinion in favor of the birth of Orosius in Tarragon "*y no Braga in Portugal*"; just as exclusively in favor of Braga, is Pius Bonifatius Gams in his *Kirchengeschichte von Spanien* (1864), II, (i) 398 ff.

The birthplace of Orosius is also discussed by Th. de Moerner (*infra*, 1844) and by Ebert (*infra*, 1889). Discussions on the biography of Orosius are also contained in J. Bosworth, *King Alfred's Anglo-Saxon Version of the Compendius History of the World by Orosius etc.* (London, 1859); in Gams (*op. cit.*, 1864); J. P. Kirsch, *Orosius* in *Cath. Encyc.*, xi, p. 322; and more recently in G. F. Browne, *King Alfred's Book* (New York, 1920).

B. GENERAL WORKS ON OROSIUS
AND HIS WRITINGS

On the historical works used by Orosius — Th. de Moerner: *De Orosii vita eiusque historiarum libris vii adversus paganos* (Berlin, 1844), — the first thorough treatment of Orosius with advantages of modern scholarship. Moerner's conclusions are debated by A. Ebert in *Allgemeine Geschichte d. Litt. des Mittelalters* (2d ed. Leipzig, 1889, I, 337–334) who differs from him on the time of the writing of the *Histories*. Karl Zangemeister also deals with the writings used by Orosius in the introduction to his text (*op. cit.*, 1882) and in his *Chorographie des Orosius* (Berlin, 1887) he treats the geographical prelude to the *Histories*. W. S. Teuffel: *Geschichte der roemischen Litteratur* (5th ed. Leipzig, 1890)

gives a comprehensive and condensed sketch of the chief
interests and questions connected with the study of Orosius. Philological aspects are treated by GRUBITZ: *Emen-
dationes Orosianae ex cod. Portensi aliusque fontibus
ductae* (Leipzig, 1836); G. Freih. v. BECK: *Diss. de Orosii font. et autoritate etc.* (Gotha, 1834); C. v. PAUCKER:
die Latinitaet des Orosius (Berlin, 1883); Karl PETSCH:
Zu Orosius in the *Neue Jahrbuch philol-pedag.*, cxlv
(1892), 219–24.

The relations of the *Histories* to German history are
dealt with especially by R. PALLMAN: *Geschichte der
Voelkerwanderung*, II, 435 ff. (Weimar, 1864); Karl
MUELLENHOFF: *Deutsche Alterthumskunde*, III, 228 ff
(Berlin, 1892); WATTENBACH: *Deutschlands Geschichts-
quellen*, 80 (6th ed., Stuttgart, 1893); C. J. H. HAYES:
*An Introduction to the Sources relating to the German
Invasions* (New York, 1909).

The most celebrated translation of Orosius is the paraphrase of the *Histories* by Alfred the Great, the more
recent texts of which are those by the *Early English Text
Society*, 1883, and by SWEET, (Oxford, 1885); G. F.
BROWNE (*op. cit.*, 1920) and J. BOSWORTH (*op. cit.*,
1859), contain texts, translations, and accounts of Orosius, his views and influences; also B. THORPE (Bohn
Library, London, 1859). A translation of Orosius is
planned for the series, *Records of Civilization*, edited by
SHOTWELL (New York, 1915 ff.) in connection with which
C. J. OGDEN is mentioned in PAETOW'S *Guide*, p.
341.

Of the 200 MSS. of the *Histories*, POTTHAST lists about
25 of the most important, at the Vatican, Paris, Chartres,
Boulogne, Montpellier, Valenciennes, St. Omer, Brussels,
Utrecht, Bourges, Breslau, Cologne, Florence, Milan and
elsewhere. POTTHAST mentions 23 printed publications
of the *Histories* from 1471 (SCHUZLER) to 1650 (VOR-
BURG); since then the most important have been HAVER-
CAMP (London, 1738, 1767, republished by Migne in PL.

with BIVARIUS' notes; reëdited with notes also by THORU-
NUS in 1857 and 1877).

The increase of interest in the " history of history "
has given a fresh importance to Orosius as the pioneer of
universal history. From Buedinger's article (*Ueber Dar-
stellungen der Allgemeinen Geschichte besonders des Mittelalters*) in 1862, to J. T. SHOTWELL'S *Introduction to
the History of History* (New York, 1922), there has
been repeated stress placed on the importance of
the Augustinian historical synthesis. Benedetto CROCE
clearly recognizes that in Augustine-Orosius for the first
time history is conceived in terms of progress. Actual
progress in historiography, however, seems to be measured by Eduard FUETER by distance from the providential view of history (CROCE: *Theory and History of
Historiography*, trans. by Douglas Ainslie, New York,
1921; FUETER: *Histoire de l'historiographie moderne*,
Paris, 1914). More discerning is Moritz RITTER, in his
Die christliche mittelalterliche Geschichte, in the *Historische Zeitschrift*, for 1911, embodied in *Die Entwicklung der Geschichtswissenschaft etc.* (Munich and Berlin,
1919).

ST. BEDE THE VENERABLE (672-735)

Rev. Francis S. Betten, S.J.
The John Carroll University, Cleveland

IN A.D. 596 the great nation of the Franks began to enter the fold of the Catholic Church. A little more than fifty years later we find St. Gregory of Tours busy writing that nation's history. When St. Gregory died in 594, the conversion of the Anglo-Saxons, the Teutonic invaders of Britain, was about to begin. In 597, St. Augustine, sent by Pope St. Gregory I, the Great, landed on the isle of Tanet in the kingdom of Kent. But the Christianization of the Anglo-Saxons was attended by much greater difficulties than had been that of the Franks. The Franks had practically only one ruler, and with his baptism by St. Remigius the work was almost done. Moreover, these new Christians simply joined the existing ecclesiastical units of Gaul. But the Anglo-Saxons had seven kingdoms and seven kings, and each ruler had to be won over individually. Nor could the neophytes join dioceses or parishes already formed; the very system of an ecclesiastical organization was to be created.

This process of conversion and organization took about eighty years. It was practically finished, when the subject of our biography, St. Bede the Venerable, was born, in 672. He was a native of the kingdom of Northumbria, and possibly his parents, certainly his grandparents, had been converted from paganism and baptized in an advanced age. When seven years old the child was entrusted to the abbot St. Benedict Biscop, who had just established the monastery of Wearmouth. To this abbey the founder later on added the monastery of Jarrow, and transferred there with a number of monks, also our young Bede. Both monasteries were considered as one, although St. Benedict Biscop put Jarrow under the special care of St. Ceolfrid. It was to this prudent and saintly superior that Bede owed his education. Of his boyhood we hear next to nothing. But Wearmouth-Jarrow must have been an abode not only of sanctity and religious regularity, but also of solid study, where the youthful inmates were schooled by expert masters in all the branches of secular as well as of sacred knowledge. When nineteen years old, St. Bede was ordained deacon. He became priest at thirty, then the canonical age.

There is little to tell about St. Bede's life beside his activity as a writer. He spent all his days — he died when sixty-two — within the precincts of his monastery. From one of his letters it appears that he visited King Wictred of Kent. Shortly before his death he traveled to York, no great distance from Jarrow, for a scientific conference with his pupil Egbert, the bishop of that city. It is also probable that he went to Lindisfarne, the famous monastery founded by St. Aidan, in order to gather material for his life of St. Cuthbert. These are the few interruptions of a life which may seem monotonous to us moderns, but which was not so to him. St. Bede was heart and soul a monk, penetrated with a firm conviction of the sublimity of these exercises to which he and his devoted brethren gave so considerable a part of their time.

He sums up his life in a few inimitable lines. Having been born on the territory of the monastery, "I was given at seven years of age to be educated by the most reverend Abbot Benedict, and afterwards by Ceolfrid; and spending all the remaining time of my life in that monastery, I wholly applied myself to the study of Scripture, and amidst the observance of regular discipline and the daily care of singing in the church, I always took delight in learning, teaching, and writing. . . . For the use of me and mine, I made it my business to compile out of the writings of the venerable Fathers, and to interpret and explain according to their meaning, the following pieces." Then he gives a list of the works he had finished when fifty-nine years of age. Four more years were granted to him, during which he faithfully continued the same manner of life and labor. Very early it seems he became popularly known as "the Venerable," but it is impossible to give a satisfactory account of the origin of this epithet.

Few lives have been spent so usefully for the Church and mankind as that of St. Bede. The productions of his indefatigable pen fill six volumes of Migne's *Latin Patrology*. He was an encyclopedic writer, that is, he tried to embrace all human knowledge as far as it had been developed down to his own time in the compass of his works. His chief attention was given to the Bible. His commentaries on the Book of Books make up something like four-fifths of his works. He also wrote much on secular matters. His writings on mathematical geography and the manner of reckoning the years, months and days, are numerous, though not extensive.

In all his writings he almost exclusively endeavored to garner the principal and most useful doctrine of the Fathers of the Church, as also of the great secular authors of classic antiquity. However, he follows his own original method in representing what he has judiciously gleaned from his authorities. As regards geography, he stands entirely upon the ground of Pliny and St. Isidore.

He is well acquainted with the sphericity of the earth, and with the way of interpreting the movements of the heavenly bodies as set forth by the Ptolemaic system. His booklets, *De Ratione Temporum* and *De Tempore*, owe their origin in large part to his desire to teach the correct way of reckoning the date of Easter, and incidentally to justify the Roman method which had dislodged the Celtic computation in the churches of Anglo-Saxon Britain.

His explanations of the Bible are composed of sentences and statements of the Fathers. These, however, he repeats only according to sense without reproducing them literally. Like all the other teachers of the monastic and cathedral schools of his country, he was extremely careful to put forth a truly correct Catholic doctrine. Hence he never deviates from the path trodden by the great men who had gone before him. It was the best thing to do, both for himself and for his countrymen. Their land had hardly been converted, and they were wise and humble enough to see that, novices as they were, they could not think of opening new vistas and starting original investigations in the field.

By these unassuming and yet laborious efforts, St. Bede like St. Isidore, though in a less degree, became one of the connecting links between ancient lore, secular as well as ecclesiastical, and medieval times. Later ages were right in looking back to him with gratitude, and in making extensive use of the treasures he had accumulated in his works.

Although we cannot here devote much time to the appreciation of his Biblical studies, we must duly emphasize the fact that his punctiliousness, far from detracting from his capacity as an historian, rather recommends him. He will show the same care and circumspection when he has to make historical statements. He will assert nothing without having proof of it. One of his smaller works in particular fills us with confidence in his historical methods. He had compiled an explanation of the Acts of the Apostles. But further study showed him that his comments could have been much better, had he paid more attention to the Greek text. So he issued a little volume in which he points to a number of texts in which either the Greek article, or the gender endings, or the more distinctive formation of the case endings of the Greek language, throw a clearer light upon the Latin text and show the meaning of the sacred writer more definitely. Similar remarks, referring to different Latin translations, are to be found here and there in other of his commentaries.

In his scientific books, too, while mainly endeavoring to put at the disposal of the reader the knowledge of former ages, he corrects, for instance, the misstatements of his Roman authorities concerning the ocean tides, of which they, living as they did on the Mediterranean Sea, could not have so clear an idea as one who knew from experience the proportions which the tides assume on the coasts of the British Isles.

St. Bede was essentially a textbook writer. He summarized, extracted, boiled down, or expanded, the information furnished him by the older authors, with an eye to making it more accessible and intelligible for his readers or rather students.[1] He could not omit grammar, Latin grammar of course, understanding the term in the wide sense it had at his time, as including the precepts of style in general. We have three books by him of this category: *De Orthographia,* a dictionary of correct Latin spelling; *De Tropis,* a treatise of metaphors and their use; and *De Arte Metrica,* on the art of poetry.

[1] St. Bede anticipated the advice given eleven hundred years later by Pope Leo XIII concerning history. "After the production of real learned books, which will necessarily be voluminous and clad in professional language, it remains to popularize their contents by issuing summaries and school books, and other publications which will appeal to a wider public."

But in the present paper we must devote our attention chiefly to St. Bede's historical works. Let us listen to his own enumeration of them:

A book on the life and passion of St. Felix I rendered in prose form from one existing in verse by Paulinus. A book on the life and passion of St. Anastasius which had been badly translated from the Greek into Latin, and still worse improved by some ignorant person, I corrected to the best of my knowledge as the sense required. I also composed, first in meter and then in prose, the life of the holy monk and Bishop Cuthbert. I wrote the history of the abbots of this our monastery, in which I rejoice to serve the Divine Goodness, namely, of Benedict (Biscop), Ceolfrid and Huetbert; and then the Ecclesiastical History of our Island and Nation, in five books, finally a Martyrology of the feast days of the holy martyrs, in which I tried with great care to set down not only on what day the various saints conquered the world, but also by what kind of combat and under what judge.

To this list drawn up by him in 731, we must add the remarkable letter to Egbert, written three or four years later, when the indefatigable author already suffered from the sickness which in 735 ended his most useful and saintly life.

As it appears, a large number of these works, though small in size, are biographical in character. His one strictly historical work is the *Historia Ecclesiastica Gentis Anglorum,* which, to use a business term, would make a dollar book. Concerning most of these works we must be satisfied with the description the venerable author gives of them in his own words. Anent his Martyrology, we may add, that, although based upon personal investigations, it no doubt also embodies the result of the labors of those who before his time had composed similar lists of Saints. Nevertheless, connoisseurs assure us that, as a whole, it was an original production. On account of its excellent qualities other authors took hold of it, and enlarged and altered it to such a degree, that nowadays it is impossible to tell which parts are Bede's and which are inserted by others. There is no doubt, however, that it exercised its influence upon similar works of the centuries that followed until under Pope Gregory XIII (1572–1585) the official Roman Martyrology was compiled by Cardinals Sirleto and Baronius.[2]

The work to which St. Bede chiefly owes his well-deserved fame as an historian is the *Church History of the Anglo-Saxons*. It begins with a description of the two great islands of the British archipelago, Britannia and Hibernia, and a few notes concerning their Celtic inhabitants. The southern part of Britannia, where the Britons lived, was subjugated by the Romans, became Christianized, and soon had its ecclesiastical hierarchy. At times this part of the Church was threatened by Pelagianism, Pelagius being a native of the country. But taken all in all, their doctrine remained uncontaminated. Then followed the terrible times of the invasions of the pagan Jutes, Angles, and Saxons, whose progress, though at times interrupted and retarded, continued

---

[2] Cf. *Kirchenlexicon*, s. v. *Acta Sanctorum.*

for a century and a half. There resulted the destruction or expulsion or enslavement of the natives, and the disappearance of Christianity in the whole eastern and central parts of the island where the barbarous invaders had settled. In 597 St. Augustine, sent by Pope St. Gregory I, the Great, began the Christianization of the Anglo-Saxons. The marriage of King Ethelbert of Kent with the Catholic princess Bertha of the Merovingian royal family of the Franks, seemed to offer an opportunity. Monastic life was to be a chief means for establishing the new religion, and the great Pope planned a hierarchy on almost the same lines on which it was eventually shaped long after his death.

St. Augustine had an interview with the bishops of the Christian Britons in the western section of the island, and tried both to gain their coöperation in his missionary work among the Anglo-Saxons, and bring them into closer union with the Roman Pontiff. The Britons flatly refused to do anything for the conversion of their hereditary foes, the Anglo-Saxons, nor would they recognize St. Augustine as the Holy Father's representative. It was a momentous decision. So far the barrier erected by the Anglo-Saxon kingdoms east of them, and the disturbances on the continent had isolated them, as it were, from the body of the Church. Now when the Church extended her hand to them, they made this isolation voluntary. On the continent the conversion of the Teutonic invaders by the old inhabitants had been completed, or at least auspiciously begun. The Britons preferred to persist in their national exclusiveness and narrow hatred of everything Anglo-Saxon. Even later on they made no difference between baptized and pagan Saxons, and their bishops refused to eat in the same house with Anglo-Saxon bishops. How different would have been the history of the next two centuries had they listened to the voice of Christian charity and to the invitation of the Supreme Shepherd at Rome.

The kingdom of Kent, however, became Catholic, and Christianity was successfully introduced in the neighboring realms. In 625 the marriage of King Edwin of Northumbria with the Kentish princess Eadberga opened the way for Christianity into the large northern kingdom. St. Paulinus, as first Bishop of York, baptized the royal family and a large number of the people. But the attack of the Christian King Cadwalla of the Britons, an ally of Penda, the pagan king of Mercia, besides causing great devastation and destruction of life, also induced very many of the newly baptized Christians to return to paganism. The result was a two years' interruption of the work of evangelizing, during which St. Paulinus with some of his companions returned to the South. But the new king of Northumbria, St. Oswald, who had made the acquaintance of the Irish monks of Iona, was no sooner firmly seated on the throne, than he requested the monks to send some of their number as missionaries to his kingdom. They sent St. Aidan as leader of a band of zealous men. St. Aidan founded an abbey on the

island of Lindisfarne, and made it a centre of new
and vigorous apostolic effort. In Northumbria they
completed the work of St. Paulinus which had been
partly destroyed by the two years of devastation
and confusion. The large kingdom of Mercia owes
its conversion entirely to them, and the same may
be said of East Anglia. The other kingdoms, too,
with the exception of Kent and Sussex, felt their
influence more or less strongly. St. Bede grows very
eloquent in sounding the praises of these missionaries, who made up for the hostile attitude of the
Britons.

It was very unfortunate that with these zealous
men an element of discord came into the new
Church. Cut off from actual communication with
Rome by the troubles of the Migration of Nations,
which upset all the conditions on the continent, and
by the barrier of pagan Saxon states, which rose on
the east and south of Britain, the Island Celts had
adhered to a reckoning of the date of Easter which
the whole Church had meanwhile abandoned. The
Catholic world, with Rome at the head, followed
another method. Southern Ireland had indeed
adopted this Roman Easter as early as 631. But the
north of the country as well as all the Irish missionaries in Scotland, headed by the great abbey at
Iona, retained the Celtic reckoning, and St. Aidan
and his companions and successors still adhered to
it. It happened consequently, that while those converted by the Roman and other continental missionaries were celebrating Easter, those converted by

the Irish were still in Lent, or the opposite. In 664 the king of Northumbria, Oswy, in whose own family the matter had become a burning question, had it discussed by learned men at Whitby, and decided that in his kingdom the Roman Easter was to be followed. His example drew with it all the other rulers and places of the Anglo-Saxon world, as far as a change was needed.

It was the only correct thing to do. It brought unity to the Anglo-Saxon Church, and prevented the confusion from assuming larger and still more threatening proportions. Although the difference was only of disciplinary character and did not touch dogma, nobody can tell to what consequences it might have led.

But the unity was dearly bought. For while the Anglo-Saxon clergy and many of the Irish submitted obediently to a clearly formulated and well-known regulation of Canon Law, Abbot-Bishop Colman of Lindisfarne, with a large number of his monks, refused to conform, and withdrew to the North, where at Iona the Celtic method was still kept up. With this the coming of Irish workers from those regions ceased.

This was a hard blow to the Church. St. Bede's feelings were evidently divided, when he wrote down the report of this event, which had taken place some nine years before his birth. On the one hand he whole-heartedly welcomed the achievement of complete Catholic unity and rejoiced over the victory of the Roman Easter, though he never lost his even historical temper. On the other hand, however, he greatly admired the virtue and ability of those who now left for good the country which was so deeply indebted to them, and he did not fail to give them a very sympathetic farewell.

Another outstanding event in the history of the Anglo-Saxon Church was the coming, in 669, only five years after the conference of Whitby, of St. Theodore, sent by Pope St. Vitalian. St. Theodore was the first real Archbishop of Canterbury (669–690). He ruled the new-born Church with kindness and firmness, visiting all its parts, assembling the bishops in canonical councils, circumscribing the dioceses more accurately, inaugurating and inspiring the establishment of new schools, and in every way giving new vigor to Christian life in all classes of the people. With the activity of St. Theodore the missionary period of the Anglo-Saxon Church came to an end. During his administration the kingdom of Sussex, the only one not yet converted, came into the fold by the efforts of the Northumbrian St. Wilfrid. True, not even at St. Theodore's death was every Anglo-Saxon actually baptized. But the country was now completely organized, and the conversion of each individual was only a question of time and would be accomplished through the agencies already established. Taken as a whole, the Anglo-Saxon Church was a full-fledged member of the Catholic world.

Although each of the five books of Bede's *Ecclesiastical History* treats of a great variety of sub-

jects, the prominent ecclesiastical fact in the first
book is the coming of St. Augustine; that of the
second book the appearance on the scene of the
Irish monks with the progress of Christianization
through the labors of both the Roman and the Irish
missionaries; the third book concludes with the
settling of the Easter question by the conference of
Whitby; the fourth is devoted to the work and times
of St. Theodore. When reading the fifth book one
feels that the age of storm and stress is over. The
author devotes much more space to the biographical
notes on the lives of saints as well as to the reports
of miraculous events. He recounts the efforts of
Anglo-Saxon missionaries in foreign countries.
Though always keeping to his strictly historical
style, the author cannot conceal the joy it gives him
to narrate the acceptance of the Roman Easter by
a great part of the clergy in northern Ireland, by
the Picts, by many of the Britons, and finally even
in the very citadel of Celtic usages, the island monastery of Iona.

To say a few words on St. Bede as an historian:
he evidently was a truly patriotic Anglo-Saxon, who
ardently loved his country and his nation. But this
never betrayed him into forgetting the historian's
duty of telling the truth, the whole truth and nothing but the truth. Where the progress of events demands it, he tells of the crimes of his countrymen,
as well as of their virtues. The Irish missionaries
he treats almost with distinction, and never omits
stating their direct or indirect influence upon the

interests of the Church. He distinguishes clearly between facts and rumors. The beautiful story of St.
Gregory and the Anglo-Saxon slaves in the Roman
market he expressly introduces as an opinion. In
his dedicatory letter to King Ceolwulf of Northumbria, who had with great interest watched the progress of the work, and even read what we should now
call the proof-sheets, the author, almost like a modern historian, gives an account of the sources on
which he had drawn. Concerning the times before
St. Augustine he followed, he says, other Christian
writers. He does not name them, but skilful com-
mentators have been able to trace nearly all his
statements, including the less important ones, to
ancient publications. The years after St. Augustine's
coming were not far removed from his own; those
were still living who had witnessed very many of
the facts embodied in his work. He says, however,
that he was careful in accepting oral testimony. He
drew largely on documents found in monasteries and
elsewhere. The monks of Lastingaeu furnished information as to the conversion of Mercia, and Abbot
Esi about the re-Christianization of East-Anglia;
Bishop St. Daniel about Wessex, the Isle of Wight,
and neighboring parts. But his most active helpers
were Abbot Albinus of Canterbury and one of his
monks, Nothelm, both of whom had been disciples
of Sts. Theodore and Hadrian. Both these men went
to great lengths to assist him. They not only inves-
tigated the archives of Canterbury and other places,
but continued their searches when in Rome. Once

Nothelm made the trip to Northumbria to bring to the writer in person documents and oral information. Concerning Northumbria, St. Bede was of course best situated. The archives gave him their treasures, the monks, the laity, the bishops and kings, communicated to him their knowledge of former days. The coöperation thus yielded to St. Bede, enabled him, among other things, to preserve for us so large a number of valuable papal and other documents, which but for him would have been lost long ago.

A very peculiar feature of St. Bede's *Ecclesiastical History* is the very large number of biographies of saints or saintly persons which are embodied in the text. They are introduced at some moment when these persons appear for the first time, or when they become more than ordinarily prominent, but chiefly when their death is reported. Sometimes they occupy but a few paragraphs, at other times they extend over several pages. Miracles play a rather extensive part in them, but this was according to the spirit and the views of the times. The author reports them only on good testimony, and although he styles them miracles, he evidently does not pretend to assert their truly supernatural character. He would be the last to object, if in a process of canonization some or even many of them were not accepted as genuine by the Roman Congregation of Rites. The insertion of these biographical notices is in accordance with his program. History, he tells us in the Introductory Letter, is to deter the reader from the bad and blameworthy of which he reads, and to stir him up to the zealous imitation of the good. Owing to these numerous lives of holy persons, the reading of St. Bede's history unfolds before us the picture of a country in which a truly Christian life was the rule. No doubt a nation, and so small a nation at that, which was able to produce such a galaxy of saintly men and women during so short a period has reason to feel proud. But on the other hand, the dark spots in the beautiful pictures are by no means glossed over or explained away, though the author never indulges in bloodcurdling descriptions of misdeeds. Only the edifying traits and facts enjoy the privilege of being represented *in extenso*. We see the kings, not only like Clovis the Frank, burn what they had adored and adore what they had burned, but no less than twenty-six kings and other personages of royal lineage exchange the pomp of the court for the poverty and menial labors of the cloister. The number of monks in many monasteries ran well up into the hundreds.

Thus, while strictly historical, as historical as the most honest efforts and the most painstaking labor could make it, the *Ecclesiastical History* is a genuine *Erbauungsbuch,* a book of religious edification and encouragement for the children of St. Bede's race and for all that peruse its pages.

To some perhaps the almost countless proper names which are scattered liberally through the whole narrative may seem bewildering. But besides testifying to the minuteness of the author's researches they were what many readers desired. These names were not unknown. They had been heard occasionally, some perhaps frequently. By putting them in the right setting, by showing the connection of these persons with the whole current of events and disclosing the causes and effects of their deeds and misdeeds, the author clarified confused ideas and joined together into a coherent system whatever fragmentary knowledge existed in the minds of his readers. It is by means of these names that the succession of bishops of various sees and the branching out of royal families can be reconstructed.

Next in merit after St. Bede's *Ecclesiastical History*, though only a pamphlet in size, is the *Vita Beatorum Benedicti, Ceolfridi, Eosterwini, Sigfridi, atque Hwaetberhti,* commonly referred to as the *History of the Abbots*. These were the first that ruled, though in different capacities, the twin monastery of Wearmouth-Jarrow, the place of the labors of St. Bede. Much of what he wrote in this booklet the author knew from personal observation, or by information obtained orally from older monks. But much is derived from smaller written sources which existed before him, though strange to say the author takes no pains even to refer to his sources. Probably all these particulars were too well known to the inmates of Wearmouth-Jarrow, for whom he wrote in the first place. One of these written sources is preserved to us, and was the work of an anony-

mous monk of the same monastery. At first sight it
may look somewhat similar, especially as it is also
known among historians as *History of the Abbots*.
But St. Bede proceeds along different lines.

As was already stated, the founder of the twin-
abbey was St. Benedict Biscop, who, however, for
a more efficient administration soon appointed St.
Ceolfrid Abbot of Jarrow, and a little later Eosterwin Abbot of Wearmouth, retaining all the time a
sort of superintendence of both institutions. Eosterwin died after four years, when St. Benedict happened to be absent on one of his six visits to Rome.
The monks of Wearmouth therefore, with the co-
operation of Abbot Ceolfrid of Jarrow, elected Sigfrid Abbot, which election Benedict cheerfully rati-
fied after his return. But both Sigfrid and Benedict
Biscop died some three years later, leaving Ceolfrid
Abbot of both monasteries. Benedict Biscop, the
founder, had ruled for sixteen years, and Ceolfrid
held the dignity after his death for thirty-five.
These are therefore the first two real abbots of the
institution; the makers of its greatness. Now the
anonymous writer of the older life makes it a biography of St. Ceolfrid, and brings in the lives of the
other three, including the founder, only briefly and
by way of further explanation. He calls his booklet
expressly *Vita Sanctissimi Ceolfridi Abbatis*.

St. Bede on the contrary begins with the life and
achievements of the founder, upon which he enlarges
greatly. Eosterwin and Sigfrid are naturally treated
much more briefly, but get their due share of con-

sideration and praise. Ceolfrid's position and long administration again requires more space. This manner of proceeding explains why St. Bede condenses the older life of Ceolfrid, and omits many of its details, although he brings in some items not mentioned by the anonymous writer. The result is a publication of modest size, all the parts of which are well proportioned, and which, for its literary qualities, and above all for its historical perfection, may deservedly be called a gem of historic literature. We wish indeed that St. Bede had told us more of the domestic life of the inmates of these two institutions. How grateful should we be for a simple description of their daily order, or of the celebration of some great ecclesiastical festival, or reception of new members. But those for whom the saintly author wrote in the first place, looked upon all this as ordinary; as something of which they needed not to be reminded. Unquestionably few monastic institutions of ancient date possess so authentic and attractive an account of their origin and the first decades of their existence, an account which is at the same time a precious contribution to the history and development of religious life in England and in the Church at large.

After all St. Bede wrote Church history. Secular events, it is true, are introduced extensively, yet always with the purpose of showing how they either furthered the progress or retarded the work of religion and piety. He dwells at great length upon the lives of the saints. The unedifying, while not omitted, is kept well in the background. The *Letter to St. Egbert,* Bishop of York, however, shows St. Bede from another side. This pious writer, this retired monk, had a keen eye for the evils of his time, and not only exposed them mercilessly, but also proposed means to counteract them. Though in the form of a letter and destined for one addressee, it is rightly numbered among St. Bede's historical writings. Egbert had been his disciple and St. Bede speaks to him with a freedom which only such a relation can excuse. The teacher first gives some private admonitions to his former pupil. Then he pictures in a language not free from indignation, several failings, and is evidently glad to have a chance of airing his mind on the subject. There were bishops, let us hope not many, who exacted the usual tribute from every place in their diocese, even from those remote villages which had not seen the bishop for many years, nay, which had not even a priest to instruct them. Some bishoprics were evidently too large, and should, with the help of the king, have been split into several dioceses. To provide the new episcopal sees with revenue, the bishops might be made abbots of some of the rich monasteries.

There were nobles who in order to avoid the tribute due the king, would establish sham monasteries and become abbots of them, without caring in the least for monastic life. Thus, adds the author with the foresight of a statesman, even the country's defensive power was being weakened, because these sham abbots were no longer bound to go to war, or furnish troops to the king.

Such language one is not accustomed to find in Bede's works. However, it is his swan song. He wrote this letter less than a year before his death.

Had he been in some highly responsible and influential position, he would no doubt have made his mark in the life of his Anglo-Saxon world, either in Church or State. But such dignities were not in the divine plan of his life. He loved to be praying and studying, teaching and writing. We can hardly doubt that as monk and scholar, teacher and writer, he has done more for the kingdoms of the Anglo-Saxons and for the Church at large than he could have achieved in any other position. What a gap would there be in ecclesiastical literature if we had no Bede. What services to the education of later centuries would have been omitted had the schools not possessed his works. We need not go into more remote centuries. St. Bede had been Egbert's instructor. St. Egbert in turn established at York a famous school of learning with a still more famous library. One of the fruits of this institution was the great Alcuin, friend, adviser, and practically minister of instruction, of Charlemagne, the man, who through the power and far-sightedness of his illustrious pupil became one of the most prominent influences in the literary and scientific life of the Middle Ages. Thus in a twofold way, namely through his books and his school, did St. Bede become one of the most influential men, not only in England, but on the Continent also, and as far as ecclesiastical learning extends over the globe.

It is not necessary to dwell on the eminent service St. Bede rendered to historical science by producing those excellent works which later writers, often unconsciously, have taken and are taking as their model; works from which they will ever derive encouragement in their vocation.

One point must not be left unmentioned, namely, his eminent service to chronology. The Christian era, that is, the counting of the years from the Birth of Christ, had been devised nearly two hundred years before his time. But its adoption was very slow. With the Roman missionaries, St. Augustine and his companions, it is supposed to have been introduced in Britain, and some instances are quoted, not without misgivings as to their genuineness, however, which would show that it was used by King Ethelbert of Kent as early as 605 and by others on later occasions during the seventh century. Whatever authority these instances may have, it is certain that St. Bede, when writing his *De Temporibus* and *De Temporum Ratione,* supposes this reckoning to be generally known among the Anglo-Saxons. But the fact that he employed it throughout in his *Ecclesiastical History* helped greatly to make its hold upon the nation still more secure. From his time on it was an established element in the dating of charters. On the Continent, however, it was not known, at any rate not practiced, at this time. But through the spread of St. Bede's books it gained admittance first in the Frankish Kingdom and Empire and thereby gradually came to be generally used. That his authority and example had a far-reaching influence on the spread of the " Christian Era " is unhesitatingly admitted by historians.

St. Bede writes an easy fluent Latin, which, with some few peculiarities, is a successful imitation of the language of the later classic period. His narrative runs on quietly, placidly, like a little brook, whose limpid waters hardly begin to foam when they run over the rocks. He simply relates the facts, and leaves it to the reader to feel and express the emotions which they may provoke.

St. Bede is not only the sole source of the history of the Anglo-Saxon lands, but he is also the organizer of this history. It was a difficult task to arrange in one continued narrative the many bits of information which were submitted to him concerning a subject which none as yet had attempted to embrace in one work. He had no predecessor in the field to point him the way; no one to furnish the outlines along which he could proceed. He had to draft the outlines himself. But he knew how to place himself upon a pinnacle so high that he was able to survey the whole of the Anglo-Saxon world; nay, his horizon was even wide enough to include also the principal events of the nations which surrounded that world and came into contact with it. The very fact that such a history was conceived and planned, throws favorable light upon the intellectuality of all the persons concerned, the author himself as well as those who suggested, encouraged, promoted and appreciated an enterprise of this kind. St. Bede's work is a monumental proof of the elevating effect Christianity had had upon the minds of the Anglo-Saxons.

His *Church History* is one of several works which profess to be histories of Germanic races. Two of these were produced in the sixth century. Cassiodorus, who died about 578 in Italy, wrote a *History of the Goths,* which unfortunately has come to us only in a rather inferior summary made by Jordanis. His contemporary, St. Gregory of Tours, who went to his reward seventeen years later, is the author of the ten books of the *History of the Franks.* This work perhaps was not without influence in encouraging Bede to resolve upon composing a history of his own Anglo-Saxons. But he surpasses St. Gregory in the succinctness of his plan. He does not begin like Gregory with the creation of the world, but with the land which was the scene of the events he was going to record; nor does he draw into the compass of his work any but those nations which were in immediate contact with his own. Critics moreover agree that he commands a more genuinely historical style and shows greater skill in handling his material. During St. Bede's later years there was born in Northern Italy the Lombard Paul Warnefried, afterwards called the Deacon, a Benedictine monk, more brilliantly gifted than Bede, but directing his attention more to the events of a secular nature. To him we owe a *History of the Lombards*. But he too interrupts his narrative by digressions into the history of other lands, especially that of the Franks.

Here again we should not omit noticing the effect of the Church's educational methods. Cassiodorus, the historian of the Ostrogoths, was no Goth himself, but the scion of an old Roman family. St. Gregory, the author of the *History of the Franks*, was no Frank, but a Gallo-Roman. These men lived in the sixth century. The seventh century passed, and the educational agencies of the Church, the bishops and the monks, kept faithfully at their task. The next national historians, St. Bede and Paul the Deacon, were sons of their own peoples, whose facts and fates they immortalized in their books. These nations had not sat in vain at the feet of their ecclesiastical teachers.

In thus concluding our brief study on St. Bede, the historian, let us offer our congratulations to the English nation, and in particular to the English Catholics, for possessing so excellent an account of the origin and growth of their Church and its organization, as also such precious notes even on their secular institutions. But we should extend our felicitations to the Church at large, and even beyond it to the whole of mankind. St. Bede has enriched Catholic literature by contributions, such as few others have been able to offer. Although his *Ecclesiastical History* does not command the popularity his other books enjoy, the large number of manuscripts of this history that have come down to our times, bears witness to the wide interest which it provoked in and out of England. His works form an essential part of historical lore, not only of the Catholic Church, but of the civilized world as well. We can only wish, though in vain, that we possessed similar accounts of the beginnings and vicissitudes of many other nations.

A word for us Americans. St. Bede wrote his history of the Anglo-Saxon Church before it was too late; before all the documents referring to these times had perished; before all those had died who could assist him by their word-of-mouth contributions. We of America are not much farther removed from the beginnings of the Catholic Church in this country than he was from those of his. We should now write our history. A good beginning has been made. But we need more than one Bede. Our country and our Church offer too great a variety of facts to be happily consolidated by any one man. God grant that St. Bede multiply himself in our midst.

We have the same wish for the Church at large and for all mankind. God grant that we find men like him working in all the parts of the wide field of history; men who produce books equally truthful, equally useful; men of whom is true what no less an historian than Theodore Mommsen said of St. Bede the Venerable: " He calls himself a *verax historicus,* a truth-loving historian, and he has a right to do so. Those who have followed him up will testify that few authors when representing facts have proceeded with the same degree of accurateness."

BIBLIOGRAPHY

A. BIOGRAPHY

There is no good medieval life of Bede. Apart from the two anonymous biographical accounts in the *Vita quorundam Anglo-Saxonum*, edited by J. A. GILES (London, 1854), there is no worthy attempt before the work of KARL WERNER, *Beda der Ehrwürdige und seine Zeit* (Vienna, 1875). This is the only serious life up to our time. RAWNSLEY, *The Venerable Bede* (Sunderland, 1903) is a superficial sketch. BROWNE, *The Venerable Bede: his Life and Writings* (New York, 1919), is written from the Anglican viewpoint and is not free from historical inaccuracy. Numerous sketches appear in various dictionaries, as for example, HUNT in the *Dictionary of National Biography*, and THURSTON in the *Catholic Encyclopedia*.

B. GENERAL WORKS ON BEDE AND HIS WRITINGS

The classic edition of Bede's works is that by CHARLES PLUMMER, *Venerabilis Baedae Historiam Ecclesiasticam Gentis Anglorum, Historiam, Epistolam ad Eggbertum, una cum Historia Abbatum Auctore Anonymo. Ad Fidem Codicum Manuscriptorum Denuo Recognovit, Commentario tam Critico quam Historico Instruxit Carolus Plummer, A.M., Colegii Corpiors Christi Socius et Capellanus Tomus Prior, Prolegomena et Textum Continens. Tomus Posterior, Commentarium et Indices Continens.* Oxford, Clarendon Press, 1896. This is an admirable work. The text has been reconstructed with an incredible amount of

patience and labor. The commentary and notes have
been composed with most loving care that does not forget
the smallest detail, and with that far-sightedness which
sees connections with numerous other literary productions. If anyone wishes to make a study on some detailed
topic of these works of Bede, let him first turn to Plummer. It will save him a great deal of useless trouble.
WERNER gives a thorough appreciation of all of St. Bede's
works. Cf. also *The Venerable Bede's Ecclesiastical History of England, also the Anglo-Saxon Chronicle* (London, 1900); F. RUHL, *Chronologie des Mittelalters und
der Neuzeit* (Berlin, 1897); REGINALD POOLE, *Medieval Reckonings of Time* (London, 1922); LINGARD, *The
Antiquities of the Anglo-Saxon Church* (London, 1848).

The best bibliography of Bede's works and commentaries thereon will be found in PLUMMER, *op. cit.*, Vol. I.

ORDERICUS VITALIS (1075–C. 1142)

CHARLES WENDELL DAVID, PH.D.
Bryn Mawr College, Bryn Mawr, Pa.

THERE are few historians of the twelfth century about whom and whose work we have such precise and satisfactory information as we possess concerning Ordericus Vitalis and his vast *Historia Ecclesiastica* and other writings. Although unmentioned by other writers of the Middle Ages, he has left on record more facts concerning himself than many of his contemporaries have done. We know much of the school in which he was trained, the monastery in which he lived and worked, the sources of information which he had at his disposal. There is no reason to suppose that any of his important works have been lost; and, what is more surprising, they have very largely survived in original autograph manuscripts. His handwriting, even, has been made the subject of special study, and has been extensively reproduced in facsimile. All his known writings are in print, and his historical works (which are the only ones of much importance) are available in editions which are in themselves monuments of erudition. There is, in fact, almost nothing which a fresh study can add to what is already known of the subject which has been assigned me in this symposium.

Ordericus Vitalis[1] was born on 16 February 1075, and was baptized on the following Easter eve (4 April) in the village of Atcham on the Severn a few miles below Shrewsbury. Ordric, the priest who administered the sacrament, acted also as godfather and gave to the child his own name. Ordericus had two brothers, both younger than himself. One of them, named Benedict, became a monk at Shrewsbury; the other, named Everard, apparently remained a layman. Of his maternal ancestry we know nothing, although it has been confidently asserted by a well-known modern writer, and it may be true, that his mother was an English woman.[2] His father, Odelerius of Orleans (son of a certain Constantius, of whom nothing is known), was a priest who had gone to England as chaplain and trusted adviser to Roger of Montgomery, Earl of Shrewsbury, one of the great barons of the Norman Conquest. Odelerius was a man of considerable distinction. His son describes him as a " sapient clerk," a man of talent, eloquence, and learning, and ascribes to him the chief credit for the foundation of the monastery of Saint Peter and Saint Paul at

[1] For all the facts concerning the life of Ordericus Vitalis, see Delisle's introduction to the *Historia Ecclesiastica*, i, pp. xxxii ff. The important autobiographical passages of the *Historia Ecclesiastica* are ii, pp. 220, 301–303, 311, 415–423, iv, pp. 272–273, v, pp. 133–137.

[2] E. A. Freeman, *History of the Norman Conquest*, 2nd ed., Oxford, 1870–76, iv, p. 494: " The French clerk had married an English wife and was the father of at least three English-born sons." This must be an inference from the fact that Ordericus Vitalis several times refers to himself as *Angligena* and that he maintained a certain loyalty to England throughout his life. English was apparently his native tongue. *Hist. Ecc.*, v, p. 135.

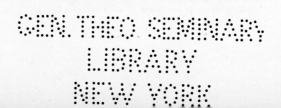

Shrewsbury. From his patron, Earl Roger, Odelerius had received an important estate outside the eastern gate of Shrewsbury, on which there was an ancient church of wood; and, while on a journey to Rome, he had taken a vow to replace this wooden structure with a more worthy edifice of stone. When he had returned to Shrewsbury and had actually begun the work, which must have far exceeded his limited resources, he succeeded in persuading Earl Roger, with the help of others, to take over the project; and so by coöperative effort the great Benedictine abbey of Shrewsbury arose. Odelerius gave to the enterprise not only his enthusiasm but practically all his worldly wealth. One of his sons, as already noted, was placed in the monastery; and after the death of Earl Roger, Odelerius himself entered the monastery and there ended his days.[3]

When Ordericus reached the age of five, he was sent by his father to school in Shrewsbury to a priest named Siward — "a noble and learned priest," he tells us — from whom he gained the rudiments of a liberal education, including a knowledge of psalms and hymns; and presently he began "the first service of his clerkship," presumably as a choir boy, in his father's church at Shrewsbury. Thus five years were passed, until, in 1085, he reached the turning point from which the whole future course of his life was to flow. Odelerius had decided that his eldest son should enter the monastic life, but, fearing the distractions of close family ties,

[3] He is probably the "Oilerius sacerdos" who figures among the early benefactors of Shrewsbury Abbey in the local foundation history. *Monasticon Anglicanum*, iii, pp. 518, 520.

he was unwilling that he should become a monk at Shrewsbury. In order that the renunciation on the part of both parent and child should be the more complete, Odelerius had determined to send him away to a far country; and so, providing him with thirty marks of silver for a gift to the society he was to enter, he committed him to a certain monk named Reginald, who conducted him over sea to the abbey of Saint-Évroul in the depths of the forest in Normandy. Father and son were never to meet again. Recalling the experience more than half a century later, Ordericus has described, in words which move us still, the painful parting scene — the tearful but determined father, the weeping but obedient child, who dared not oppose a father's wishes, the tearful relatives and friends.

Arrived in Normandy, " like Joseph in Egypt " Ordericus heard a language which he knew not. Yet by the grace of God he met with a most cordial reception at the hands of the strangers who were soon to regard him as one of themselves. He was given the tonsure according to clerical rite and received into the monastic life at Saint-Évroul by Abbot Mainer on Sunday, 21 September 1085; and next day, since " Ordric," his English name, sounded harsh in the ears of the Normans, they changed it to " Vitalis," the name of one of the companions of Saint Mauritius whose martyrdom they were then commemorating.[4]

---

[4] The exact dates of these events are really not certain. Ordericus Vitalis seems to speak of his reception, tonsure, and renaming as if they all came together on Sunday, 21 September; but Saint Mauritius' day is 22 September. I have ventured to

The rest of the life of Ordericus Vitalis was spent
in the profound calm of religious devotion and
scholarly labor which only the monastic life made
possible in that age of feudal violence, and there
are but few more facts to record about him. He
was ordained subdeacon by Gilbert, bishop of Li-
sieux, on 15 March 1091, deacon by Serlo, bishop
of Séez, on 26 March 1093, and finally priest by
Archbishop William of Rouen on 21 December
1107. This last event must have been one of the
most memorable of his career. He was ordered to
Rouen for the occasion by his abbot, Roger du Sap,
and there he joined with a company of some seven
hundred men, including an abbot elect of Fécamp,
who were simultaneously raised to one or another
rank of the priesthood. The pomp and circumstance
of the occasion moved him to commemorate it in
verse.

On some other occasions, also, we know that
Ordericus Vitalis was permitted to go beyond the
confines of his abbey. Twice, at least, he visited
England: once when he spent five weeks at Croyland abbey,[5] making an abridgment of an obscure
life of a little known saint; and again, when at
Worcester he was able to examine the universal
chronicle of Marianus Scotus in its continuation by

---

remove the inconsistency by supposing that the renaming took
place on Monday. By a slip Delisle has placed these events in
October instead of September. *Hist. Ecc.*, i, p. xxxiv.

[5] Croyland was then presided over by Geoffrey of Orleans, a
former monk of Saint-Évroul. Delisle supposes the date to have
been about 1115. *Hist. Ecc.*, i, p. xxxvi.

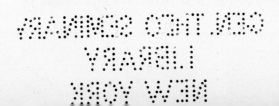

Florence and John of Worcester.[6] On another occasion he was at Cambray and saw in the abbey of
Saint-Sépulchre a copy of the chronicle of Sigebert
of Gemblours. He was probably present at the
Council of Rheims in October 1119;[7] and he certainly took part on 20 March 1132 in the great
gathering at Cluny of more than twelve hundred
monks of the Cluniac order with which his own
house of Saint-Évroul was affiliated. These were
not the only times when he went beyond the cloister,[8] but such occasions must have been few. The
life of Ordericus Vitalis was not spent upon the road
or at the courts of princes. It was for the most part
spent in the quiet seclusion of his abbey. It was
there that he received the major portion of his education, there that his talent was formed, and there
that he accomplished his prodigious work in the
service of history.

[6] *Hist. Ecc.*, ii, pp. 159–161. Ordericus Vitalis names John of
Worcester as the continuator and makes no mention of Florence.
Le Prévost (followed by Delisle) has proposed to correct him by
substituting Florence for John. This seems hardly necessary. The
work, which Ordericus describes in some detail, was clearly that of
Florence; but Florence died in 1118, and the work was there-
after carried on by John. If Ordericus visited Worcester after
1118, as he presumably did, it would not be unnatural for him
to refer to the work as John's. The work of John of Worcester
is now available in a satisfactory edition by J. R. H. Weaver (Oxford, 1908), who, however, seems not to know of this passage in
Ordericus Vitalis.

[7] This is the opinion of Le Prévost and Delisle, based on the
fullness and accuracy of the description which Ordericus Vitalis
has given of the council. *Hist. Ecc.*, i, p. xxxvi, iv, p. 372.

[8] He was in France in 1105. He was at Merlerault, in Normandy, on the occasion of a severe storm on 9 August 1134, and
next day he went to the nearby village of Planches in order to
observe at first hand the destruction wrought by the lightning.
Hist. Ecc., i, p. xxxvi.

The monastery of Saint-Évroul was in many respects an excellent school for the work which lay
before him. As a centre of intellectual life it did
not, of course, compare with the famous school
which Lanfranc and Anselm had created at Bec —
a monastery, says Ordericus, in which " almost all
the monks would seem to be philosophers, and fluent grammarians might profit from conversation
with even the most unlearned among them." [9] Yet
Saint-Évroul must certainly be counted among the
most important centres of civilization in Normandy
in the eleventh and twelfth centuries, and it is notable for the variety of intellectual interests which
it fostered. Theodoric, the first abbot after its re-
foundation in 1050, was a skilful and active copyist
of manuscripts. He brought with him from Jumièges
several disciples who were also skilled in the art of
writing. And he proceeded at once to establish at
Saint-Évroul a school of copyists, which, under the
fostering care of himself and later abbots, remained
active for many years, and enriched the abbey's
library with many precious volumes. Still other volumes were obtained elsewhere, and so the library
grew into a very substantial collection. We are so
fortunate as to possess a catalogue of this library,
which was drawn up about the middle of the twelfth
century, and shows us with some certainty the books
which Ordericus Vitalis and his fellow workers had
regularly at their disposal. It was such a library as
we should expect. It was mainly filled with liturgi-

[9] *Hist. Ecc.*, ii, p. 246.

cal works which were needed in the services, the Holy Scriptures and commentaries thereon, writings of the fathers, and lives of the saints. It was practically devoid of the classical literatures of Greece and Rome. There were a number of history books, such as those of Eusebius and Orosius, Bede and Paul the Deacon. There was a book of Hippocrates and there were volumes of Isidore of Seville *On Synonyms* and *On the Nature of Things*. The literary achievements of the monks of Saint-Évroul were considerable, as Delisle has shown, though no one else produced a work in any way comparable with that of Ordericus Vitalis. The art of music was also much cultivated, as the numerous references to it by Ordericus testify. One of the monks of Saint-Évroul was a competent architect, who supervised the building of a new church for the community. Another was a master of the difficult art of ornamenting precious books with gold and silver and precious stones. Still others were skilled in the art of illumination. And one of the abbots, Osbern, combined with remarkable literary gifts a talent for sculpture and perhaps also for work in metal. Finally, Saint-Évroul was in some degree a centre of interest in medicine. As noted above, the library contained a book of Hippocrates, and two notable physicians were numbered among the monks.[10]

Ordericus Vitalis made good use of the opportunities which his life at Saint-Évroul afforded. His fame as a historian has overshadowed his other

[10] For the intellectual life of Saint-Évroul, its library, etc., see Delisle's introduction in *Hist. Ecc.*, i, pp. iii ff.

achievements, but it must not be forgotten that he was a skilful copyist of manuscript as well as something of a poet, and, if I am not mistaken, he was also something of a musician.

The interest which Ordericus Vitalis took in the copying of manuscripts is proved by the full and precise information which he gives us concerning the school of copyists at Saint-Évroul and the work of copying which was carried on there. It is also well illustrated by the evident relish with which he records a favorite story which Abbot Theodoric used to tell when he wished to stimulate the industry of young novices in the art of writing. It is the story of a monk who in his lifetime had been guilty of many transgressions but who had copied a great volume of the Scriptures and who at the final judgment was spared because it was found on examination that the number of letters in the volume which he had written exceeded by one the number of his sins.[11] But we do not have to depend upon such evidence as this for proof of the interest which Ordericus took in the art of the copyist. A considerable number of manuscripts written in his own hand has come down to us. These include three of the four volumes of the manuscript of the *Historia Ecclesiastica* and manuscripts of his other historical work and of some of his poems, as well as manuscripts of a number of works of which he was only the copyist, not the author.[12] Taken together they

[11] *Hist. Ecc.*, ii, pp. 49–50.
[12] For extensive reproductions of these manuscripts in facsimile, see *Matériaux pour l'Édition de Guillaume de Jumièges*

compel us to recognize him as one of the most skilful and active copyists of his epoch. No one can
look at a page of his manuscript without admiration. The characters are, as a rule, large, clear, and
elegant. The writing is comparable with that of the
very best professional scribes; "and yet," says
Delisle, "it has a character which is always peculiar and, so to say, individual, a character which
makes it possible to distinguish it from the great
mass of the writing of the period; numerous traits
denote a hand which is steady and very experienced,
which has been trained to a rigorous and constant
system of letters and abbreviations, without arriving
at the banal uniformity of much of the writing of
the period, which makes it resemble something
printed from type." [13] In short, the personality of
Ordericus Vitalis is apparent even in his handwriting.

In some way, we know not how, Ordericus developed a taste for profane literature, and Delisle has
compiled a substantial list of pagan authors whom
he cites.[14] But he never allowed his poetical impulse
to tempt him into writing light verses in the pagan
manner. Those who have taken the trouble to read

---

préparée par Jules Lair, [Paris], 1910. The preface to this work,
by Léopold Delisle, was reprinted in *Bibliothèque de l'École des
Chartes*, lxxi (1910), pp. 481–526. The references *infra* are to the
reprint. For a description of the hand and of the autograph
manuscripts of Ordericus Vitalis, see the foregoing preface, *Bibl.
de l'Éc. des Chartes*, lxxi, pp. 481, 506. Cf. also Delisle, in *Annuaire-Bulletin de la Soc. de l'Hist. de France*, 1863, Part II, pp.
1–3, and in *Bibl. de l'Éc. des Chartes*, xxxiv, pp. 267–276.

[13] *Ibid.*, lxxi, p. 492.
[14] *Hist. Ecc.*, i, pp. xxxviii–xxxix.

the versified epitaphs which he has scattered through
the *Historia Ecclesiastica,* and of which he was
manifestly very proud, will not, I imagine, be inclined to admit that he had a poetical impulse in
his nature. But he was the author of a number of
other poetical compositions upon which our judgment may be more favorable. I do not insist upon
the merits of a lament upon the abasement and desolation of the church (*Conquestus de Abieccione
et Desolatione Sancte Dei Ecclesie*),[15] about the
authorship of which there is in fact some doubt,
although the manuscript is wholly in the hand of
Ordericus Vitalis and the sentiments are such as we
would expect him to express. Nor do I insist upon
the merits of another poem in similar vein which
begins

Mundi forma veterascit, evanescit gloria,[16]

about the authorship of which there can be no doubt.
The manuscript is wholly in the hand of Ordericus
Vitalis and bears the author's own corrections; and
Delisle has noted close parallels both in thought
and language between this poem and certain passages of the *Historia Ecclesiastica.* It is a violent
satire upon the evil days in which the author lived
and may well refer to the disorders which prevailed
in Normandy under the weak rule of Robert Curthose. Of a higher order are two other poems which
seem designed for use in religious worship and

[15] *Bibl. de l'Éc. des Chartes,* lxxi, pp. 505–506.
[16] *Annuaire-Bulletin de la Soc. de l'Hist. de France,* 1863,
Part II, pp. 3–7; cf. *Bibl. de l'Éc. des Chartes,* lxxi, pp. 497–499.

which in their deep religious feeling reveal our author at his best.[17] The first is a prayer, of which the opening stanza is as follows:

> *Summe pater, coeli rector, qui es sine tempore,*
> *Cui non est pietatis modus nec clementiae,*
> *Te personis celo trinum, unius substantiae.*

The second is a sort of litany in verse, which was pretty surely used in the service at Saint-Évroul, and which begins:

> *O Maria, gloriosa angelorum domina,*
> *Maria stella, vincens cuncta claritate sidera,*
> *Virgo pulchra, virgo casta, me clementer adiuva.*[18]

The three poems which have just been described, that is the satire, the prayer, and the litany, stand together in a single autograph manuscript; and the first three verses of the satire are accompanied by a musical notation, which raises an interesting question as to the knowledge of music which Ordericus Vitalis possessed. We cannot, of course, assume that he was the composer of the music here recorded, though it would be no matter for surprise if he were, for we have other evidence that he was well versed in the musical art. It will be recalled that his musical education had begun at Shrewsbury when he reached the age of five. Delisle has col-

---

[17] *Annuaire-Bulletin*, pp. 7–13; cf. *Bibl. de l'Éc. des Chartes*, lxxi, pp. 499–500.

[18] Still another poem, on Richard of Ilchester, abbot of Saint-Évroul, may be by Ordericus Vitalis, but the attribution is doubtful. It is published by Delisle in *Bibl. de l'Éc. des Chartes*, xxxiv, pp. 273–282; cf. *Hist. Ecc.*, i, p. xxvii.

lected the numerous passages in which he has described the progress of music at Saint-Évroul.[19] I
will quote from one of them: " The aforesaid monk
[Witmund] was an accomplished musician as well
as grammarian, of which he has left us evidence in
the antiphons and responses which he composed,
consisting of some delightful chants in the antiphonary and troper. He completed the history of the
life of Saint Évroul by adding nine antiphons and
three responses. He composed four antiphons to the
psalms at vespers, and added the three last for the
second nocturn, with the fourth, eighth, and twelfth
responses, and an antiphon at the canticles, and
produced a most beautiful antiphon for the canticle
at the gospel in the second vespers. The history of
the life of Saint Évroul had already been composed
by Arnulph, precentor of Chartres, a pupil of Bishop
Fulbert, at the request of Abbot Robert, for the
use of his monks, and it was first sung by two
young monks, Hubert and Ralph, sent for that purpose by the bishop of Chartres. Afterwards Reginald the Bald composed the response ' To the Glory
of God,' sung at vespers, with seven antiphons
which still appear in the service books of the monks
of Saint-Évroul. Roger du Sap, also, and other studious brethren produced, with pious devotion, several hymns having the same holy father for their
subject, and placed them in the library of the abbey
for the use of their successors." [20] It seems evident

[19] *Hist. Ecc.*, i, pp. xxviii–xxx.
[20] *Hist. Ecc.*, ii, pp. 95–96.

that the author of such a passage as this must have
been a well-informed and practiced musician, if he
was not himself an original composer.

All the other accomplishments of Ordericus Vitalis
are, of course, as nothing compared with his achievements as a historian. And here it is to be noted that,
whatever the other literary interests of the school in
which he was trained, there was at Saint-Évroul no
previous tradition of historical writing, and Ordericus had no local model to point the way and give
him inspiration.

His historical works consist of (1) a portion of
the meagre annals of Saint-Évroul,[21] which is unimportant and need not concern us further, (2) a
group of interpolations in the *Gesta Normannorum
Ducum* of William of Jumièges, and (3) the voluminous *Historia Ecclesiastica*, which has been well
described as " the *chef-d'oeuvre* of Norman historiography and the most important historical work
written in France in the twelfth century." [22]

It is only in recent years that it has become possible to speak with any certainty concerning the interpolations of Ordericus Vitalis in the *Gesta Normannorum Ducum* of William of Jumièges. It has
long been known that the work of William of Jumièges was several times revised and enlarged after
its author's death and that much of what passed for
his work in medieval manuscripts and modern edi-

---

[21] Published as an appendix in *Hist. Ecc.*, v, pp. 139–173. On
Ordericus' part in them see Delisle in *Bibl. de l'Éc. des Chartes*,
lxxi, p. 493.
[22] Haskins, *Normans in European History*, p. 180.

tions was really not his at all. In 1873 Léopold Delisle recognized the hand of Ordericus Vitalis in the
original manuscript of one of the most important of
these revisions and thereby proved him to be its
author. This manuscript was reproduced in facsimile
in 1910; [23] and the publication in 1914 of a definitive
edition of the *Gesta Normannorum Ducum*,[24] in all
its parts, has finally made it possible to see precisely
of what the work of Ordericus Vitalis consisted. As
was to be expected, he made no great changes in the
original text of William of Jumièges. He confined
himself almost wholly to interpolations, and these
are of slight importance throughout the earlier and
by far the greater portion of the work. They amount
to but four or five pages in the whole of the first six
books. But the seventh book is greatly enlarged, it
is in fact more than doubled, so that we have here
to deal with an important contribution to history.
As sources Ordericus undoubtedly used William of
Poitiers and the archives of Saint-Évroul and perhaps also some Norman family genealogies; but in
the main he depended upon information gathered
from oral report and tradition. Though there are
constant references to later events, the work really
closes with the Norman Conquest and cannot be
regarded as a contemporary authority. This, however, is not to condemn it as valueless. The author
was drawing upon living sources which were even

[23] *Matériaux pour l'édition de Guillaume de Jumièges préparée
par Jules Lair.*

[24] By Jean Marx on the basis of materials prepared by Jules
Lair.

then passing away; and he already reveals the same
insatiable curiosity about men and events, the same
desire for full and intimate knowledge which characterize his later work and which enabled him to
write the vivid narratives with which all readers
of the *Historia Ecclesiastica* are familiar. The work
is not without interest for the affairs of the great
world — for the Norman conquest of England and
the Norman exploits in southern Italy — but, for
the most part, it is a work of local history, concerned with the affairs of Saint-Évroul and with the
histories of great baronial families such as those of
Bellême, Géré, Toeny, and Grandmesnil. These last
make a record of private war and violence, not to
say of savagery, which would seem incredible, had
not our previous study of feudal society in the
eleventh century prepared us to believe that it is
essentially reliable.[25] From internal evidence it is
possible to say that Ordericus Vitalis composed his
interpolations in the work of William of Jumièges
in, or not long before, 1109. They are therefore his
earliest historical work by more than a decade, and
they may very well have drawn the attention of his
superiors to his historical talent and caused them to
set him to work upon his *magnum opus*.[26]

It is difficult to describe in brief compass the vast
work which Ordericus Vitalis finally decided to call

[25] For a good example see *Interpolations d'Orderic Vital* in
William of Jumièges, *Gesta Normannorum Ducum*, pp. 161–163.
[26] For all that concerns the interpolations of Ordericus
Vitalis in William of Jumièges, see Marx's introduction to the
Gesta Normannorum Ducum.

the *Historia Ecclesiastica*. Begun in, or not long before, 1123, at the express command of Abbot Roger du Sap, it must have occupied his working time for almost a score of years, until old age and infirmity compelled him to lay down his task in 1141. At first, it would seem, his intention was to write no more than a history of his own monastery from the time of its restoration in 1050, but, as the work progressed, his plan changed; and what he finally produced may be described as a general history of the world from the beginning of the Christian era to his own day, written from a Norman, ecclesiastical, monastic, and modern viewpoint. So indefatigable was he in his search for knowledge that he found no time to recast and revise the work as a whole in view of his altered plan; and so it remains in its present form almost without a general plan. Indeed, it must be confessed that the author never had a very definite, clear-cut plan, and that plans seemed to him on the whole unimportant. What he did have was interests, and it is by understanding his interests that one can best comprehend the character of his work. Once he described his work as a history of " Norman deeds and events for the use of Normans," and again he described it as a modern history of Christendom (*modernos Christianorum eventus*); and he was evidently speaking the simple truth when he said: " I labor . . . to unfold simply and truthfully for the instruction of posterity events which I have seen happen in my own time or which have come to my knowledge as

happening in neighboring countries." What fascinated him was modern history, especially Norman
history — the men and deeds, especially of the Norman race, of his own age and of the recent and
related past. The more general portion of his work,
dealing with the distant past, is comparatively brief,
and was doubtless included as a concession to the
new taste for universal history which had sprung
up in his own generation. That he should have entitled his work an "Ecclesiastical History" is com-
prehensible only when one recalls the predominant
rôle which the church played in the life of the
Middle Ages.[27]

The thirteen books of the *Historia Ecclesiastica*
were not written in the order in which the author
finally arranged them. The researches of Léopold
Delisle have thrown a flood of light upon their
order and date of composition. Books III to VI and
VIII to X were produced one after the other in the
order named between about 1123 and 1136; and
apparently the scheme on which the author was then
working was completed by the addition of Book XI
in 1136, Book XII in 1137 or 1138, and Book XIII
in 1141, making a complete work in ten books. But
before Ordericus had completed this plan, he turned
aside from his main theme and composed in 1136
two books of more general scope on the whole of
the Christian era, and these, somewhat retouched
in 1141, he placed at the beginning of his work as
Books I and II. Book VII also formed no part of

[27] Cf. *Hist. Ecc.*, i, pp. 2–4, ii, 300–301, iii, p. 255.

his original scheme, but was composed and added after 1135. It resembles Books I and II in that it contains a long and almost valueless section of early history (dealing with the Carolingian and early Capetian monarchies), but the later portions deal with the more immediate past and are valuable.[28]

From the point of view of the modern researcher, the way in which Ordericus Vitalis used his sources must be reckoned one of his merits. I do not mean that he maintained a critical attitude towards his sources, for of course he did not. He often used legendary and apocryphal sources without a suspicion as to their character. But he is candid and conceals nothing. Very often, when he turns to a new subject, he frankly announces the source on which he proposes to draw. For example, at the beginning of his account of the First Crusade, he gives notice that its history has already been written by Fulcher of Chartres and by Baldric, Archbishop of Dol; and at the end he says: " Thus far I have followed the steps of the venerable Baldric in giving a true account of the noble army of Christ. . . . In many places I have quoted the very words used by that writer, not daring to alter his language, as I did not think I could improve it." [29] He does not always designate his sources in this specific manner, but his usual practice of following them closely has made it comparatively easy to discover them when he leaves

[28] For full details and references see Delisle in *Hist. Ecc.*, i, pp. xlvi–l.
[29] *Ibid.*, iii, pp. 622–623.

them unnamed. Delisle has compiled a list of his
sources which may be regarded as practically complete, but it is, unfortunately, too long to be included
here.[30] It has made it possible to discriminate with
ease between those parts of the *Historia Ecclesiatica*
which are derived and, therefore, as a rule, of small
value and those other and greater portions which
are original, or at least are based upon the author's
investigations among living men, and which give to
his work its great interest and importance.

It is to this portion of the *Historia Ecclesiastica,*
which was extracted not from books, but from the
author's own living age, that I would especially direct your attention. The abbey of Saint-Évroul was,
of course, an excellent centre for the gathering of
the information which Ordericus Vitalis required.
Its possessions were widely scattered in Normandy
and England. It had interests at the Norman and
English courts as well as at the papal curia. Some
of the monks had often to be abroad upon the
abbey's business, and they doubtless often returned
with much information which the historian could
turn to account. The community numbered among
its members men who were connected with great
families in Normandy, England, and southern Italy.
Often these were old men who had entered the
monastery to spend their declining years, and who
in their prime had played their part in the affairs of
the great world and knew much of past events.

[30] *Ibid.,* i, pp. lxiii–xciii.

Monks from Saint-Évroul had founded other monasteries in southern Italy, and frequent intercourse with these daughter houses kept the parent abbey in touch with that distant land of Norman enterprise. The abbey was also, of course, a frequent place of hospitality for merchants and pilgrims and other travelers from distant parts. Thus Ordericus Vitalis had much information at his disposal without going beyond the confines of his abbey,[31] and yet it must ever remain a matter for wonder that he was able to gather the vast mass of facts with which he has filled his volumes.

His handling of this mass of facts is sometimes highly perplexing, for, as the *Historia Ecclesiastica* as a whole is almost without a general plan, so its minor parts are often sadly in want of arrangement. The narrative is often interrupted by long and distracting digressions. Sometimes the same event is recorded twice in widely separate parts of the work. Sometimes a single series of events is recorded twice in such a way as to make it appear that there are two series of events in question, and the reader is left in doubt as to the real truth. Occasionally the difficulty is increased by egregious blunders in chronology. For the dates which Ordericus Vitalis gives, numerous and helpful as they are, are not infrequently erroneous, and they are not really dependable unless they can be checked from other sources.

[31] *Ibid.*, pp. xxxvii–xxxviii; Haskins, *Normans in European History*, pp. 181–182.

His literary style, too, is at times labored and pedantic and leaves much to be desired. Without any knowledge of Greek, he attempts on occasion the use of a Greek word with unfortunate and sometimes surprising results.[32] More often he uses classical Latin words in unreal and misleading senses to designate medieval institutions. In imitation of ancient historians he adorns his text with elaborate speeches of his own composition in direct discourse. The long-winded discourses of William the Conqueror and of Robert Guiscard, when they were both *in articulo mortis,* will be recalled by all readers.

But these blemishes, great as they are, are slight when compared with the great merits of Ordericus Vitalis as a historian. His Latin style, though sometimes affected, is usually clear, and it is often fine and flexible and full of charm. As a thinker he has not the philosophical grasp of his younger German contemporary, Otto of Freising, perhaps not of his English contemporary, William of Malmesbury. But no other historian of his time had his breadth of human interest or his zeal for full and detailed knowledge. All things modern and human interested him, whether the local affairs of his abbey or distant events in England, Italy, or the Orient, whether military, ecclesiastical, religious, or literary and artistic. Especially was he interested in people; and no other work of his time contains such a collection of portraits of both men and women. He was a fair

[32] Cf. Delisle in *Hist. Ecc.,* i, pp. xli–xliii.

judge of character, also, and he was not without insight into the meaning of events. He saw and comprehended the life of all classes. And he observed not externals merely, he had a keen eye for the intimate and personal. No other writer of his time is so rich in what is called local color. The affairs of the clergy and nobility naturally fill the centre of his picture, but he did not overlook the peasantry and he felt keenly for their sufferings in time of war.

With respect to the proper attitude of a historian towards the great issues of the day, he expressed his ideal when he said, " I shall relate the melancholy vicissitudes of the English and Normans without flattery, seeking no reward from either victors or vanquished." [33] In practice he was, as a rule, not able to rise quite to this high level. But such prejudices as he had were honest prejudices, openly held, and they need mislead no one. As a monk and a churchman, he had a strong interest in peace and orderly government. Feudal violence, the inevitable accompaniment of weak government, was the thing above all else to be dreaded. For this reason his sympathies were, for example, very strongly on the side of Henry I, as against Robert Curthose, and he probably does the latter less than justice. Again, he was thoroughly loyal to his own religious house and order and to the Benedictine rule as observed by his order. He had very little of the temper of an ascetic and he had a great fondness for ancient and

[33] *Hist. Ecc.*, ii, p. 161.

established ways. For this reason while he gives a fine account of the early history of the Cistercians, who had recently sprung into fame, he is content to express a formal admiration for them which does not conceal a certain prejudice against them. Innovations in dress or in the fashion of wearing the hair also shocked him, and his outbursts on these subjects are very well known. But on the whole he managed to maintain the tempered equanimity which ought to characterize the historian; and he succeeded in producing not only a marvelous record of events, but, in the words of his latest judge, " the most faithful and living picture which has reached us of the society of his age." [34]

It is a strange fact that the great work of Ordericus Vitalis was so little known and appreciated in the Middle Ages and that it was so long neglected in modern times. Ordericus, the historian, had no successor among the monks of Saint-Évroul, and his work, so to say, died with him. His precious volumes lay for centuries in the abbey library almost unnoticed. Apart from the original manuscript of some six-sevenths of the work in the author's own fine hand and a fortunate copy of the remainder and a copy of three other short fragments, we know of no manuscript of the *Historia Ecclesiastica* which is older than the fifteenth century.[35] The work is un-

[34] Haskins, *The Normans in European History*, p. 183.
[35] The manuscripts are described and dated by Delisle in *Hist. Ecc.*, i, pp. xciii–cix. See also *Bibl. de l'Éc. des Chartes*, xxxvii, pp. 491–494, lxxi, pp. 485 ff., and Delisle's introduction to *Chronique de Robert de Torigni*, i, pp. xix–xxii.

mentioned by any medieval author, and appears to
have been almost unknown to the Middle Ages.
Robert of Torigny was the only writer of the twelfth
century who made any extensive use of it, perhaps
he was the only writer of that period who used it
at all. He drew upon it for his continuations of the
Gesta Normannorum Ducum of William of Jumièges
and for his continuation of the universal chronicle
of Sigebert of Gemblours and also for his treatise on
monastic orders and the abbeys of Normandy. It
may be conjectured that he used it for all these purposes while he was still a monk of Bec, that is, before he became abbot of Mont-Saint-Michel in 1154.
The *Historia Ecclesiastica* was also used in the composition of an unimportant chronicle of Bec, which
is not yet available in any satisfactory edition, and
which is not independent of Robert of Torigny. It
was also used in the fourteenth century in the com-
pilation of an unimportant anonymous catalogue of
Norman and English bishops.[36]

The *Historia Ecclesiastica* began to be appreciated in the sixteenth century, and two unsuccessful
attempts were then made to publish it. But it remained for André Duchesne to produce the *editio
princeps* in 1619 as a part of his *Historiae Normannorum Scriptores*. Most of it was again published
... eighteenth century by the Benedictines of
Saint-Maur in their collection entitled *Recueil des*

[36] See Delisle in *Hist. Ecc.*, i, pp. lix–lx, and in *Chronique
de Robert de Torigni*, ii, pp. xiii–xvi, and i, pp. xix–xxii, liv;
and Marx in Wm. of Jumièges, *Gesta Normannorum Ducum*, pp.
xxvii–xxix.

Historiens des Gaules et de la France.[37] But a really satisfactory edition was still wanting until in the middle of the nineteenth century the monumental edition of the *Société de l'Histoire de France* was produced by the combined efforts of Auguste Le Prévost and Léopold Delisle [38] — a work which in its text, notes, introduction, and index represents very nearly the perfection of modern scholarship and makes the reader forget almost all the shortcomings of Ordericus Vitalis.

BIBLIOGRAPHY

A. WRITINGS

Historia Ecclesiastica, ed. Auguste Le Prévost and Léopold Delisle, for the Société de l'Histoire de France, 5 volumes, Paris, 1838–55. This supersedes all previous editions.

Annales Uticenses, of which Ordericus Vitalis was in part the author, published as an appendix in *Historia Ecclesiastica,* ed. Le Prévost and Delisle, v. pp. 139–173.

Interpolations in the *Gesta Normannorum Ducum* of William of Jumièges, ed. Jean Marx, Paris and Rouen, 1914, pp. 151–198.

Three poems without title, published by Léopold Delisle in *Annuaire-Bulletin* of the Société de l'Histoire de France, 1863, Part II, pp. 1–13. The first two were previously printed by Edélestand du Méril, *Poésies Populaires Latines du Moyen Age,* Paris, 1847, pp. 102–107.

A poem entitled *Conquestus de Abieccione et Desolatione Sancte Dei Ecclesie,* published by Léopold Delisle in *Bibliothèque de l'École des Chartes,* LXXI, pp. 505–506.

A poem on Richard of Ilchester, abbot of Saint-Évroul, published by Delisle, *ibid.*, XXXIV, pp. 276–282. Doubtfully attributed to Ordericus Vitalis.

B. TRANSLATIONS OF THE HISTORIA ECCLESIASTICA

Into French by L. F. DuBois, in Guizot's *Collection des Mémoires relatifs à l'Histoire de France*, XXV–XXVIII, Paris, 1825–27. Based on the edition of Duchesne with some comparison with the original manuscript.

Into English by Thos. Forester, *The Ecclesiastical History of England and Normandy*, 4 vols., London, 1853–56. Based on the edition of Le Prévost and Delisle, but a poor translation.

C. BIOGRAPHY AND COMMENTARIES

The following works by Léopold Delisle are of fundamental importance, and the foregoing paper is very largely based upon them: " Notice sur Orderic Vital," in *Historia Ecclesiastica*, I, pp. i–cvi (1855), reprinted with a " note additionnelle " by the Société Historique et Archéologique de l'Orne, *Orderic Vital et l'Abbaye de Saint-Évroul* (Alençon, 1912), pp. 1–78; " Vers Attribués à Orderic Vital," in *Annuaire-Bulletin* of the Société de l'Histoire de France, 1863, Part II, p. 1–13; " Lettre à M. Jules Lair sur un Exemplaire de Guillaume de Jumièges copié par Orderic Vital," in *Bibliothèque de l'École des Chartes*, XXXIV (1873), pp. 267–282; preface to *Matériaux pour l'Édition de Guillaume de Jumièges préparée par Jules Lair* (Paris, 1910), reprinted in *Bibliothèque de l'École des Chartes*, LXXI, pp. 481–526. Also important is the introduction to the edition by Jean Marx of the *Gesta Normannorum Ducum* of William of Jumièges (Paris and Rouen, 1914). See also F. P. G. Guizot, " Notice sur Orderic Vital," in Vol.

I of DuBois' translation (*supra*), pp. i–xiii; T. D. Hardy, *Descriptive Catalogue of Materials relating to the History of Great Britain and Ireland* (London, 1865), II, pp. 217–223; R. W. Church, *Saint Anselm* (London, 1870), Ch. VI; E. A. Freeman, *History of the Norman Conquest* (2nd ed., Oxford, 1870–76), IV, pp. 494 ff.; Jules Tessier, *De Orderico Vitali* (Poitiers, 1872); *Fêtes de Saint-Évroul: Comte-Rendu et Discours* (the inauguration of a monument to Ordericus Vitalis, 27 August 1912), in *Bulletin* of the Société Historique et Archéologique de l'Orne, XXXI, pp. 476–566; C. H. Haskins, *The Normans in European History* (Boston and New York, 1915), pp. 180–183.

LAS CASAS (c. 1474–1566)

FRANCIS J. TSCHAN, PH.D.
Pennsylvania State College

FEW men that were prominently identified with the Spanish conquest of the New World are as esteemed as Las Casas. His personality as well as the principles for which he stood and fought command the admiration of men who can see little if any good in the makers of early Latin American history. "The painful narrative" of Spanish relations with the Indians, declares Mr. George Ellis in the essay which he contributed to Justin Winsor's *Narrative and Critical History of America,* " is to be relieved by a tribute of admiration and reverential homage to a saintly man of signal virtues and heroic services, one of the grandest and most august characters in the world's history. . . . Truly was he a remarkable and conspicuous personage, — unique, as rather the anomaly than the product of his age and land, his race and fellowship. His character impresses us alike by its loveliness and its ruggedness, its tenderness and its vigor, its melting sympathies and its robust energies. His mental and moral endowments were of the strongest and the richest, and his spiritual insight and fervor well-nigh etherealized him. His gifts and abilities gave him a rich versatility in capacity and resource. He

was immensely in advance of his age, so as to be
actually in antagonism with it. He was free alike
from its prejudices, its limitations, and many of its
superstitions, as well as from its barbarities. He
was single-hearted, courageous, fervent, and persistent, bold and daring as a venturesome voyager
over new seas and mysterious depths of virgin wilderness, missionary, scholar, theologian, acute logi-
cian, historian, curious observer of Nature, the peer
of St. Paul in wisdom and zeal." He was " the only
Spaniard who stands out luminously, in the heroism
and glory of true sanctity, amid these gory scenes,
himself a true soldier of Christ."

More temperate is the estimate of Las Casas
which A. F. Bandelier, the well-known archae-
ologist, contributed to the *Catholic Encyclopedia*.
"In his active sympathy for the American aborigines Las Casas had not stood alone. He had on his
side, in principle, the sovereigns and the most influential men and women in Spain. He was sincerely
admired for his absolute devotion to the cause of
humanity, his untiring activity and zeal. He stood
out among the men of his day as an exceptionally
noble personality. But the more perspicacious
among his admirers saw, also, that he was eminently
unpractical, and, while they supported within reason,
they could not approve the extremes which he per-
emptorily demanded. His very popularity spoiled
his character. . . . Everywhere he found abuses,
and everywhere painted them in the blackest colors,
making no allowances for local conditions or for the

dark side of the Indian character. . . . He addressed to the King a memorial, couched in violent terms, on Peruvian affairs, of which he had not the least personal knowledge. . . . By no means thoroughly acquainted with the character of his Indian wards, he idealized them, but never took time to study them. . . . Neither was he in any exact sense a missionary or a teacher . . . the life of constant personal sacrifice among the aborigines was not to his taste. . . . He did almost nothing to educate the Indians. The name, Apostle of the Indies, which has been given him, was not deserved; whereas there were men opposed to his views who richly merited it, but who had neither the gifts nor the inclination for that noisy propaganda in which Las Casas was so eminently successful."

I

Interesting as a review of the life of Las Casas, and inviting as a study of the merits of the estimates we have cited, might be, we shall not undertake to present either of them directly. The life of Las Casas has been many times written, and his writings many times discussed, both so thoroughly and so critically that now he who runs may read. Our concern may more profitably be about the question: Is Las Casas the father of American historiography? We might limit our question to this — is he the father of Spanish American historiography, but for the fact that we like to think of

America as a whole and not piecemeal; that is, of an English America that became our country and the dominions north of us, of a Spanish America that was shattered into over a dozen fragments when Spain was forced to withdraw from the regions south of us, and of a Portuguese America that became Brazil. The rise and evolution of historical writing in all these Americas was conditioned by factors that are analogous, if not identical. The Old World lingered long in the New. The traditions, the ideas, the attitudes — all that is comprehended by the term culture — of the parent peoples came to the Americas with the colonists and were modified, in some regions more quickly and more thoroughly than in others, by the new environment. The study of the development of one section throws light on the study of the evolution of the others. In the twentieth century Canada may profitably consider how we solved problems that met us in the nineteenth century and even in the eighteenth. The historian of Argentina can see the reasons for our sectional strife, even the causes of our financial crises, repeated in the story of his country. There is, then, no good reason why we should not let our question stand as it is: Is Las Casas the father of American historiography?

II

Our answer to this question depends, however, on the answer which we give to another — When may a country that traces its origin to colonies planted by a state, the inhabitants of which had already attained a high cultural level at the time the colonies were settled, be said to have an historiography that is indisputably its own? What criterion, or criteria have we by which we may say that this cultural activity or that institution is essentially American and not European? The solidarity of our modern world makes compounds of all our works and increases the difficulty of our search for distinguishing criteria.

Sometimes the line between that which is European and that which is American seems very plainly drawn. Politically, for example, the distinction is apparently very clearly marked. The colonies rebel. Their rebellion is so far successful that one or more states possessing independent standing in the estimation of civilized nations recognize the independence of the colonies and, perhaps, even aid them in forcing the metropolitan or mother country to accord them like recognition. The year 1778, in which France recognized our independence, or the year 1783, in which England reluctantly consented to regard us as a sovereign and independent congeries of states, might dispute the claim of the year 1776, to being our natal year. These years, however, fix in time our formal, not our actual independence. Ultimately our revolution came because we had developed a political philosophy which was incompatible with that of England. We desired to regulate our governmental agencies according to principles that were not acceptable to England. One of the principles, in some respects the most fundamental, was that of sovereignty within spheres. We held that though the English King and Parliament were supreme in matters of internal, of imperial concern, our legislatures were supreme in matters of external, of colonial concern. To Englishmen this doctrine seemed an abuse of their cherished ideas of sovereignty. We had developed a political philosophy which was heretical in their estimation. As a matter of fact we had made a real contribution to the political thought of mankind. This contribution was, moreover, characteristic of ourselves. We had evolved it out of our environment and circumstances and, except in so far as we were indebted to English political thought for our basis, not out of the environment of England. We had, without doubt, reached the *creative* level of political intelligence. Whether our Revolution was successful or not, we had achieved real political independence. The compelling others to recognize our political majority was dependent on a multitude of other forces, some external, some internal, on which it is not essential to our thesis to dwell.

Sometimes colonial peoples have independence, so to speak, thrust upon them before they have reached this creative level of political intelligence. The interest of some power, for example, may demand their recognition as a sovereign state and may compel the metropolitan country to surrender its authority over them. Such a people are likely to have a stormy political future. Not having attained their political majority, they are likely to imitate too closely the successful political institutions of other peoples, and this imitating almost invariably calls for many adjustments each of them more or less costly and painful. Are we right, for example, in regarding the innumerable Latin American revolutions as disturbances caused by the lusting of ambitious and unscrupulous men for power or for loot? Are not these revolutions in reality so many efforts to adjust institutions to conditions that were not correctly appreciated in the beginning of the national existence of the Latin American peoples or that have arisen in the course of their national lives? One man's coat rarely fits another. It must be taken in here and let out there, and every change involves the trouble of taking off the garment and trying it on again.

Without straining for final exactness of statement, we may conclude that a declaration of independence of the mother country by the colonies, even the reification of that declaration does not clearly mark the real political independence of the colonies. Real political independence comes with the development of the ability of a colonial people, that is, the politically conscious part of that people, to think creatively in political matters in a manner that is characteristic of themselves. Seldom is the year of the real political majority of a people distinctly marked. With nations, as with individuals, the definitely recorded day on which they came into the world is far less important than that on which they first reasoned, independently of others, their own way to a conclusion on some cultural topic, whether or not that conclusion had been reached by some one else before they came to it.

III

The criterion of creative ability, which determines the political independence of a colonial people with greater finality than do the norms that are commonly accepted, determines also that people's artistic and intellectual independence. The creation of a new art or of a new philosophy, taking that term in its widest sense, presupposes the colonial people to have been so much affected by their New World environment that, notwithstanding their ancestry and cultural heritage, their emotional and intellectual being or soul has become different. Other factors, the consideration of which would lead us far afield, contribute to this difference in the cultural being of the colonial and the parent people. Among these factors we may count the bitterness which the colonists feel toward the metropolitan people in consequence of wrongs, real or fancied, that led, or may lead, them into rebellion. The production that manifests this new soul need not be a *magnum opus*. The earliest efforts of a people's art, indeed, often seem too trivial for the artists of later years to notice. Long before Grieg interpreted for us the soul of his northland home, his people had expressed themselves in their characteristic songs and dances. Long before MacDowell's compositions were hailed by critics as distinctively American, relatively obscure singers had given voice to the soul of this new land. *Pari passu* the first efforts of a colonial people to interpret old truths in new terms, characteristic of themselves, or to thrust forward the frontier of knowledge at the expense of the seemingly impenetrable wilderness of human ignorance and inexperience may be very modest. However trivial and however modest the early characteristic efforts of the colonial people in art or philosophy may be, these efforts constitute the achievement of their artistic or intellectual independence.

IV

In particularizing these observations with respect to historical studies, several distinctions must be made. In history two elements call for consideration — the literary and the scientific. We expect the historian to be able not only to carry on original investigations in his subject, but also to describe the process of his investigations and to state his conclusions in a pleasing manner. Few universities fail to demand of the writers of dissertations the ability to set forth their matter in a style that passes as good English, or that is at least appropriate to the subject on which they are writing. No university will, however, accept a dissertation, no matter how well written, that does not meet the scientific requirements expected for the degree to which the candidate is aspiring. The universities regard primarily the substance of the paper, and secondarily its form. The workaday world and people who are only literary in their tastes are likely to stress the form rather than the substance of an historical composition. This emphasis accounts, along with advertising, for the presence on so many bookshelves of such lucubrations as — to mention only the more notorious perennials — Lord's *Beacon Lights*, Ridpath's *History*, and Wells' *Outline*. Elegance of form and style may give a work about historical matter rank as a literary production, but, unless it also qualifies scientifically, not as an historical production. We shall not, then, in our groping for the beginnings of colonial historiography consider a work primal because its literary qualities mark it as being of the New World and not of the Old.

Our criterion finds application in the scientific element in history, the element that is essential, that makes history history and not necessarily literature. In this element there is an apparatus of research of which the historian, whose work would entitle him to primacy in the new historiography, must be master. Let it be conceded that this apparatus was not perfected in the days when the Spaniards and the Portuguese, and even when the English and the French, came to America. Still the sense that demands of the historian that he consult, if possible, eye-witnesses and evaluate what they say was not dormant. The days of the Spanish conquest were also the days of Lorenzo Valla and Nicolo Macchiavelli.

The apparatus of research, however, is in a sense only material. Skill and infinite patience in its use may win for one fame as a compiler. The analysis which this apparatus makes possible must be enlivened by that historical imagination, or insight which enables the historian properly to interpret the events and movements that are occurring in his presence or the accounts the worth of which he has evaluated.

This historical imagination has been defined by Thompson in his *Reference Studies* as " the faculty that enables the student to put himself in thought in the time and place about which he is reading." This imagination is the *sine qua non* of sound historical writing. In this element our criterion finds application.

Difficulties, however, at once arise. We assume at the outset that the father of the new historiography is one of the colonial people, one who, whether born in the Old World or in the New, has identified himself with the younger country and its population. Obviously an historian of the parent stock who writes the history of the colonies will have done only what is required of everyone of his craft if his work qualifies with respect to this historical imagination. With his work the historiography of the new people cannot be said to begin. The colonial historian, too, will not have done more than is expected of one in his profession if he writes in har-

mony with this historical imagination. If he be the
first to do so, however, he may be regarded as the
father of the new historiography. His work may be
on the history of his own people, or on that of some
other people. In either event he will have demon-
strated that the colonial people has attained the
creative level of historical intelligence.

His task will have been by no means easy of
execution if he write the story of his own people.
He must know intimately both the parent stock and
its offspring. The Old World does linger long in the
New, but there is a time when the Old begins to
fade from the New. That time is at the beginning
of the colonial era. The moment the colonists establish themselves in the New World they begin to
be different. They are then on the other side of the
ocean. They are then in a different environment.
They need to make adjustments of which the metropolitan people and their officials cannot reasonably be expected to comprehend the necessity. As a
matter of fact the mother country almost invariably
regarded the colonists as so many workers for its
advantage. Some of the English colonists were relatively free from this condition. Yet these colonists
had other difficulties which could not but make
them feel that in becoming colonists they had meas-
urably exchanged a state of economic mastery for
a state of economic dependence. From the foundation of the new states, then, their people are different. This difference is slight. In its slightness lies
the difficulty of the historian. Few men have ears

so keen as to be able to distinguish the tones between the half steps of the musical scale. The colonial historian may not be able to catch the quarter
tones by which his people vary from the accepted
pitches set by the parent voice. His scientific imagination, his ability to interpret his own people may
not be subtle enough to perceive the essential distinctions. His body may be in the colonies, but his
spirit is still in the motherland. His work, then,
belongs to the historiography of the metropolis. If,
however, our historian's scientific imagination be
colored by the environment of the New World, if
his work show that he has lived, or is living in the
New World, and has not been, or is not merely
dwelling therein, if he interpret his data in terms
of the culture of the New World, however crude
that culture may be, then may we say that in him
the colonial people have achieved independence in
the field of historical endeavor. Whether the ana-
lytical processes which entered into its making were
performed in Europe or in America matters not.
What does matter is the spirit of his synthesis. If
this spirit is of the colonies, their historiography
has begun.

V

In considering the claims of Las Casas to being
the father of American historiography, we could
reasonably invoke the rule that the honor can belong only to a colonist. Las Casas can hardly be
called a colonist. He did not identify himself with

the New World. What he might have done, if he
had been successful in his mission, obviously does
not matter. Let us, however, give him the benefit of
any doubt that may exist. Are the writings of Las
Casas of America or of Europe? Are they instinct
with the spirit of the New World, or are they animated by that of the Old? Sympathetic as we may
be with Las Casas, we cannot say that there is anything either in his career or in his writings that is
peculiarly suggestive of the New World.

Las Casas was a Spaniard who, like many spir-
ited Spaniards of his day, came to the New World.
His father had crossed the ocean with Columbus on
his second voyage and had brought back for his
son, then a law student at Salamanca, a young Indian slave, who, along with other natives that had
been carried to Spain, was liberated by the order
of the Queen, Isabella. Possibly this act gave the
young Las Casas inspiration for his career. When
he himself came to the Indies, in 1502, his training
in law stood him in good stead, for we find him
acting soon after his arrival as the adviser of Gov-
ernors Ovando and Velasquez. The first "gold
rush" of our history, greater than any Europe had
before experienced, was then taking place in the
Indies. The legally-minded — and at this time perhaps also religiously-minded — Las Casas was
caught in the whirl of events in which he lost his
bearings. All that he could see were the evils of the
times — and there were many of them — particularly the abuse which the natives suffered in con-

sequence of the cupidity of his countrymen. Other Spaniards in the Indies also commiserated the Indians, but there is record of none who more completely devoted himself to the cause of the relief and the saving of this unfortunate folk. Las Casas became a priest and so gained, as Bandelier states in his article in the *Catholic Encyclopedia,* two important points: almost complete freedom of speech and material independence. Of both advantages he made the fullest use.

He was never idle. Travels in America and voyages to Europe filled the years of his missionary life. In 1515 he was in Spain telling King Ferdinand of conditions in the colonies. His words did not fall on deaf ears, but Ferdinand died. Las Casas found, however, other helpers, among whom the most powerful was the famous Cardinal Ximines. In 1517 Las Casas went to Spain a second time to urge that men of family settle in the Indies and till the soil instead of demanding that work from the natives. Spaniards, however, were averse to going across seas to be husbandmen, and the project failed. Las Casas also joined those who advocated the exportation of negroes to the Indies to replace the Indians, and he begged for means to establish a model Indian settlement. Charles I, the new sovereign, assigned without delay an asiento to one of his court officials, and made ample provision for an Indian settlement which was to be located at Cumana in Venezuela. Negro slavery in America got such an impetus that, later in life, Las Casas much regretted his having advocated it. The settlement, unfortunately, failed through the fault of the Indians. Las Casas, however, plausibly laid the blame for the catastrophe on the Spanish adventurers. Nevertheless the failure of this project sorely tried his soul. He sought solace as one of the brethren of a quiet Dominican friary in Santo Domingo. For eight years he studied and meditated. Regaining his courage, he left this haven in 1530, and, there is some reason to believe, went to Spain. Presently we find him in Mexico and in Central America, where he stayed seven or eight years, not, however, without interrupting the period by another voyage to Spain in the interest of his cause. In 1539 he sailed for Spain again, this time in behalf of a plan for another Indian settlement from which all laymen were to be excluded. His hopes for its success were high, and he would, no doubt, have returned to America immediately after he had secured authority and means for the enterprise if he had not been detained by the Council of the Indies. That Council then had under consideration a body of laws which it hoped would better the government of the colonies and remedy the grossest evils in the Indian situation. This code, promulgated in 1542 and generally known as the " New Laws," made Las Casas the most unpopular man in the Indies. The colonists were not mistaken in their belief that it was in part at least the result of his agitation. Two years later, Las Casas, still in Spain, was consecrated Bishop of Chiapa. He did not aspire to episcopal honors. He accepted them only because he thought they would help him carry out his reform programme. He learned, however, that even bishops can be helpless. In vain did he issue a diocesan order that absolution be refused to men who held Indians in bondage contrary to the provisions of the " New Laws." In 1547 he went to Spain again, this time never to return. He died in Madrid in 1566.

VI

Las Casas' writings are as was his life. He was a man of one purpose; apparently he could not turn from this purpose even for a moment. His cause blurred his historical vision. His writings, voluminous as they are, are all on one theme. In the years that were filled with the long voyages between Spain and America, with tedious waitings for interviews with Spanish officials, lay and ecclesiastical, with endless conferences with these dignitaries about how his much desired reforms might be effected, either in general or in particular, or with respect to projects he had in mind or had begun, Las Casas found time to preach and to write. Bibliographers cannot agree on the number of his major writings. Sabin was of the opinion that thirteen tracts of his were still in manuscript, but Field reduced this number to five. In 1854 Stevens printed six papers from original manuscripts in his possession. Three of these papers are without doubt from Las Casas' pen. Nine tracts, known under the title of the first and most important, *Breuissima relacion de la destruycion de las Indias*, were printed in Seville in the years 1552–1553, and reprinted in 1646 under the general caption, *Las Obras*, etc., but with the original date, 1552–1553. The title of the first tract speaks for itself. The second tells of the cruelties which the Indians endured, as observed by a Spanish traveller. The ninth proves the right of the sovereigns of Castile and Leon to absolute supremacy in the Indies, and, therefore, their competence to execute the reforms which he proposed for the natives. The eighth lays down the principles on which his defense of the rights of the Indians are based. The third discusses twenty reasons why the natives ought not to be enslaved. The fourth and seventh deal with his confessional enforcement of the " New Laws " in the diocese of Chiapa. The fifth has to do with Las Casas' controversy with Sepulveda, the canonist who sought to lead him into the toils of the Inquisition on the score of statements he made in behalf of the Indians. The sixth gives reasons why the natives should be restored to freedom. There is also a tenth tract written in Latin and printed in Germany five years after Las Casas' death, that should very probably be credited to him.

Besides these tracts Las Casas also wrote a fiercely polemical defense of the lives and characters of the Indians, the *Apologética Historia de las Indias*, and *Historia de las Indias* in three volumes. The latter work he probably began in the Dominican convent in which he took refuge when the In-

dians foiled his efforts to establish a settlement for
them at Cumana. Some of his biographers, among
them Helps, think that he did not begin this work
until he returned to Spain for the last time. Be
that as it may, the book occupied him as late as
1561. He never finished it; and probably forecast-
ing the reception it would receive if it were printed,
he enjoined his brethren not to permit anyone to
make use of it within forty years of his death. His
wishes, however, were not respected. Herrera, appointed official historiographer by Philip II, copied
much of it into the *Historia General* which he published in 1601. Las Casas' *Historia* lay in manuscript until the Royal Academy of History at
Madrid issued it in five volumes in 1875–1876.
With the *Historia,* too, were printed parts of the
Apologética Historia.

The *Historia de las Indias* is Las Casas' *magnum
opus.* It is invaluable for the documents imbedded
in it, the originals of which have apparently been
lost forever. Much of what we know about Columbus and the early years of Spanish expansion in
America is derived from the *Historia.* Yet the work
has never been completely translated into English,
and it is not frequently seen in Spanish. It was long
the hope of the writer that the late Knights of
Columbus Historical Commission would undertake
the production of a critical edition of the *Historia,*
if not of all the extant writings, of Las Casas. The
work is valuable, too, because it is so highly auto-
biographic.

VII

The published writings of Las Casas were issued in Spain. This fact is due not merely to the accident that in his day publishing facilities in Spanish America were meagre or non-existent, but also to the conviction of Las Casas that he must reform the New World from the Old. From the first this was his plan; hence, his many visits to Spain. That his plan of campaign in behalf of Indian freedom should have been so oriented was but natural. The Spanish colonies were ruled from Spain. Reforms in the colonies should, therefore, originate in Spain. The most that could be done in the colonies was to prepare the way for the favorable reception of the reform proposals when they came from Spain, or to inaugurate such enterprises as clearly fell within the scope of regulations already established. His plan, moreover, possessed the merit of winning for his reforms the favor of men who were less directly interested economically in their results than were the colonists. This orientation is indicative, also, of the working of Las Casas' mind. He wisely made his appeal to the audience which he knew best how to sway. For several years he had pleaded with the Spaniards of the Indies, he had scolded them, he had denounced them — all with little or no effect. One is reminded of the vain efforts of the wind in the old story of its contest with the sun to decide which was the stronger. Las Casas knew not how to fall in with the Spanish American public, because he could never get its point of view. His nearest approach to its viewpoint was the proposal to substitute negroes for the Indian toilers. This idea, however, was not original with him. Negro slavery had been introduced into Spanish America before Las Casas began his crusade. Negro slavery had met with approval in Portugal and Spain in the days of Henry the Navigator. In reality, therefore, Las Casas' proposal only carries us back to the Old World, though it did fall in with American needs. There seems no escape from the conclusion that Las Casas' campaign was ultimately based on Spain because among other reasons his mind was of Spain and not of Spanish America.

This conclusion, however, assumes the existence of a Spanish American mind at a time when such a mind presumably had not evolved. The mind of a colonial people is not formed in a day. Nearly all the Spaniards who were active in America in the early years of Las Casas' activity had come from Spain. Las Casas himself, born in 1474, was but eighteen or nineteen years old when Columbus discovered the Indies. In a new country, however, the economic pressure is ordinarily great enough to change in a very short time the attitude of men with respect to questions of the hour. Colonists may cling for years without number to the ideas and ways of their motherland in matters not of immediate, vital concern. In Spanish America the economic pressure was not ordinary; it was extraordinary. Europe needed nothing so much as gold and silver. In

America there was this gold and silver. Enough treasure had been filched from the Indians, or found in readily accessible locations, to warrant the staking of life itself on the possibility of finding more. Labor only was necessary to make real the dreams of the adventurers, but in the New World labor was the scarcest of all things unless the idle native could be put to work.

When, therefore, Las Casas preached against the employment of the Indian in the gold diggings, he as much as told the Spanish Americans: Here, indeed, is treasure untold; it is yours for the trouble of getting it, but you may not use the only means of securing it. Such propaganda will promptly develop a colonial mind. Las Casas' inability to appreciate the psychology of a gold-rush (and who can criticize him for his inability to understand? Was he not by profession a leader of men on their way to a world in which the idea of gold is superfluous?) and his " big stick " methods of effecting his programme very quickly created a Spanish American mind that would not receive his preachings whether delivered in person or in the guise of the " New Laws." So determined became this colonial mind that even the Bishop of Chiapa left the See which was the last resort in his campaign. It was the same mind that could ignore all the commercial regulations of the metropolis and trade cheerfully with its most implacable enemies, even to the ultimate ruin of the empire. This mind Las Casas should have confronted with thinking of its own kind. This mind he should have been able to interpret. Unfortunately the individual is sometimes less plastic than the group. Las Casas could not think in terms of the American mind; indeed, his agitation negatively contributed not a little to its formation and determined character.

Even a casual reading of his writings confirms the conclusion that Las Casas was non-American in his thinking. As an historian he belonged to the same school as Herrera in the seventeenth century and Muñoz in the eighteenth. All three men saw the New World as something objective to themselves, as something to be described, not so much in terms of itself, as in terms of a particular cause or of the culture of the motherland. The works of Las Casas and Herrera unmistakenly belong to the literature of Spanish expansion. As well might we say that Hakluyt is the father of English American historiography because he so earnestly urged his countrymen to people the new lands. The honor of being the father of American historiography, in the sense which we have defined, must, then, be accorded to some other historian, devoted not to a cause, but to the understanding of the colonial people.

Still there are good reasons why for good and for ill Las Casas should be better known. Without his works, particularly the *Historia,* the beginnings of Europe in America would indeed be shrouded in darkness. Without his writings we should probably know little of a singularly noble character. Without his writings the English, the Dutch, and the French would have experienced great difficulty in justifying their courses with respect to Spain. As the most recent writer on the history of Spain in Europe and America has put it: " . . . things so fell out, in the years after his [Las Casas'] death, when the power of Spain was the nightmare of Europe, that the various tracts, in which the Apostle had exaggerated the sufferings of the Indians, for the purpose of securing their alleviation, were greedily seized upon by Spain's numerous enemies as affording a true picture of conditions in the Spanish colonies. They made excellent propaganda, and were used to the limit of their possibilities. Thus the most permanent result of the work of the Apostle was not the accomplishment of the end he had in view, but rather the perpetuation of the legend of Spanish cruelty." This legend clearly accounts for the difference in the estimates of Las Casas with which we began this paper.

BIBLIOGRAPHY

A. BIOGRAPHY

The earliest biographies of Las Casas were written by two friars of his own Order: REMESAL, in his *Historia general de las Indias etc.* (Madrid, 1619), and DÁVILA Y PADILLA, *Historia de la Fundación y Discurso de la Provincia de Santiago de Mexico* (Madrid, 1596; Brussels, 1625). QUINTANA in his *Vidas de Españoles célebres* (Madrid, 1837) writes a panegyric of the great Dominican. Cf. FABRE, *Vida de Las Casas,* in the *Colección de Documentos inéditos,* t. lxx (Madrid, 1895); ORTUETA, *Fray Bartolomé de Las Casas* (Madrid, 1920). The best guide to the ever-increasing literature on Las Casas is GRACE GARDNER GRIFFIN's *Writings on American History,* which is published annually by the American Historical Association.

B. GENERAL WORKS ON LAS CASAS AND HIS WRITINGS

Up to the year 1880, WINSOR's *Narrative and Critical History of America* may be trusted for bibliographical references to the literature on Las Casas's writings. Useful information will be found in BÉCKER, *La Política Española en Las Indias* (Madrid, 1920). The voluminous collection, *Documentos ineditos de Indias,* contains many documents on Las Casas and his historical compositions. The most recent evaluation of his works will be found in WALDMAN, *Americana: the Literature of American History* (New York, 1926).

BARONIUS (1538–1607)

VERY REV. THOMAS PLASSMANN, O.F.M., PH.D., S.T.D.
St. Bonaventure's College and Seminary, Allegany, N. Y.

IN language no less forceful than truthful, the Anglican Bishop, Montagu, pledged to Cesare Baronio the title of Father of Modern Church History when he declared that the great Annalist had accomplished his work " plane novo et inaudito exemplo ab omni retro antiquitate, heroico conatu et praedicando." [1] In other words, Baronius broke with the past; he set out to write the universal History of the Church according to an entirely new plan, and with prodigious learning and heroic energy carried out his plan. Hence it is that the " Annales Ecclesiastici " stand on the verge of the sixteenth century like a great archway which not only overtowers in its colossal magnitude the entire past but opens straight and wide into the vast field of Modern Church History. The astounding fact is that the twelve great tomes of this work were written single-handed by one man who devoted over two score years of his life to this tremendous task. As a result the history of the author's life will be in a large measure the history of the book.

---

[1] Hurter, *Nomenclator*, III, p. 535.

153

1. His Life

Cesare Baronio was born October 30,[2] 1538, at Sora in the Kingdom of Naples. His parents were of noble lineage but not blessed with riches. His father, Camillo, was vigorous of character; his mother, Portia by name, was of a tender and pious disposition. She dedicated her child even before his birth to the Blessed Virgin, and when little Cesare, at the age of three, was dangerously ill she confirmed her early offering by a vow which her son was happy to ratify in after years. Of the many virtues which his mother instilled into his tender heart, charity towards the poor was undoubtedly the most favored and one which lent a special charm to the career of her son.

His biographers tell us of his early love for solitude and for the charms of nature, and how the grand panorama of beautiful Sora was his delight in his boyhood days. Perhaps this explains his abiding love for Art and Poetry of which his sacred hymns give ample proof.[3] But whatever influence the natural surroundings of his early days may have exercised upon his character, it is above all the very marked and almost opposite characteristics of his parents, that blended so harmoniously and expressively in Baronio the man; his strength of will, tenacity of purpose, unflinching energy and straight-

[2] This date is found in Baronius' own hand. See Laemmer, *De Caesaris B. etc.*, p. 8. Other biographers give Oct. 31, and still others Aug. 30.

[3] F. F. Guelfi in *Per Cesare Baronio Scritti vari etc.*, p. 312.

forward manner on the one hand, and on the other, a tender piety and childlike humility, stayed with him to the last. Such were the qualities that in later years, St. Philip Neri rejoiced to recognize in young Cesare when finally, after submitting him to a long and severe test, he singled him out for his life work.

Cesare studied at Veruli, Naples and Rome. He was nineteen when he arrived in the Eternal City to continue the study of jurisprudence and little did he fancy that here was to be his abode for the rest of his life. Cesare loved Rome, and all that he possessed in sanctity and learning he attributed to this " sedula morum magi͟͟tra ac literarum." [4]

Not long after his arrival a friend introduced him to St. Philip Neri. Almost instantly the indescribable spell of Rome's Apostle wrought a complete change in young Cesare. With characteristic energy he started on the narrow road to perfection and he is not known to have ever deviated from it. His earnest, straightforward and thorough-going nature suffered no alternative and no medium course; henceforth an utter contempt for the world and an equally strong desire for things spiritual marked his every thought and action. So sincere was his conversion that, as his first offering to God, he tore into shreds all his poems which in his youthful years he had taken such delight in composing.

Then came the struggle for his vocation. He felt a strong desire to enter the Order of St. Francis either as a Capuchin or as an Observantine. St.

[4] Barnabeo, *Vita,* I, 1, c, 2,

Philip bade him wait, and for three long years he waited, not without much internal suffering. But his spiritual father stood by him and prudently directed his energies upon the ardent pursuit of study and works of charity.

His father became furious when he learned of his son's new manner of life, and employed drastic measures to change his mind, but to no avail. The noble-minded Paravicino received Cesare as tutor into his domestic circle until at last the youth was satisfied that his vocation was not the religious state but the secular priesthood. Meanwhile, the Oratory of San Girolamo had so captivated his soul that without further hesitation he took the vows of poverty, of chastity, of obedience to St. Philip, and, to satisfy the craving of his inmost soul, the fourth vow of humility. When Tonsure and Minor Orders were conferred upon him he chose God literally as " the portion of his inheritance " and to prove it, he tore up the Degree of Doctor of Laws which had been awarded to him in spite of his youth. He was now twenty-two years of age. Before taking Major Orders another severe struggle with his relentless father had to be fought but the equally persistent son came forth victorious. He was ordained a priest in 1564.

During all these struggles the vigilant eye of St. Philip was forced upon Baronius. From their first meeting there had grown up between these two men the most beautiful relationship. No one has revealed to us the words that were spoken at that meeting;

most likely they were very few, but from that moment their souls were welded together in mutual affection and admiration. If we may draw a bold parallel, we should surmise that this meeting was much alike to the first meeting between the Divine Master and St. Peter. Even there, few words were exchanged but the Master looked upon Simon Peter long and affectionately. And indeed there is a striking resemblance between Peter and Baronius in character and temperament. Both were impetuous and sanguine; enthusiastic almost to a fault; strong-willed if not obstinate in striving after what they considered to be right, yet docile and pliable as children under correction, and withal loyal unto death to their masters.

Philip's influence over Baronius was overpowering and irresistible from the first. On one occasion the Historian beautifully alludes to this in our Saviour's words: " My father who is in me doth the works." And whatever may have been his own personal endowments, certain it is that Baronius, the man and the Church Historian, owes much to St. Philip. From the very first, Philip knew that his disciple was to be " a Vessel of Election " in the Church of God, and the more he studied him the stronger grew his conviction that he was the man of the hour, and that the work which he was planning in his own mind could be entrusted to no one worthier than Baronius.

The immediate occasion which shaped Philip's design into a definite resolve was the publication in

1559 of the Magdeburg *Centuries*. In this work,
Flacius Illyricus and his collaborators had attempted to force the battles of the Reformation
upon the field of history. The Church of Rome,
they claimed, was not the Church of Christ; not
the Apostolic Church. The Roman Pontiffs had
gained their supremacy by intrigues and had deliberately distorted the primitive type of the Church
which the Reformers, as the legitimate successors of
the Apostles and the Fathers, were endeavoring to
reëstablish in doctrine, ritual and government. We
can imagine how such novel tenets must have
wounded the heart of Rome's Apostle, St. Philip
Neri. Not that he felt alarm or that he feared for
the safety of the Church which he knew was built
upon the indestructible Rock, but with many prominent ecclesiastics he feared lest the Little Ones of
Christ's Flock suffer scandal, and being a man of
action he realized that it would not do to stand
idly by but rather to forge weapons which would
bear out the Saviour's prophecy: " And the gates
of hell shall not prevail against it."

By this time he had picked out the man who was
to wield the new weapon in the conflict. But as was
his custom, he did not for a long time reveal his
real objective. One day he summoned " his Cesare "
as he was wont to call him affectionately and said,
" Cesare, it is my wish that in the sermons which
you preach to the people, you narrate to them the
whole history of the Church." Baronius felt like
Peter when the Master bade him cast out his net,

after fishing all night in vain, and like Peter he remonstrated vehemently, but like Peter he also obeyed.

He set out with his wonted energy upon this new field of labor and when after two years he had finished the proposed course of historical instruction, Philip calmly bade him do the same thing over again. This happened seven times. In this way, this master pedagogue with his wonderful intuition and practical sense attained a two-fold object: he forced his disciple to penetrate farther and farther into the vast field of unexplored historical lore, each time coming forth burdened with new but as yet ill-ordered material, and he compelled him to present it in simple language appropriate to devout listeners in the House of God. Hence the two outstanding merits of the *Annals*, thoroughness and reverence. But Baronius also claimed a gain which was all his own; what had been hard and bitter to him in the beginning was now converted into supreme delight and joy. He epitomizes the work of these years in the preface to the fifth volume where he apostrophizes his father, who had then joined the Saints in Heaven, as follows: " This I began in obedience to thee, and persevering for thirty years, I went through the history of the Church seven times." Had he been acquainted with modern pedagogical methods he would have told us how St. Philip had designed for him a rather unique but eminently efficient seminar course in which his mind was constantly enriched with new information, his judgment sharpened, his vision broadened and his heart made to glow with genuine love for the work.

Possibly such procedure is branded with cynical sarcasm by those who proclaim that their standards are purely intellectual and that historical truth should be sought after with an absolutely unpre-possessed mind, yet, whatever the merits of such declarations, we owe it to every historian that we seek to understand clearly his mind and purpose. Many have misread and misjudged the *Annals* be-cause they failed to realize that this work was con-ceived and prompted by a Saint, that its contents were first explained in simple language in the Ora-tory of San Girolamo before the Altar of Eternal Truth, and that it was committed to writing by a man whose sole aim was the untarnished truth and who had a deep appreciation of what in our own day the scholarly Cardinal Capecelatro demands of the Church historian. On the occasion of the Third Centenary of Baronius, this learned Churchman wrote: "The History of the Church must soar to great heights on the wings of faith, and must be written with an intuition so broad and reassuring as to make it the history of Divine Providence among men. He who writes this history must pene-trate this life's inexpressible mystery by means of which the doctrine of our faith and the heresies, virtue and vice, peace and persecutions, joys and sorrows; all this fabric of good and evil, tends to the glory of God. And from this glory as from the fountain of all good, there proceeds the onward march of the human race towards truth and charity, or rather towards Christ and His Religion." [5]

It seems to have been Philip's wish that Baronius should not set himself to writing before he had finished his seventh course of lectures on Church history. This was characteristic of Philip for undoubtedly he judged that as Josue had marched seven times around the city of Jericho before launching his attack, so Baronius was now prepared to enter upon his work. However, confusion filled Baronius' soul when he received the command. He begged, remonstrated and entreated his superior to appoint in his stead the learned Ottavio Panvinio, but every interview ended with the gentle but firm command of Philip: " As to the Church History, it is you, Cesare, who have to write it."

And yet there remained some anxiety in Philip's mind. He knew well that his disciple would shed lustre upon Mother Church, and while he ardently loved the glory of the House of God, he loved the immortal soul of his Cesare not less. The docile disciple who had placed his soul in his hands, who had been his faithful associate in their earthly paradise, the Oratory, must needs be his associate also in the heavenly paradise. And yet he feared lest the tremendous labors should extinguish in him the spirit of devotion and lest the praises and adulations of men should blur the deep humility of his soul. How was he to reach his double objective? This

[5] *S. Philippo Neri e gli Annali del Baronio,* in *Per Cesare Baronio etc.,* p. 5.

was the problem that confronted Philip. He settled
it by firmly resolving: first, that the Church History must be written and secondly, that the writer
must become a saint. The former resolution he carried out with unshaken firmness, the latter with un-
relenting severity. This alone explains why during
these years of arduous and unremitting labors, of
severe sufferings and almost cruel humiliations for
Baronius, the gentle Philip should have played the
part of the " stern exactor " as his disciple was wont
to call him.

In spite of the tremendous burden placed upon
his shoulders which forced him to search for, to
collect and work through an unwieldy mass of
books, documents and manuscripts, hidden away in
the various libraries of Rome and elsewhere; to
carry on a large correspondence on historical questions; to wait patiently on printers and obstinate
correctors; to write and rewrite every single line
of the twelve folio volumes, Baronius was not relieved of a single community exercise, or his daily
visits to the sick and the prisons, nor of the duties
connected with the various offices he held during
this time. And constantly, his " stern exactor "
found new work for him of a most distracting nature, so much so that the humble disciple was almost scandalized at his spiritual father who so
tormented him. Cardinal Capecelatro [6] and Lady
Amabel Kerr [7] have given us vivid descriptions of

[6] *The Life of Saint Philip Neri*, II, pp. 1-31.
[7] *The Life of Cesare Cardinal Baronius.*

these years of toil and struggle, and when reading
these fascinating pages one is constantly put in
mind of the familiar scene where Peter, drowning,
cries out in dismay: " Domine, salva me," and
where the Master gently raises him by the hand
saying, " Modicae fidei, quare dubitasti? " It would
almost seem as if Philip had made the disciple live
the life of the Church Militant in his own soul before he was permitted to write her history. However, he attained his double object and the results
were marvellous in both the book and the writer.
Without intending it, Baronius set a perennial monument to his humility and obedience when he wrote
on the chimney-piece in the kitchen at Vallicella:
Baronius Coquus perpetuus. It forcefully reminds
us of another parallel in history, Petrus Piscator.
And later when the whole world, popes, princes, and
scholars of all the nations, sang his praises, Philip
alone remained silent. The only reward he extended
to the man whom the world acclaimed as the *Parens
Historiae Ecclesiasticae* was: " Go and serve thirty
masses." Perhaps the historian's heart was wounded,
but still he understood his master. Such is the way
of the saints. When Philip's end was near, he called
his disciple to his bedside and said, " Cesare, you
have a great many reasons for thinking lowly of
yourself and the chief of them is that you have
written the Annals; for you know it was not by
your own industry and toil that you wrote them,
but by the singular grace of God." And Baronius
replied: " Yes, my dearest father, I know it well;

all that I have written I owe to God and to your prayers." These touching words which remind us so much of a similar conversation on the shore of the lake of Galilee, was repeated three times by both master and disciple.

Before speaking of the *Annals* in detail it is well to mark the chief events of the historian's life. Having been promoted to the Holy Priesthood in 1564, he was given charge of the Church of St. John the Baptist of the Florentines where he performed his pastoral duties with his wonted fervor and energy. When in 1575 the Oratory was officially established at the Church of Santa Maria in Vallicella, Baronius was transferred thither. This appointment afforded him great spiritual joy, especially when in 1583 St. Philip was commanded by the Pope to take up his residence at the new Oratory. It was during his residence at Santa Maria in Vallicella that Baronius, under the vigilant eyes of St. Philip put forth several smaller writings as well as the revised Martyrology and the first five volumes of the *Annals*. Baronius remained at the Oratory until 1593. In that year Philip resigned as Superior of the Congregation and Baronius, after his usual vehement remonstrances, was finally induced to take his place. Pope Clement VIII appointed him in 1595 his Confessor. It seems that whenever Baronius was forced into an office at the risk, as he thought of his humility, he generally found an ingenious way of taking revenge by obtaining some spiritual favor. This time the revenge consisted in demanding of the Pontiff the absolu-

tion of Henry IV of France. In the same year the
Pope conferred upon him almost by dint of physical
force, the insignia of Protonotary Apostolic. In the
following year Baronius who had thrice refused the
mitre, had to face what he termed a tragedy, for
the Pope bestowed upon him under pain of excommunication " the dreaded purple." With many tears
he entreated the Pontiff to allow him to return to
his beloved Oratory and when he was consistently
refused he found some relief in taking the vow of
never aspiring to the Papacy. Later he confessed
that of all the burdens ever placed upon his shoulders, the heaviest was the Cardinalate.

His appointment in 1597 to the office of Librarian
of the Vatican [8] was at least more congenial to his
nature. But the clouds gathered thickly over his
head during the two conclaves in 1605. In the second one, following the premature death of Leo XI,
Baronius' election seemed a certainty when to his
great satisfaction the Spanish delegates protested on
account of the stand Baronius had taken in the
Sicilian question.[9]

The last eleven years of his life Baronius was
forced to spend at the Papal Court. His many
duties impeded his literary work, yet he had the
consolation of seeing the twelfth volume of the
Annals completed before his holy death which occurred at the beloved Oratory on June 30, 1607.

Our common impression of Baronius is, and the

[8] G. Mercati, *Per la Storia della Bibliotheca Vaticana*, in *Per
Cesare Baronio*, pp. 85–178.
[9] F. Ruffini, *Perchè Cesare Baronio non fu Papa*, in *Per
Cesare Baronio*, pp. 355–430.

preceding as well as the following pages bear it out, that he was of a very stern disposition. Some authors go so far as to say that he was never known to laugh. However this may be, in his correspondence with intimate friends we find many witticisms and humorous pleasantries, which go to show that he was capable of occasionally assuming a more congenial air.[10]

Enough has been said about his deep piety and profound spirituality. The world was not surprised when Benedict XIV adorned him with the title of "Venerable." But if God should please to promote the process of his beatification by signs and miracles, the student of history will always regard the *Annals* as the greatest miracle of this eminent "Servus Mariae," as he would style himself.

2. HIS WRITINGS

Besides the *Annals*, Baronius published several smaller writings which in their very titles reveal to us in some measure what was closest to his heart, namely, the Saints and the Popes. As the reader of the *Annals* will readily observe, when the life of a saint or the trials of a martyr are to be narrated the pen of Baronius waxes eloquent, and one feels that he was telling the truth when he wrote: " O Lord, behold I come, ready, if Thy grace permitted it, to

[10] See the interesting correspondence between him and Card. Fred. Borromeo: A. Ratti (Pius XI), *Opuscolo inedito e sconosciuto del Card. Cesare Bar. etc.*, in *Per Cesare Baronio*, pp. 178–245.

testify to the truth of Thy Church with my blood rather than with my pen."

Hence it was that at the request of friends he wrote in 1580 the *Vita Gregorii Nazianzeni*, the first fruits of his literary labors, and presented it to Pope Gregory XIII.[11] It seems that a few years later he revised this little work, for according to his own statement [12] he completed it in 1584 as also the *Vita S. Ambrosii* and the *Martyrologium Romanum*. The revision of the *Martyrology*, imposed upon him by Pontifical orders, proved to be an undertaking of painstaking research. Cardinal Sirleto and other prominent scholars lent their assistance to this task which, when finished, was acclaimed a great success, but none of the earlier editions and prints satisfied Baronius. At last the edition of 1589 by Platinus of Antwerp met with his approval.[13]

Amid all his labors Baronius found time to wield his pen in defense of the Papacy. It could not be otherwise, for his devotion to the Successor of Peter was at once profoundly spiritual and thoroughly practical. The man who daily visited St. Peter's where he could be seen to pour out his soul before the " Confessio " and reverently kiss the foot of the bronze statue of the Prince of the Apostles; who had taken a vow never to aspire to the Papacy and yet wanted to die facing an image of the

11 Laemmer, *De Caesaris Baronii Lit. Commercio Diatriba*, pp. 8, 55.

12 Laemmer, *op. cit.*, p. 8.

13 Laemmer, *op. cit.*, pp. 8, 53, 62, 91.

Apostles, and the name " Papist " to be written on his tombstone; — such a one could not remain silent when the rights of the Vicar of Christ were attacked. It has been rightly said that, " Loyalty to the Church and devotion to the Holy See was the key-note of his life." [14] The author's unalterable if not defiant attitude in this regard was the principal reason why the *Annals* aroused such ire among his enemies. Pits observes, not altogether unjustly, " It should have been called, the *Annals* of the papal power rather than the *Annals* of the Church." [15] And yet, notwithstanding his strong sentiments and convictions, Baronius never allowed his judgment to be swayed in discussing the rights of the Holy See on the merits of historical facts or documents. Instances of this are his *Tractatus de Monarchia Sicula, Paraenesis ad Rempublicam Venetam* and *Votum contra Rempublicam Venetam* which were written to set forth the rights of the Holy See in its litigations with Spain and Venice, respectively. While setting forth with remarkable force and lucidity the relations between Church and State these treatises may be considered, as Professor Guelfi remarks, " model historical monographs." [16]

Naturally these smaller writings, but especially the *Martyrology*, retarded the progress of the *Annals*, upon which Baronius spent his best years and

---

[14] Kerr, *op. cit.*, p. 353.
[15] Kerr, *op. cit.*, p. 338.
[16] F. Filomusi-Guelfi, *Su alcuni punti delle dottrine filosophiche e giuridiche del Card. Ces. Bar.*, in *Per Cesare Baronio*, pp. 313, 315, sqq.

best efforts. Capecelatro tells us that St. Philip had
charged his disciple with the task of lecturing exclusively on Church history as early as 1559, which
is the date of the publication of the *Magdeburg
Centuries*. From this we may infer that Baronius
devoted almost fifty years of his life to the study of
Church history. He himself informs us that he gave
seven such courses of conferences, but it is not certain at what time he actually started work on the
Annals. Tiraboschi [17] and others state that he began
this work as early as 1568. In a letter to Cardinal
Sirleto, dated May 16, 1577,[18] Baronius speaks definitely of his plan to write the entire history of the
Church, and in a letter dated April 25, 1579, he
joyfully informs his father that the first volume is
completed but that for various reasons it cannot be
printed immediately.[19] It came from the press in
1588. St. Philip had ordered him to put out one
volume each year. This order was fairly well carried out up to the seventh volume, which appeared
in 1596, but it took the Cardinal the remaining
eleven years of his life to bring out the last five
volumes of the work.

Historians have often wondered how Baronius,
although he worked, as Cave puts it, " with ada-
mantine courage and superhuman labor," [20] was
able to master and keep in order the " mare magnum et spatiosum " of the material gathered during

[17] *Storia della Letteratura Ital.*, VII, I, p. 363.
[18] Laemmer, *op. cit.*, p. 46.
[19] Laemmer, *op. cit.*, p. 48.
[20] Kerr, *op. cit.*, p. 337.

all these years. In a valuable contribution to the
collection of writings published at the third centenary of the Annalist, our gloriously reigning Pontiff throws some interesting side-lights on his method
of working.[21] The eminent writer acquaints us with
an unpublished Italian treatise, probably written
about 1595, in which Baronius tells his friend Cardinal Frederico Borromeo that he was in the habit
of taking down notes " in un indice confuso." We
are further advised that Cardinal Borromeo saw
this remarkable note-book which he calls, " volumen
quoddam inconditum." His comment upon it is interesting inasmuch as it allows us at least to catch
a glimpse of Baronius' workshop. Setting Baronius
up as an example, he continues, " qui vel instinctu
divino, vel admonitu fortasse cujuspiam, quo primum tempore ad Ecclesiasticam Historiam ani-
mum adjecit, notaverat, exceperatque multa, et volumen quoddam inconditum rerum diversarum sibi
praepararat, cujus quotidie crescente mole, potuit
deinde ditissimus copiosissimusque videri, sicuti
vere erat." [22]

The style of Baronius is the candid expression of
his soul. One feels that his pen is impelled by that
" carità serafica " to which his Italian biographers
refer so often, and yet withal his language is simple,
direct, unlabored and dignified. The text of his
works is saturated with Biblical quotations, allusions and sentiments, but these are always appropriate and never descend to merely puerile inven-

[21] A. Ratti, *op. cit.*, pp. 181, 237, sqq.   [22] *Ibid.*, p. 231.

tions. Frequently one is at a loss whether to marvel at his profound and comprehensive knowledge of Holy Scripture, or at his dexterity in crystallizing with a scriptural phrase his own intimate and personal appreciation of a historical event or period.[23]

Baronius chose the chronological and annalistic form of presentation for very definite reasons. Certainly this method of writing had serious disadvantages but we cannot agree with Fueter,[24] who, without taking the trouble of investigating those reasons, dismisses the subject summarily by blaming the great historian for having opened the way to what he terms, "die Moderne Vertuschungsmethode." Even a casual glance at the situation should have convinced him that if the *Annals* were to be an answer to the *Centuries*, period for period, then the arrangement of the *Annals* naturally had to have the general outline of the *Centuries*. This, Baronius has done with scrupulous consistency. And there is the difference between the two works. Lady Amabel Kerr writes, "The one object he had in view was to bring to light by this chronological chain of ungarbled facts, the evident and undeniable existence, from the beginning, of one unfailing Church under one visible and supreme head." [25]

---

[23] Some of his Biblical allusions have almost become proverbial. Thus, when asked who were his helpers on the *Annals*, he replied: "Torcular calcavi solus." He had intended to call his twelfth volume "Benoni" on account of the great strain he suffered while compiling it, but he adds in a more cheerful vein. Now I shall call it "Benjamin, Paulo nostro jam in dextera collocatus."

[24] *Geschichte der Neueren Historiographie*, pp. 263–265.

[25] *Op. cit.*, p. 76.

If by the rather obscure term, " Vertuschungs-methode," Fueter means the obscuring of facts and dates, then certainly Baronius is not guilty for it was just the opposite that he intended and accomplished. We do not maintain that Baronius' method would be suitable in modern historiography, yet we cannot deny the truth of what Cardinal Capecelatro has to say on this head. "Chronology," he writes, " removes the obscurity which hangs round many events; it puts together the disjoined, scattered members of the body of history and gives it its due form and proportions." [26]

Baronius looked upon everything from a spiritual viewpoint. Divine Providence was for him the supreme law and as he faithfully recorded, day by day, and year by year, the " Mirabilia Dei " and the glorious names of Saints and Christian scholars, not of course without their shadows and counterparts, he must have felt a supreme delight in the Saviour's prophecy, " Behold, I am with you all days." In this sense the *Annals* may be termed, as Professor Guelfi [27] suggests, a Philosophy of Church History.

In his preface to the first volume, [28] the author describes in his own direct and forceful way the name and scope of the *Annals*. He calls his work advisedly, *Annales*, and not *Historia* because the former term is consecrated by ancient usage, and

[26] *Op. cit.*, p. 14.
[27] *Op. cit.*, p. 313.
[28] We quote from the *Annales Ecclesiastici* (ed. Venice, 1705 sqq.).

introduces the story of the Ancient Church wherein truth needs no apology or vindication. He choses this plan and method because it is more in conformity with the Saviour's words: " Sit sermo vester, est, est, non, non, quod autem his abundantius est, a malo est."

One cannot forego the pleasure of quoting the following sentence which we believe comes straight from Baronius' heart and reveals to us his own personal conception of the subject: " Et quod ecclesiasticam majestatem ac gravitatem maxime decet dicendi genus sectantes; quae dicenda sunt, sancte, pure, sincereque absque ullo prorsus fuco, vel figmento, prout gesta sunt, per annos singulos degesta narrabimus." [29]

In the matter of sources, Baronius revealed a true historical instinct. He searched for history everywhere: friend or foe, stone or parchment, sacred objects or secular; all were alike to him as long as they could serve him as trustful witnesses of the past. His first endeavor was, as F. Barnabeo tells us, to study and collate all the historians that had ever written before him. We can appreciate the tremendous difficulty of this task when we remember that there existed no universal history of the Church before Baronius, but that he had to cull his information from an almost infinite variety and multiplicity of chronicles, manuscripts and fragments.

With holy avidity he perused the Acts of the

[29] *Ibid.*

Martyrs, for they were an inspiration to his fervor and zeal. " I quoted them at full length," he writes, " out of reverence for such antiquity, though I know that I run the risk of being accused of prolixity." [30] Fueter [31] misses this point entirely when he accuses Baronius of intentionally thereby diverting the attention of the reader from the main point. This is a crude insinuation when we know the true motive and remember that every drop of blood shed for our Holy Faith was sacred in the eyes of the writer, who sedulously gathered up all the fragments that told the wonderful story.

He next turned to the Fathers of the Church, both Greek and Latin. When he started, his linguistic knowledge was very limited, but as he toiled along he acquired no small proficiency in the Greek tongue, and even had the courage to acquaint himself with Hebrew in order to master the original text of the Old Testament.

He studied profane history with deep interest, especially the many chronicles bearing on the history of Italy, and anything pertaining to the Holy Roman Empire. The City of Rome offered Baronius ample opportunities for archæological studies. Possibly for the first time, were many ancient monuments, arches, buildings, columns, and coins called upon to mingle their silent voices with the triumphant strains, not of the Caesars, but of the Nazarene. Day after day, Baronius wended his way to

[30] Kerr, *op. cit.*, p. 77.
[31] *Geschichte der Neueren Historiographie,* p. 264.

the Roman libraries. If he had no other merit than
that of rendering accessible to the world the wealth
of information gathered from the manuscripts of
the Vatican library and the archives of St. Angelo,
he would have earned the world's gratitude.[32] Nor
was he satisfied with the written word. In search
for the truth he enlisted the counsel of men who,
he knew, could enlighten him, among them, Pietro
Morino, Jacopo Sismondo, Cardinal Sirleto, Nicholas Faber of Paris, Henry Gravius of Louvain,
F. Soria, S.J., and Fronto Ducaeus. A great bulk
of correspondence left after him,[33] reveals the fact
that frequently he wrote lengthy monographs either
to elucidate a point for the benefit of an inquirer,
or to ascertain another's opinion on a matter of
doubt.

The critical value of the *Annals* is naturally relative. Gauged by contemporary standards, however,
the work is far ahead of its time. Historiography
has progressed much since the days of Baronius,
but that has nothing to do with what may be termed
the absolute critical value of any book of any age,
and this value does not deteriorate in spite of any
scientific progress, provided the author has the will,
the means and the ability to tell the whole truth.

Baronius started out and persevered with the unshaken will to find and write the truth. No critic
has ever succeeded in convicting him of garbling a
single date or fact. On the contrary, he generously

[32] Mercati, *op. cit.*, *passim*.
[33] See the collections of Albericius, Laemmer and Ratti.

invited both friend and foe to criticize his work in accordance with St. Augustine's axiom: " Verum et severum diligo correctorem meum." His constant request to his at times rather eager critics was: " Touch boldly, speak freely, and know that you will thereby give me real pleasure." The solution of chronological intricacies afforded him perhaps the greatest natural pleasure that his austere temperament would allow him to indulge in. It may be truly said that the *Historica Veritas* was never committed to a trustier charge than to this eminent Oratorian whose sincere, frank, straightforward nature shrank from the very suggestion of an untruth and whose inmost heart constantly breathed the prayer, " Domine, ne auferas de ore meo verbum veritatis usquequaque." [34]

His passionate love for truth coupled with his severe and unyielding disposition made him a formidable opponent. Casaubon expresses it well in the phrase, " Gigantem istum debellare." [35] And yet it was the same love for truth that made him at once so humble and so charitable. This explains how both through the written word and personal contact he made many converts to the faith. [36]

In Fueter's [37] opinion the *Annals* do not mark any progress beyond the critical standards created by the Humanists, though he admits that Baronius re-

[34] In an intimate letter to Card. F. Borromeo he remarks casually: " non ho mai havuto animo di adulare." Ratti, *op. cit.*, p. 245.
[35] N. Festa, *Note per un capitulo della biografia d'Isacco Casaboun*, in *Per Cesare Bar.*, p. 292.
[36] Hurter, *Nomenclator*, p. 534.   [37] *Op. cit., loc. cit.*

veals closer contact with the methods of the school
of Blondus than did the Centuriators. Objectively
speaking, this declaration attaches no blame to
Baronius or to the Magdeburg editors, for it stands
to reason that monumental works of this kind must
necessarily depend upon the monographic studies
that have preceded them. Without such, our modern historiography could not have stepped beyond
even sixteenth century standards. And yet the same
Fueter has only scant praise for the great outstanding merit of the *Annals,* which raises their value
high above all contemporary writings, namely, the
careful and abundant use of the wealth of hitherto
unpublished documents.

Here it must be stated that Baronius does not by
any means employ his sources indiscriminately.
Many, indeed, have sneered at the large number of
errors that modern criticism has discovered in the
Annals, but few have pointed out the astounding
array of errors detected by Baronius in the sources,
old and new, that he had to collate and master
single-handed. Fueter reluctantly admits his careful
scrutiny of modern and medieval sources, but seems
to take for granted a lack of criticism in reference to
the early Christian writers. This statement sounds
almost ridiculous when we read the instructive article, " Eusebio guidicato dal Baronio " by Professor Benjamino Satoro.[38] As this writer points out,
the Annalist traces, with merciless logic, error upon
error and marks them with language which is by

[38] In *Per Cesare Baronio,* pp. 331–353.

no means complimentary to the Father of Church History, such as, "multa mentitus est," "corrigendus est Eusebius," and even goes so far as to accuse him of a "turpe mendacium" or a "dolus malus." His love for truth no less than his critical judgment are especially apparent when he corrects Eusebius in reference to Constantine the Great, the first Christian Emperor, who is the leading figure in Volume III of the *Annals,* and who in his Eusebian dress would have lent himself wonderfully to a grand picturization of the ideal Christian Ruler. Since this volume was dedicated to Philip II, Baronius would have welcomed such an opportunity had he been a dramatist and not a historian. What Eusebius had passed by in silence Baronius stigmatizes as "dolendum facinus." In this connection Baronius lays down in forceful and characteristic language what appears to have been his ruling principle throughout his work, namely that it is far from his mind to write apologies or cover vice with false excuses, lest, "privatus affectus nos in sinuosos impellat anfractus," and he continues, "sed recto tramite, via regia ac libera incedentes praevia veritate, quae ipsa ingerit, quae sola monet ac docet, nostris scriptis tantummodo complectemur." [39] However, we cannot blame him for not feeling justified in questioning the authenticity of the pseudo-Isidorian decretals, for after all Blondel's famous reply to Torres appeared only twenty-one years after Baronius' death. As to the

[39] *Annales,* III, 84.

celebrated *Donatio Constantini* Baronius resolutely declares the traditional text of the document corrupt. This was an important step in advance when we realize that only in the nineteenth century was sufficient evidence found to disprove the authenticity of the document.

Baronius also rejects the correspondence between Seneca and St. Paul on the authority, not of Erasmus and the Centuriators, but of abundant intrinsic and extrinsic evidence of his own finding.[40] With remarkable ingenuity he traces not only the proofs against its genuineness but also the reasons for the long-standing popularity of these letters.

Always ready to yield to the verdict of historical truth Baronius surrenders even those traditions which had entwined themselves with the faith of his forefathers. However, he does not employ the iconoclastic methods of the Centuriators, but rather proceeds with due reverence for those who in ages past may have found inspiration and spiritual comfort in such traditions. A characteristic example is the fictitious correspondence between Christ and King Abgar. While the Centuriators firmly cling to its genuineness, Baronius, after giving the letters in full, and clearly pointing out their doubtful origin, adds with his characteristic tactfulness, that he thought it wise to embody them " tum nequid lectorem praetereat; tum etiam ne ea quis omnino contemnenda existimet, quae majores complures venerati esse noscuntur." [41]

[40] Ad annum, 66, xi, xii, xiii.   [41] Ad annum, 31, lx.

The merits of the *Annals* are probably seen to their best advantage if gauged in relation to the Magdeburg *Centuries*. No one will gainsay that the latter work gave a powerful impetus to historical research and that it was responsible at least indirectly for a striking array of historical works written either in refutation or confirmation. It would not be presumptuous, however, to say that its greatest merit lay in bringing about the writing of the *Annals* of Baronius. The material accumulated and arranged in the order of centuries by the several authors of the Protestant work should not be underestimated; yet it stands no comparison with the wealth of hitherto unknown and most valuable information that was sifted, sorted, and synthesized by Baronius single-handed. In the matter of historical material the usefulness of the *Centuries* has long since spent itself, while the *Annals* have proved their permanent and abiding value to this day. So true is this that even Protestant writers have no hesitation in calling it, " Eine Fundgrube kirchenhistorischen Wissens." [42] As to the critical value of either, Fueter [43] declares that the *Centuries* mark a step backward in every regard, while the *Annals* hardly mark a step forward. What he really means is that the Catholic historian was incapable of moving forward owing to his religious convictions. If religious convictions constitute an impediment to critical judgment, then we certainly must not look

[42] C. Mirbt in *Realencyklopedie f. prot. Th. und Kirche,* s. v.

[43] *Op. cit., loc. cit.*

for it in Baronius nor for that matter in the Centuriators. But the real question at issue is to what
extent these writers allow their religious beliefs to
influence the treatment of their subject. Baronius,
it is true, does walk along the royal highway, as
he terms it, in the broad mid-day sun of his faith
and gathers up with childlike eagerness and deep
reverence, the fragments of the past scattered by
the roadside. But never does he consciously beguile
himself or others into error, and that, after all, is
the most important requisite in a historian. On the
other hand, it is admitted by friend and foe that
the Centuriators under the spell of the destructive
culter Flacianus wilfully garbled historical facts
and evaluated all sacred traditions, miracles, relics,
etc., by the standard of their religious tenets; if
these favored their anti-papist tendencies, they were
true and genuine; if not, they were relegated among
the " signa mendacia." Baronius never attacks them
openly, his policy was rather to let the facts speak
for themselves. Yet, occasionally he betrays his feelings in such remarks as, " the Centuries of Satan "
or " quaecumque ignorant, blasphemant." [44]

It stands to reason, of course, that the Centuriators had a more difficult task before them. The
burden of their thesis was to prove that from the
sixth century down, the Church of Christ had gone
wrong and that its default was due, not to a natural
development of things but to the wicked machina-
tions of men. Had they been schooled in modern

[44] Apparatus ad ann., 96.

rationalism their task might have been easier and
the usefulness of their work might have reached at
least the threshold of modern criticism. As it is,
their children being much wiser than they, charge
them with confessional fanaticism and look upon
their tremendous efforts as an interesting but valueless relic of the past.

Baronius, however, appeals even to the modern
world for the dignity, earnestness and solidity of
his work. In spite of the superhuman efforts demanded by his colossal undertaking, his was the
easier task. As Fueter [45] very naïvely remarks, " he
had to do less violence to the sources, because the
Fathers of the Church can more easily be harmonized with Catholic doctrine than with the Protestant beliefs." But had Fueter perused the correspondence between Baronius and Father Talpa and
his other confrères at Naples, he might have had
reason to admire the most scrupulous and painstaking accuracy employed by Baronius in every
single quotation from the Fathers,[46] and perhaps he
would not have dismissed the subject with the hasty
predicate, " ganz kritiklos."

There is another aspect of the question in which
Baronius occupies a more advantageous position
than his opponents. It was their purpose to show
that all the defects in the Church since the sixth
century proved a departure from the original type,
and tended towards a novel organization conceived

[45] *Op. cit., loc. cit.*
[46] Kerr, *op. cit.*, p. 104; Laemmer, p. 82.

by human selfishness or, as Casaubon terms it,
" Romani Papae tyrannis." [47] They further proceeded to show that the Reformation of the sixteenth century was patterned after the old Church
and was linked directly to the sixth century. Baronius started out with the conviction that "evils
must come" in the Church of God; that they are a
natural outgrowth of an organism which consists of
a human as well as a Divine element. In other
words, he simply sought for the truth, whether good
or evil, while the Centuriators were bound to find
evil, whether it was there or not. Thus it happened
that where his critics suspected formidable snares
for him and causes for self-deceit, there precisely lay
his greatest strength. The reason was because they
did not grasp his lofty and yet very practical concept of the Church; they forgot that for the picture
he was designing of the Bride of Christ, he needed
both light and dark colors; that every dark spot in
her history served him as another proof of her
supernatural character, of the abiding presence of
Christ in His Church and of the power of Divine
Providence.

What gives the *Annals* a special charm is the tone
of humility and reverence that marks every sentence
of the great work. It seems as if the saying of St.
Philip had at all times resounded in the author's
ears, " God does not need men." Baronius considered himself a worthless tool in the hands of the
Great Architect who built the Church whose history

[47] See his *Diary*, in N. Festa, *op. cit.*, p. 293.

he was writing. His zeal may have at times prompted him to point out the finger of God in certain things which may easily admit of a natural explanation, but never did the same zeal beguile him deliberately to falsify or misinterpret a single iota. If the latter were true we should have to accuse Baronius of blind partisanship; the former makes him guilty of nothing else than an ardent devotion to the Church of Christ. For the rest, the errors and mistakes that historical critics have discovered in the *Annals* of Baronius must be ascribed to the tremendous difficulties with which the undertaking was beset.

A work that contains the best and most comprehensive criticism of Baronius and which should always be found with the *Annals,* is the *Critica Historico-Chronologica* of the two eminent sons of St. Francis, Anthony Pagi, O.M.C., and his nephew, Francis Pagi, O.M.C. It is prefaced by a eulogy of the Annalist whose sole aim was " quae una primum est Historicae decus ac lumen, Veritas." Furthermore the author remarks with good sense, " Haerent, vel post supremam artificis manum, tersissimis quibusque artis operibus, sui naevi."

How different is the criticism of Fueter! A few of his statements will suffice to reveal the spirit that prompted him. According to Fueter,[48] Baronius found all the institutions of the Catholic Church set down in the Gospel accounts. Thus the Confession of Peter is given as the unchangeable type of General Councils. But when we read the *Annals,* it is

[48] *Op. cit., loc. cit.*

altogether different.[49] After a clear explanation of the momentous event based upon the Biblical texts and Josephus, Baronius begs his readers to pause for a while and take note: " Ejusmodi namque tanti ponderis et auctoritatis actio Christi, typum quemdam exprimit celebrandi concilium." The reader who agrees that the Confession of Peter was not a mere exchange of compliments but an act of far-reaching results, will readily admit that Baronius' point is well taken and that his mild inference is based on sound exegesis and good reasoning. To say the least a " typus quidam " is by no means " ein unveraenderliches Muster."

Again, Fueter makes Baronius infer from the ceremonies at St. Stephen's death that the commemoration of the thirtieth day is based upon Apostolic tradition, and that these ceremonies prove indirectly the Apostolic origin of the belief in Purgatory. Baronius treats of this matter not in section 308 as Fueter surmises, but in sections 313 and 314.[50] Furthermore there is question, not of the thirtieth day, as Fueter again falsely imagines, but the seventieth day. Had Fueter taken the trouble to read the *Annals* carefully he would have found that Baronius draws the inference not from the Bible but rather from the accumulative testimony of the first four centuries, and that even then, notwithstanding the long array of witnesses, he is contented with the cautious remark, " Apostolica traditione in ecclesia etiam consuetudo illa probata videtur."

---

[49] Ad annum, 33, xvi, xvii.   [50] Ad annum, 34.

With regard to the belief in Purgatory Baronius says this, " Res enim est non recens in ecclesia adinventa sed quae ex eisdem apostolicarum traditionum fontibus manat." He then proceeds to prove his assertion with an astounding wealth of quotations from Tertullian, St. Cyprian, Origen, St. Epiphanius, St. Chrysostom, St. Cyril of Jerusalem, St. Gregory of Nyssa, St. Jerome, St. Ambrose, St. John Damascene, and above all from St. Augustine. Whoever reads these testimonies carefully need not make a " salto mortale," as Fueter insinuates, in order to be convinced that, after all, there is some truth in St. Augustine's words, " Hoc enim a patribus traditum universa tenet ecclesia."

There is a feeling of well-merited satisfaction in the preface to the twelfth volume. " Behold," the Annalist writes, " with God's help, we are about to bring into the church the twelfth volume of the *Annals*. It has been our endeavor that these twelve tomes, one and all, should endure like unto twelve columns adorned with writing and which, being grounded on the firmness of truth, should preserve intact the Church against the unremitting strokes of her persecutors, while at the same time, by the writing which is upon them, they proclaim everywhere in God's vast Kingdom His glory which must not pass into oblivion but rather must be set forth upon thousands of monuments and sung by the tongues of men and angels for all eternity."

In a large measure this prophecy has been fulfilled. Baronius avoided the mistake of his antagonists who had raised thirteen columns of support along the outer walls of the Church, feigning that the clerestory of the edifice was about to collapse. Baronius proved himself a more expert architect. In what his antagonists had pointed out as faulty workmanship, Baronius saw the well-defined design, no matter whether in the course of centuries it bore the stamp of the Basilica, the Romanesque, the Gothic or Renaissance style; and trusting in the solidity of the massive walls he calmly set about his work, and starting from the very sanctuary he moved down the spacious nave and built his mighty columns, one by one, reaching from the solid foundation to the highest arches of the edifice. And while today his columns stand firm and solid, the work of his opponents has gradually crumbled into ruins around the walls of the Ancient Church.

BIBLIOGRAPHY

A. BIOGRAPHY

BUCCIO, *Vita* (MS., Roman Oratory); H. SPONDÉ, *Epitome* (Paris, 1612); GIR. BARNABEO, *Vita Caesaris Baronii* (Rome, 1651); RICCI, *Vita* (Rome, 1745); RAYM. ALBERICIUS, *Ven. Caesaris Baronii . . . Epistolae, Opuscula . . . Vita* (Rome, 1759–1770); SARRA, *Vita del Ven. Ces. Baronio* (Rome, 1882); LE FEVRE, *Vie de Card. Baronius* (Douai, 1868); R. BAUER, S.J., art. *Baronius* in *Kirchenlexikon;* C. MIRBT, art. *Baronius* in *Realencyklopedie fuer Protestantische Theologie und Kirche;* LADY AMABEL KERR, *The Life of Cesare Cardinal Baronius of the Roman Oratory* (London, 1898); A. WEBER,

art. *Baronius* in *Kirchl. Handlexikon* (Buchberger);
JOHN B. PETERSON, art. *Baronius* in *Cath. Encyclopedia;*
GENEROSO CALENZIO, ORAT., *La Vita e gli Scritti del Cardinale Cesare Baronio* (Rome, 1907); *Per Cesare Baronio Scritti Vari nel Terzo Centenario della sua morte* (Rome, 1911); HUGO LAEMMER, *De Caesaris Baronii Literarum Commercio Diatriba* (Freiburg i. B., 1903).

B. GENERAL WORKS ON BARONIUS
AND HIS WRITINGS

GIR. TIRABOSCHI, *Storia della Letteratura Italiana* (Florence, 1805–1813), VII, I, pp. 401–404; VILLOROSA, *Memorie etc.* (Naples, 1837); ALFONSO CAPECELATRO, *The Life of St. Philip Neri* (trans. by T. A. Pope, London, 1882); II, pp. 1–31; E. FUETER, *Geschichte der Neueren Historiographie* (Munich and Berlin, 1911), pp. 263–265; H. HURTER, S.J., *Nomenclator Literarius*, III, pp. 526–539; RAUSCHEN, *Jahrbücher der Christlichen Kirche unter dem Kaiser Theodosius dem Grossen: Versuch einer Erneuerung der Annales Ecclesiastici des Baronius für die Jahre 378–395* (Freiburg i. B., 1897); POTTHAST, I (2nd ed.), xxvii sqq. For adverse criticism see: CASAUBON, *Exercitationes* (Geneva, 1654); cf. *Per Cesare Baronio* (v.s.), pp. 261–294, and PATTISON, *Isaac Casaubon* (Oxford, 1892), pp. 315–341; CAVE, *Historia Literaria Script. Ecclesiasticorum* (London, 1868), xxv–xxvi; DOWLING, *Introduction to Critical Study of Ecclesiastical History* (London, 1838), pp. 105–128.

As stated in the text, the *Annals* were first printed in Rome, 1588–1607. Each of the volumes extends over a century, the twelfth ending with the year 1198. There are several continuators of the *Annals*, but none brings the work down to our age and none equals the original author. Among them three Oratorians occupy the first place: RAYNALDUS covered the period 1198–1566; LADERCHI,

the period 1566–1571; THEINER, the period 1572–1585.
Another, less valuable, continuation covering the period
1198–1572 was brought out by the Dominican BZOVIUS,
and a third, 1198–1646, by Bishop SPONDÉ. There are
numerous translations and epitomes of the work. The best
criticism was published by the two Conventuals AN-
THONY and FRANCIS PAGI, *Critica historico-chronologica
in Annales Baronii*, 4 vols. (Antwerp, 1705 and 1727).
The best among the many editions of the *Annals* are
those of MANSI (Lucca, 1728–1759, 38 vols.), who inserted Pagi's corrections and added a valuable Index, and
THEINER (Bar-le-Duc, 1864–1883, 37 vols.).

BOLLANDUS (1596–1665)

Rev. Francis Mannhardt, S.J.
University of St. Louis

" Die Bollandisten, eroeffneten die gelehrte historische Kritik." Fueter, *Geschichte der neueren Historiographie.*

THE modern trend in historical studies has often resulted in restating the facts of the past. For whatever their theory, all scholars are agreed that history must aim to find and to spread the truth. This was not always the case. Excepting perhaps Thucydides and Tacitus, the Classics saw little difference between history and rhetoric,[1] while the Middle Ages sought edification and were naïve enough to lend belief to every written word. If these views differed much from our own, they nevertheless invited excuse rather than blame. A change came about with the rise of Humanism. The spirit of criticism cultivated by Valla († 1457), Guicciardini († 1540), and Erasmus († 1536), meant indeed an advance upon the naïve credulity of the previous centuries, but was inspired by unworthy motives and could never achieve the best results. Under the conditions existing at that time, it prepared the way for the pseudo-history of the following three centuries, which, in spite of all its pretensions, has been defined as " a conspiracy

---

[1] Cf. Cic., *De leg.*, 1:2, 5, *Orat.*, 20:66. Quint., *Instit.*, 10:1, 31.

against truth." However, de Maistre spoke of historical narratives, not of historical studies, for
challenged by the hostile polemics of Humanists
and Reformers, Catholic scholars soon recognized
the need of checking up the writings of their opponents. They felt the jarring discords existing between traditional accounts and contemporary objections, but admitted that the Catholic past had
been too uncritical in many beliefs to permit them
to assert without hesitation the historical truth of
those which were attacked. They had every reason
to think that honest research would vindicate the
Church, which was of divine origin and held the
promise of Christ's vigilant care, but it was obvious
that their opponents had to be met on purely historical grounds. Hence they determined to return to
the sources, in the interests both of a legitimate defense and of true scholarship.

The situation became acute under the stress of
the Protestant Revolution. It will suffice to mention
the Magdeburg Centuriators (1559–1574), whose
partisanship was promptly recognized by their Catholic contemporaries, but whose pretentious erudition
misled many. Even Fueter [2] admits that the attacks
of the early Protestant writers were based on weak
foundations, a fact clearly proved by Canisius
(† 1597), and Baronius († 1607). These controversies, though regrettable and at times disgusting,
begot our modern historiography, because under
their stress much effective work was done for his-

[2] Fueter, *l. c.*, p. 311.

tory. It is admitted that this was of very unequal value and that it was, in general, of the nature of preparatory studies and the gathering of material. The *Annals* of Baronius (1588–1593), planned as a corrective of the Magdeburg *Centuries,* had shown the need of a fuller disclosure of the sources, and their " immediate influence was the creation of a new school of Catholic historiography, devoted to the publication of source material rather than to the actual narrative of Church History." [3] The leaders of this school were the Maurists and the Bollandists, followed by a number of individual scholars, such as Muratori († 1750), J. S. Assemani († 1768), Tillemont († 1698), and Mansi († 1769). The most important work was done by the two groups of religious, the Benedictines and the Jesuits, not merely because a religious order alone could at that time insure the personnel, the organization and the sustained effort demanded by a great work, but also because it alone could protect its writers against the whims of princes and the caprices of the public. There is this distinction, however, between the two groups, that, whereas the Maurists were interpreters rather than critics of the sources, the Bollandists were pioneers and leaders in their critical evalua- tion. Such is the opinion of a recent writer,[4] and such is the admission of Fueter himself, who, in spite of his disdain of Catholic scholarship, is forced to admit that the Bollandists inaugurated modern his-

---

[3] Guilday, *l. c.,* p. 274.
[4] Guilday, *l. c.,* p. 275. Fueter, *l. c.,* p. 312.

torical criticism. We readily understand, therefore, why the name of Bollandus must appear on every list of Catholic historians and why a discussion of his work must include a brief account of its bearing on modern historiography.[5]

A. THE SEVENTEENTH CENTURY

I. ROSWEYDE

In speaking of the *Acta Sanctorum* we may deal briefly with historical data, for there is no need to repeat a twice-told tale. The original conception of the *Acta* is due to a Belgian Jesuit, Heribert Rosweyde (1569–1629) whose researches in the libraries of Flanders had drawn his attention to the glaring contrasts existing between the current lives of the saints and the readings of the original manuscripts. He secured the approval of his superiors as early as 1603, but could not propose his scheme to the learned until 1607, when he published his *Fasti Sanctorum quorum vitae in belgicis bibliothecis manuscriptae*. His plan called for the publication of eighteen folio volumes, of which the first three were to treat of the feasts of Christ, of the Blessed Virgin and of the saints in general, while the last three were to contain the necessary notes and dissertations. The bulk of the work was to consist of twelve volumes or months, giving the lives of the saints, classified according to the calendar. This program of eighteen volumes was simple and modest

[5] Fueter, *l. c.*, p. 325. Dunin-Borkowski, *l. c.*, p. 410.

if compared to the actual work later published, but seemed chimerical to Bellarmine and to many contemporaries. Rosweyde, however, was not discouraged and continued his search for manuscripts. He further exemplified his proposal by the publication of his *Vitae Patrum* (1615) for which he used twenty-three manuscripts and twenty printed works, and to which he added an introduction, notes and indexes. His method was, therefore, substantially that of the later Bollandists and consisted in the gathering of sources, the collation and correction of manuscripts, the addition of introductions, notes and explanations and the enrichment of the whole with pertinent dissertations. It is granted that there exists a wide difference between the tentative method of Rosweyde, the assured procedure of Bollandus and Papebroch and the scientific thoroughness of De Smedt and Delehaye, but the difference is one of degree, not of principle. How Rosweyde's ideas would have taken concrete shape in the actual publication of a volume of the *Acta*, cannot be known, for he died before he had been able to publish a single fascicle (1629).

2. BOLLANDUS

His vast collections were committed to John Bollandus (1596–1665) then about thirty-four years of age, a man of penetrating intellect, marvelous memory, prodigious industry and broad sympathies. After due reflection, Bollandus determined to adopt the plan of Rosweyde but to expand its scope. He explained his plan and method in the preface to the first volume of January, which preface, it has been said, " must always have a place in the history of historical method." [6] The *Acta Sanctorum* were, therefore, to provide the best and the amplest material for the student of hagiography; they were to include all the saints, even those little known and those without a cult; and were accordingly to give the full texts of all the manuscripts. It may be added, however, that though this last principle was ever upheld, it was not always rigidly enforced before the nineteenth century. Bollandus intended, furthermore, that only the best sources were to be used in the critical evaluation of the manuscripts; but while all necessary information about the origin and condition of the text was to be supplied together with the necessary critical apparatus, the sources were to be published as they were found, including even palpable forgeries, fables and apocrypha. Certainly an ambitious scheme, which might have been utterly wrecked had Bollandus and his Provincial fully grasped its implications.[7]

We may abstract from many of the obstacles which confronted Bollandus in order to mention only three which have since his day been removed from the path of the modern scholar. We refer to the absence of central libraries and bibliographical aids, to the undeveloped state of textual criticism

---

[6] Collis in *Cath. Hist. Rev., l. c.,* p. 307.
[7] *Acta SS.,* Jan., Vol. I., Praef. c3.

and to the necessity of patronage and financial support. The last proved to be the least of these difficulties, for by the liberality of friends, as well as by the shrewd business capacity of such men as Henschen († 1681), and Janninck († 1723), the *Acta Sanctorum* were not exposed to straitened circumstances until after the suppression of the Society of Jesus in 1773.

The undeveloped state of textual criticism was a more serious difficulty and explains the shortcomings of the earlier volumes, but its discussion may be reserved for a later paragraph. Suffice it to say that the very method of Bollandus and his followers must be said to have established this science.

If the dream of Bollandus was not to remain a hagiographic Utopia the extensive use of libraries was a necessity. But, alas, in the early seventeenth century there were few large depositories of books similar to our national, municipal and university libraries. This meant that the hagiographic material was dispersed in countless private libraries, for instance in those of monasteries and of individual scholars. Moreover, there were no catalogues of manuscripts and printed works, such as those of Potthast and Chevalier; or, if such existed, they listed none but the manuscripts of one library and were inaccessible except on the spot. There were no historical periodicals with bibliographies of local saints or current hagiographical publications, such as the *Catholic Historical Review,* the *Analecta Bollandiana,* and the *Revue d'Histoire Ecclésiastique.*

There were at that time few, if any, collections of
sources such as those of d'Achéry and Mabillon,
Muratori and Migne. But Bollandus was an excep-
tional man, cast in the mould of heroes and of saints.
As the manuscripts must be used, ways and means
must be found to reach them. Hence the creation of
the Bollandist Museum or Library, hence the many
scientific journeys of his assistants and followers,
hence the vast scientific correspondence maintained
with all the learned world. The nucleus of the Bollandist Library was the transcripts of Rosweyde,
continually and extensively augmented by later
transcripts, purchases and donations, so much so
that within fifty years it was the richest hagiographic library in Europe. During the period of the
French Revolution it was completely scattered and
largely destroyed, but it numbers today more than
fifteen hundred thousand volumes and about six
hundred periodicals.

The rapid growth of the Library was a partial
result of the many journeys undertaken by the Bollandists, who, like the proverbial busy bee, did not
return from abroad without being heavily laden.
Abstracting from the shorter expeditions of Rosweyde and Bollandus, these scientific journeys may
be said to have begun in 1660, when Henschen and
Papebroch visited the libraries of the Rhineland,
Bavaria, Austria, Italy and France. Their journey
of twenty-nine months had enabled them not only to
acquire an enormous mass of documents, transcribed
either by themselves or by copyists, but had also put

them in touch with local correspondents and with the most learned men of that time. At Rome alone they garnered a harvest of seven hundred transcripts. Thus did the Bollandists help to establish the modern principle that there is no excuse for ignoring an important manuscript.

Because of the many bibliographical aids at the service of the modern scholars, not only for general but also for local and particular history, scientific correspondences have lost much of their former importance. In the days of the early Bollandists they were an absolutely necessary means for scholarly work. The correspondence of Bollandus was immense, though accurate data concerning it are wanting; of Du Sollier († 1740), we know that his list numbered twelve thousand letters.

3. THE COLLEGE OF BOLLANDISTS

A winsome and interesting characteristic of Bollandus was his enlightened prudence and genial sympathy. Not many years had elapsed before he recognized that his work could not be done by one generation and that he was called not only to begin a great work, but to found a school. The result was the establishment of " The College of the Bollandists." This consists of a select group of scholars, never more than four or five, totally devoted to hagiography, and bound together, less by the bonds of discipline than by devotion to their work. According to the wishes of Bollandus, there was to be no position of superiority among them and, though there is a division of work, all questions of publication were to be dealt with in common. It has been aptly said by a living Bollandist that " to be certain of founding a school, Bollandus formed a family." [8]

Such were the ideas of Bollandus, such the means employed. It would be a mistake to ascribe the success of the *Acta Sanctorum* exclusively to him, but to him must be given the credit of having well begun, of having firmly established and of having wisely provided for the whole enterprise. Still, as true scholars are wont to be, he was extremely humble and modest, and greatly rejoiced at the mature judgment, the industry and the keenness of Henschen († 1681), and the initiative, the critical acumen and the facile style of Papebroch († 1714). Both were his pupils in their youth, his assistants in their prime and proved his competent successors after his death. Together with him, they dominate the golden age of the Bollandists. When Bollandus died, in 1665, six large folio volumes had been published to the delight of the learned world. Henschen and Papebroch continued and intensified the work, so that when Papebroch came to die, in 1714, the *Acta* covered the first six months of the year and comprised twenty-four volumes.

A critique of the work of Bollandus will, therefore, acknowledge its imperfections, but will also recognize that these were due, not to incompetence, lack of industry or mistaken apologetics, but to the

[8] Delehaye, *The Bollandists*, p. 46.

condition of historical studies at that time. The earlier volumes are not the equals of the latest, for historical criticism needs historical sources and these were at that time not sufficiently available. That they were placed within reach of later scholars is, in great measure, the merit of the Maurists and the Bollandists, that they were critically sifted and prepared for use being above all the merit of the latter. Their seventeenth-century work was not as far advanced as that of the nineteenth, but even of the former it remains true that the *Acta Sanctorum* are one of the greatest monuments of sound erudition, of patient research, and of critical taste that science knows.

B. The Eighteenth and Nineteenth Centuries

The earliest productions of great writers are often the best and it might seem that the same observation is to be made of the Bollandists. The eighteenth-century Bollandists no doubt maintained the high standard of erudition and painstaking accuracy set by their predecessors, but were to some extent affected by the diffusiveness of the age and its religious controversies. However, Bollandus had planned well and his spirit had descended upon his successors, so that they continued to make noteworthy contributions to history and to historical studies. An advantage was derived from the fact that the work had been undertaken by a religious

Order, which not only provided competent and well-trained workers, but insured also consistent methods and an established tradition, — an advantage of no little moment in the production of a work of centuries. A second advantage was more directly due to Bollandus since it flowed from the organization and the *esprit de corps* which he had bequeathed to his successors. This in fact was so close-knit and strong that the Bollandists outlived the suppression of the Society by twenty-one years. But we know the dreary story of the end: the contempt of the *Acta* as out of harmony with the age, the last wanderings of the older Bollandists, the final catastrophe in 1794 and the scattering of the Bollandist collections.

However, storms do not last, and even the French Revolution became an event of history. A brighter day seemed to dawn for the *Acta* with the opening years of the nineteenth century. The Society of Jesus had been restored in 1814, Belgium had achieved its independence in 1830, the Belgian Province of the Society had been organized in 1832, and Catholic scholars everywhere urged the resumption of the *Acta Sanctorum*. The danger of others undertaking this work brought matters to a head, and in 1838 the Neo-Bollandists published their prospectus *De prosecutione operis Bollandiani*. The event was hailed with joy by all the learned, and though the difficulties were many, the work has since then progressed at a steady, albeit slow, pace. Between 1837 and 1910 ten volumes of the *Acta* have been published and three volumes of supplements, so that the work now comprises sixty-three volumes and gives the lives of all the saints from January 1 to November 8. The fourth volume of November has just been published.

It may seem strange that the older Bollandists should have published the first twenty-four volumes of the *Acta* within seventy years, and that the Neo-Bollandists, in spite of all modern aids, should not have been able to publish more than ten volumes within the same space of time. The explanation is to be sought in the more exacting demands of scholarship, the fewness of writers, and the need of supplementing the earlier volumes.

Father Charles De Smedt († 1911), the Papebroch of the nineteenth century, found it necessary to adapt the old methods to the new conditions, and not only to avail himself of a far more ample source-material, but also to subject it to a much more searching criticism. Scientific historiography has made notable progress during the nineteenth century, new branches of knowledge had been introduced, such as the study of comparative religions and literatures, and the auxiliary sciences of history were being intensely cultivated. If the *Acta* were to be true to themselves, they must necessarily meet the most severe tests, whether these were the rules of the auxiliary sciences or the cavilings of an unsympathetic critic. Moreover, the need had arisen of supplementing the earlier volumes of the *Acta*, as well as of finding a means of publishing separate and lengthier studies. These considerations led to the publication of the *Analecta Bollandiana*. Appearing quarterly since 1882, this periodical enables the Bollandists to supply corrections and supplements to the published volumes of the *Acta*,[9] to hasten the publication of important manuscripts,[10] and to publish special hagiographic studies and catalogues.[11] In short, it serves in a general way as the subsidiary companion-publication of the larger work. Its scholarly papers are deservedly admired and its contributions to Catholic scholarship are of great importance.

The fewness of writers has at all times been a serious difficulty, but never so much as during the last decades. It is easily understood if we bear in mind the varied and stupendous activities of the Belgian Jesuits and the many years spent in training by a Bollandist. In 1922 the College of the Bollandists consisted of three members, Fathers Delehaye, Peeters, and Lechat, but four younger men were in training, one specializing in Gaelic hagiography, two others in medieval and early Christian, while the fourth was to succeed Father Peeters as authority on the Greek and the Oriental saints.

[9] E.g. cf. *Analecta Bollandiana*, Vol. III. *Historia S. Ursulae ex codice Bruxellensi 831–834.* Vol. I. *Vita S. Bonifacii auctore Willibaldo.*

[10] E.g. cf. Vol. I. *Vita S. Patricii auctore Muirchu Maccumachthani.*

[11] E.g. cf. Vol. XXIII. *S. Ambroise et l'empereur Theodose. Catalogus Hagiographicus Bibliothecae Regiae Bruxellensis. Bibliotheca Hagiographica Latina*, 1898–1901. *Supplementum*, 1911. — *Bibliotheca Hagiographica Graeca*, 1895. 2a ed. 1909. — *Bulletin des publications hagiographiques.*

We must abstract from the "subsidia" and the other publications of the Bollandists, important though some of these are, in order to give a brief estimate of the work of Bollandus and of its place in modern historiography.

C. The "Acta Sanctorum" and Modern Historiography

Leibniz († 1716) had said in reference to the *Acta Sanctorum,* "If the Jesuits had produced nothing but this work, that alone would be a sufficient reason for their existence and would entitle the Society to our esteem." His opinion will not seem strange to those who have a more intimate acquaintance with the *Acta.* They must indeed be considered as one of the most important historical undertakings of the last three centuries, not merely because of their material contributions to historical knowledge, but also because of their systematic application of critical methods. Historical criticism was not unknown before, but never had it been so searchingly applied to the sources found and so extensively and consistently continued. The motives for this intensive criticism are to be found in the aim and purpose of Bollandus, which was to find and to publish the truth. He was of opinion, we may admit, that the truth, if frankly presented, would speak for itself, but there is no excuse for the insinuations of Fueter which betray bias rather than knowledge.[12] To say without adequate proof, that the Bollandists developed historical criticism only to that degree which was compatible with the principles of their Order, has no meaning for one acquainted with the Jesuit Rule and deserves only contempt. Nor does another statement of his square with the facts. We are told that the Bollandists wrote for the apologetic purpose of saving the Catholic veneration of saints, and that they sought to meet the attacks of Protestants by a bolder scepticism of hagiographic legends.[13] The truth of the matter is that they were scientific historians and considered it their duty as such to examine the connection of a current version with the real facts, not its connection with traditional beliefs, legends and popular devotions. This is proved to evidence by their very method,[14] which did not consist in writing the lives of the saints, but in publishing every ancient *vita*, every scrap of record, every bit of pertinent erudition, which would enable the reader, the scholar and the writer to construct the story himself. The introductions and notes were their own, but were suggested by the text of the manuscripts, and were of such a scholarly and objective nature that any other aim than that of the quest of truth is inadmissible. The assumption, therefore, that the *Acta Sanctorum* are a cleverly disguised apology must be waived aside, though the sheer force of their sincere candor often enough attained this end.

[12] Fueter, *l. c.*, p. 325.   [13] *Ib.*, p. 310.
[14] *Acta SS*. Jan. Tom. I. Praef., and Collis in *Catholic Historical Review*, Oct. 1920, p. 294.

There is nothing which supports this conclusion
more strongly than the influence exerted by the
Acta upon modern historiography, an influence
which even Fueter is compelled to concede to
them.[15]

The contributions of the Bollandists to modern
historiography are of three kinds: source-material,
special studies, and critical methods. For the publication of source-material they were not the only
workers in the field of history, even during the
seventeenth century, nor was the mass of material
published so much larger than that published by
others. Still it has been said by a competent scholar
that there is no work " which has given to the world
such a wealth of admirably edited historical material." [16] Abstracting for the present from the introductions and commentaries on the texts, we must
remind ourselves that the critical collation of manuscripts was in its infancy in the early seventeenth
century and that catalogues of codices did not exist.
Hence it was that the Bollandist publication of
sources took two forms: a critical and carefully col-
lated publication of the primary sources with their
variant readings, and the publications of bibliographical catalogues, martyrologies and menologies.

However, the texts published in the *Acta Sanctorum* form only a small part of the work. Taking
a broader view, the Bollandists have not narrowed
their field of vision to hagiography, but have discussed all incidental questions, even in their rela-

[15] Cf. Fueter, *l. c.*, p. 312.
[16] Thurston in *The Month*, 1891, p. 20.

tion to general history. The result has been that the *Acta* are a storehouse of historical information, and that there are few points of ecclesiastical history upon which they have not shed new light. This collateral information and erudition is found as a rule in the introductory and explanatory notes accompanying the text, but above all in the masterly dissertations often interspersed or, of late in particular, published separately. As instances of this literary activity we might mention Bollandus' preface on the writing of history,[17] Papebroch's discussion of the Carmelite Legend,[18] and so forth throughout the past three centuries until Delehaye's publications on the Cult and Martyrs and the Stylite Saints.[19] As a rule these special studies were exhaustive, and we of the twentieth century will find a strong proof of their unprejudiced and independent scholarship in the controversies which many of them caused at the time of their publication. Times have changed; in our day we are not terrified by the rejection of a belief which has persisted perhaps for a thousand years, such as the Lateran baptism of Constantine, or the exposure of a forgery upon which during eight hundred years many authors have based papal rights, as for instance the False Decretals. We might almost say that we have become accustomed to such revelations, since the

[17] *Acta SS.* Jan. Tom. I. Praef.; Collis, in *Cath. Hist. Rev.*, *l. c.*

[18] *Acta SS.* Apr. Tom. I., p. 769; Delehaye, *The Bollandists*, p. 123 sqq.

[19] Delehaye, *Les Passions des martyrs et les genres littéraires.* Bruxelles, 1921. Delehaye, *Les saints stylites.* Bruxelles, 1923.

naïve credulity of the Middle Ages and the hostile perversions of anti-Catholic writers have both tended to make us slow to put faith in legends and cautious in the acceptance of popular traditions.

From the viewpoint of the professional historian, however, the Bollandists have nowhere done more surprising work than in the field of historical criticism. From the first prospectus of Rosweyde, 1607, and Bollandus' preface to the first volume of January, 1643, down to De Smedt's *Principes de la critique historique*, 1883, and Delehaye's *Les legendes hagiographiques*, 1906 (Engl. ed. 1907), the Bollandists have emphatically advocated historical criticism in theory and in practice. Building on the foundation of solid and profound knowledge, which they had acquired by unwearied labor at the sources themselves, they carefully distinguished between the various traditions, apostolic, historical, and popular. Setting aside the first as less within the purview of the historian than of the theologian, they applied the laws of science to historical and popular traditions. Historical traditions go back to the events themselves, and hence, if securely established, are true history; popular traditions often arise several centuries later, but by their catchy details and concrete additions often supplant the former or totally envelop them. The .distinction is of vital importance and has legitimately disposed of a mass of hagiographic fungi without tampering with healthy hagiography itself. Needless to say, the Bollandists had continually to deal with tradition, be it written, oral, pictorial or monumental, but while subjecting the evidence to a searching probe, they have not handled it in a preconceived or iconoclastic spirit. Though they have been reproached with having wrought havoc among the traditions of hagiography, they must in reality be acquitted of the charge of leaning to either extreme. Their condemnation of hagiographic errors was prompted by love of truth, not by carping jealousy or the desire of novelty. And it would seem superfluous to add that this statement remains true even of such aggressive scholars as Papebroch, De Buck, Van Ortroy, De Smedt and Delehaye.

Unbending love of truth was, therefore, the outstanding characteristic of the Bollandist historians. This naturally determined their methods. They made the most extensive use of the so-called auxiliary sciences of history, not indeed in the seventeenth century with that conscious facility which marks their work in the twentieth, but yet with such intelligent persistence that most of these sciences owe much of their existence and development to the *Acta Sanctorum*. Philological criticism was applied by the Bollandists to the analysis of the sources and of the authority of authors. Their chronological and topographical discussions are justly admired and, while not meeting present demands, are yet worthy of the age of Petau († 1652). In critical studies they were usually the leaders, though they were always ready to admit the good work of others. For instance, Papebroch's venture upon the uncharted main of diplomatics,[20] called forth Mabillon's classic work *De re diplomatica,* and with genuine humility the Jesuit admitted his own mistake, while he rejoiced at the gain for historical scholarship.

As true scholars, however, the Bollandists have ever kept themselves free from the craze of conjecture and hypothesis which afflicts so many lesser lights in our day. "As a rule they (the Bollandists) have abstained from attempting to solve insoluble problems, holding it to be a sufficient task to classify the hagiographic texts, to print them with scrupulous care, to make known with all attainable exactitude their origin, their source, their style, and, if possible, to pronounce upon the talent, the morality, and the literary probity of their authors." [21] It would seem, therefore, that the Bollandists were ahead of their age, and it could not be otherwise if, as even their enemies admit, they have made such important contributions to critical history. Would that they were more justly appreciated; would that they were frequently consulted.

BIBLIOGRAPHY

A. BIOGRAPHY

No complete biography of John Bollandus has yet been written. Apart from the sketches in the various encyclopedias and dictionaries — one of the best of which is the

---

[20] *Acta SS.* Apr. Tom. II., pp. i-xxxi. cf. also Delehaye, *Legends of the Saints,* p. 122 sq.

[21] Delehaye, *Legends of the Saints,* p. 218.

article *Bollandists* in the *Cath. Encycl.*, by Charles De-Smedt, S.J. — the student will find biographical data in the *Prefaces* to Vols. I (Jan.), II (April), V (May), VI (June), VII (October), and in particular Vol. I (March), which contains Papebroch's notice: *De Vita, operibus et virtutibus Joannis Bollandi, S.J.* Delehaye's recent volume: *L'oeuvre des Bollandistes (1615–1915)*, an English translation of which was published (Princeton, 1922), is the most complete account up to the present time of Bollandus.

B. GENERAL WORKS ON THE BOLLANDISTS

PITRA, *Études sur la Collection des Actes des Saints* (Paris, 1856).

RENAN, *Études d'Histoire Religieuse* (Paris, 1860).

HURTER, *Nomenclator Litterarius*, II, 222–233, 557, 883 (Innsbruck, 1903).

PELSTER, *Die Bollandisten und ihr Werk*, in *Stimmen der Zeit*, July, 1920.

LECHAT, *Les "Acta Sanctorum" des Bollandistes*, in the *Catholic Historical Review*, for October, 1920, pp. 334–342.

COLLIS, *The Preface of the "Acta Sanctorum,"* ibid., pp. 294, 307.

PALMIERI, *The Bollandists*, ibid., Oct., 1923, pp. 341–357.

THURSTON, *The Bollandists*, in the *Tablet* for April 8, 1922.

GUILDAY, *Introduction to Church History*, pp. 145, 183, 221, 274–275 (St. Louis, 1925).

FEDER, *Lehrbuch der historischen Methodik*, p. 72. (Ratisbon, 1924).

DUNIN-BORKOWSKI, *Aus den Werkstaetten zur Erforschung der neueren Geschichtschreibung*, in *Stimmen der Zeit*, 1912.

MURATORI (1672–1750)

RIGHT REVEREND THOMAS J. SHAHAN, D.D., RECTOR
Catholic University of America

THE greatest of Italy's historians, Ludovico Antonio Muratori, was born October 31, 1672, at Vignola, near Modena, better known as the birthplace also of the famous architect, Jacopo Barozzi. His parents were in modest circumstances, but kept the boy at school, first in his native village, and later in the Jesuit college at Modena, where by dint of severe studies he acquired a more than ordinary knowledge, particularly of Latin, and laid the foundation of his almost incredible erudition. He inclined from early youth toward the priesthood, and for that reason pursued the usual studies of philosophy, moral and dogmatic theology, and canon law, but his tastes soon led him to an intimate acquaintance with the masters of style, both classical and Italian. Soon he acquired a solid knowledge of Greek. Meantime he developed a taste for ancient inscriptions and read widely in that field, little thinking that he would one day rank among the great masters of Latin and Greek epigraphy. Indeed, his youthful admiration and tastes were all for classical antiquities, history, and letters, and his idols were Carlo Sigonio and Justus Lipsius. He looked originally on the medieval world as a long stretch of intolerable barbarism.

From a Franciscan friar he obtained an excellent training in logic and soon fell in with a remarkable scholar, Dom Benedetto Bachini, the Benedictine librarian of the Duke of Modena, under whom he made great progress in the reading and the science of medieval manuscripts. He was scarcely twenty-one when his phenomenal learning was brought to the attention of Count Carlo Borromeo, who appointed him (1693) on the staff of the Ambrosiana Library at Milan, founded a century earlier by Cardinal Federico Borromeo, of all places the best suited for his peculiar genius. That year he published his first dissertation, on the value and excellence of the Greek tongue, also a study on the rise and fall of the barometer, while the next year (1694) he wrote a treatise on the earliest Christian churches and obtained his degrees in civil and canon law. He was ordained a priest in 1695. For seven years he lived amid the manuscripts and printed books of the Ambrosiana, hiving in his twenties the vast erudition that was to stand him in such good stead for fifty years.

I

In 1697 he published the first volume of his *Anecdota Latina*, i.e. twenty-two dissertations on certain important discoveries he had made in the Ambrosiana, among them four hitherto unknown poems of St. Paulinus of Nola. In 1698 a second volume of similar researches appeared, and his name was henceforth pronounced in Europe with respect.

Incidentally, among the Bobbio manuscripts he came across the famous second century list of the books of the New Testament now known as the Muratorian Canon, and the Latin Antiphonary of ancient Irish Bangor. In this young priest of twenty-five the erudite world of Europe welcomed a new scholar and a critic whose insight, judgment, good sense, and correct feeling were thenceforth seldom at fault, though he was destined to range freely through every province of learning.

The natural sciences, philosophy, ethics, classical antiquities, particularly Italian letters, attracted him in turn, and along all these lines he read enormously and retained his readings in an impeccable memory. He would probably have become the Magliabecchi of the Ambrosiana, if the Duke of Modena had not induced him to accept the office of archivist and librarian of the Este collection of manuscripts and books saved a century earlier from the wreck of their Ferrara fortunes.

Muratori remained always deeply attached to the Borromeo family and to Milan, which he was wont to call "la città del buon cuore," and which later stood by him splendidly at the turning-point of his hopes and ambition.

Literary interests seem to have absorbed his attention after his return to Modena. Two volumes (1700) entitled *Della perfetta poesia italiana*, critical of the "Marinismo" of the time, even of the divine Petrarch, and two years later a somewhat similar work: *Reflessioni sopra il buon gusto nelle*

scienze e nelle arti, made both friends and enemies
for him. He returned later to the *Rime* of Petrarch,
and composed also two works on popular eloquence.
To his literary tastes and interests may be ascribed
the biographies of Maggi, Castelvetro, Orsi, Torti,
Giacobini, and of his fellow townsmen, Sigonio and
Tassoni. For a while he dreamed of creating a literary republic in Italy, and drew up a constitution
for it (1703) over the pseudonym of "Lamindo
Pritanio," which literary disguise he favored for
some time, chiefly on account of his youth. Meanwhile he found leisure to publish his *Epistola Ex-
hortatoria ad Superiores et Lectores Italiae pro
emendatione studiorum monasticorum,* a severe but
friendly criticism of the content and methods of
education in the monastic houses of the peninsula,
particularly of the dry and unattractive teaching of
dogmatic theology.

During the next ten years the little city of Comacchio, amid the salt marshes of the Adriatic,
looms up largely in the life of Muratori. In medieval
times the Este family held it as an imperial fief. It
lay, however, in the territory of Ferrara, and when
in 1598 that city was taken over by the Holy See as
a fief of the Church, Comacchio shared the same
fate and became papal. In 1708 on occasion of the
War of the Spanish succession, Emperor Joseph I
seized Comacchio but eventually returned it to the
Pope. Meantime Muratori, as archivist and librarian of the House of Este, asserted sharply, but in
vain, its juridical rights, not only to Comacchio but

also to Ferrara. The papal canonists replied, and
the conflict, a purely literary one, dragged along
through a decade. Though he wrote with dignity and
calm, Muratori was accused, not without reason, of
hostility to the temporal power of the Holy See, and
the controversy probably prevented the ecclesiastical advancement which might later have been offered
to him.

Amid these distractions he brought out in 1709 a
volume of *Anecdota Graeca,* two hundred and
twenty-eight unedited epigrams of St. Gregory
Nazianzen, forty-five letters of Saint Firmus of Caesarea, four of Julian the Apostate and one falsely
ascribed to Pope Julius I. The same volume contained also *De Synisactis et Agapetis, de Agapis
sublatis,* and *De Antiquis Christianorum Sepulcris.*
Two other volumes of *Anecdota Latina,* from the
manuscripts of the Ambrosiana and other libraries,
appeared in 1713, — letters, discourses, fragments,
etc. About this time he published a work of much
importance, *De Ingeniorum Moderatione in reli-
gionis negotio,* a plea for a fair and reasonable treatment of Catholic writers by the Holy Office. It soon
went through several editions and was much read
in Germany, where his sane and not unreasonable
criticism of certain religious practices and customs
aroused some controversy. Meantime he had become (1716) provost or parish priest of a church
in Modena, Santa Maria in Pomposa, and as such
soon introduced the Spiritual Exercises of St. Ignatius under the direction of Padre Segneri, nephew

of the famous orator. His account of these devotions (1728) contains some sharp criticism of certain abuses connected with the veneration of the Saints. In 1714, fearing an outbreak of the pest, he published at Modena his famous *Del Governo della peste* from political, medical, and ecclesiastical viewpoints. It went through many editions, rendered notable service in cities afflicted by the pest, and won the approval of the best physicians. Meantime he was busily engaged on the two volumes of his *Antichità Estensi ed Italiane* (1714–1720), the first of his great historical works, and a model of genealogical research. Through original documents and scientific commentary it traces back the famous House of Este to the tenth century, and establishes a common Lombard origin for the Houses of Este and Brunswick. He attracted thereby the favorable notice of George I of England, and entered into personal relations with Leibnitz who made use of these researches in his epochal work on the history of the Brunswick dynasty. He also wrote on grace, on paradise, on fasting, on lessening the holidays of obligation, and on popular devotions, and was ever ready to defend with his pen whatever thesis he set forth. Perhaps the most notable of his numerous controversies was that known as *De Voto Sanguinario*, waged with ecclesiastics of Sicily who had popularized a vow to defend, even at the risk of one's life, the Immaculate Conception of Mary.

Muratori had all the instincts of a born teacher, and was never at rest until he had thrown his concepts into some handy and practical manual, and had given them a publicity that often took on large proportions. Feeling the need for the schools and the general public of an up-to-date manual of ethics, he composed a *Filosofia Morale* (1736) that was cordially welcomed and widely used. He composed also two works on Human Intelligence (1735) and on the Imagination (1745). He is always a Catholic philosopher, sane, practical, and logical, though hostile enough to Scholasticism, or rather to the aged and arid forms in which it yet appeared.

Francesco de Sanctis calls Muratori the Bayle of Italy. It is true that he was easily stirred by the sight of ignorance and superstition in religious life, and was active and courageous in denouncing them. It must not be forgotten that the eighteenth century was the "siècle de Voltaire," and that every weakness of popular religion was for the first time noisily proclaimed to all Europe, every abuse and excess caricatured, and all defects parodied. On the other hand his domestic adversaries were many, but they served to popularize the reformatory writings of this historical sage. More than once he was denounced at Rome, but always found papal protection. "Benedict XIV," says Kirsch, "wrote to him (1748) with the intention of easing his mind troubled by the attacks of adversaries, and Cardinal Ganganelli, later Clement XIV, wrote him in the same year, assuring him of his great esteem and respect." Muratori fought always with his own hand, and from the ramparts of his books and manuscripts put up a very creditable defense of Catholic faith and discipline, based on truth and reason.[1]

Pietro Giannone (1668–1744) and his Neapolitan followers were filling Italy at this time with a malicious misrepresentation of the origins of Catholic discipline and government, and flattering the Bourbon princes by their hostility to the temporal power of the Popes, more venerable in its origin and milder in its administration than any government of Europe. It is true that able ecclesiastical apologists were not rare when such names as Pallavicini, Tommasi, Gotti, Bianchini, Noris, and Merati were everywhere held in esteem, not to speak of the scholarly layman Scipione Maffei (1655–1755). But not all had the courage of Muratori or his burning zeal for religion, much less the good sense to see that the new irreligion had to be fought with its own weapons and on its own ground. This Muratori did, with so much frankness and fairness, so much public spirit, and such a command of facts that he may be looked upon as a forerunner of our

[1] " E dalla lotta co' protestanti uscirono, in opposizione alle *Centuriae magdeburgenses* (1588–1607), i poderosi volumi in cui Cesare Baronio condusse fino al 1198 gli *Annales ecclesiastici,* e dalla rinnovazione del sentimento religioso e della devozione alla podestà della Chiesa uscì l' *Italia sacra* di Ferdinando Ughelli tra il 1644 e il 1648: due grandi opere, non senza difetti di critica la prima e di eguaglianza la seconda, ma che per la vastità e novità del disegno, la grandiosità del lavoro, la copia dei documenti comunicati, furono esempio e diedero impulsi efficaci alle raccolte storiche posteriori, come i due lavoratori che le fecero preannunziarono in altro campo l'ingegno e le fatiche di L. A. Muratori." — CARDUCCI, Preface, p. xxx.

modern Catholic journalism. We may add that his burden was all the more difficult by reason of the strange weakness of French apologetics at a time when France was the chief source of all the philosophers, philanthropists, and " esprits forts " who were flooding Italy with their wares.

Though the comfort and leisure of this great scholar were seriously affected for many years by the war which Spain and France and the Empire fought out, largely on the unhappy soil of Central Italy, he never lost sight of patriotic interests, while he retained the esteem of the foreign masters of the peninsula. His work on the public welfare, *Della felicità pubblica* (1749), merited and secured universal approval, as did another work, *Dei difetti della giurisprudenza,* with which he incorporated a code of laws (*De Codice Carolino*), drawn up for Emperor Charles VI of Austria, but never promulgated. He denounced the current belief in magic, and wrote against the duel, as also against the use of torture and the abuse of capital punishment, against class privileges and special tribunals, and other relics of an undemocratic age.

II

When Muratori began to plan a collection of all materials for Italian medieval history that had escaped the wreckage of medieval life, he could not consider himself a pioneer in the field of great historical collections. German scholars had long since roused the envy of learned Europe by the documentary collections of Freher, Goldast, Meibom and Leibnitz, to say nothing of earlier names. England offered the national collections of Savile, Twysden, Camden, Fell and Gale. France honored the names of two Jesuits, Sírmond and Labbe, and of a great layman, André Du Chesne (1584–1640), author of thirty-four historical works, and who left one hundred folio volumes written with his own hand. Two French Benedictines, D'Achéry and Mabillon, had pillaged the archives and libraries of their ancient order; the latter, in particular, had published his immortal *De re diplomatica* (Paris, 1681) and the nine folio volumes of his *Acta Sanctorum O. S. B.* (1688–1702), models of erudition and good method, rich in notes, dissertations and prefaces. They stirred to action the lonely scholar in the grand-ducal library of Modena, and fed his patriotic ambition. The enormous folios of Gronovius, Graevius, and Burmann, englobing so much erudition, medieval and modern, concerning Italy were his despair as he reflected that foreigner, devoted themselves to its honor and glory, "while Italians themselves slept or rather snored." Doubtless also, he remembered that various attempts had been made in the course of the seventeenth century to publish the national historical materials of Spain, Russia, Poland, Bohemia, and Belgium. And he was probably not ignorant of the fine historical work, outlined, begun or accomplished, in favor of Ireland by Franciscans at Louvain, Hugh Ward, Michael

O'Clery, John Colgan, Patrick Fleming, and in honor of his own order by Luke Wadding at Rome. Nevertheless, Italy of the sixteenth and seventeenth centuries did not lack all sense of its national historical wealth in the way of annals and chronicles. The famous humanist, Carlo Sigonio (1520–1584), townsman of Muratori, published (1574) a history of Italy from 570 to 1276, based on original materials, and two years later (1576) his *Catalogus historiarum et archiviorum Italiae,* which Muratori himself calls " insigne profecto opus." Carducci says of Sigonio that he was " il vero scopritore ed apritore del medio evo," and Muratori wrote a life of that great scholar.

Vincenzo Borghini (1515–1580), a Tuscan man of letters, art-critic, sculptor, and historian, treated the history of Florence in dissertations not unworthy of Muratori, and kept alive that " senso e sapienza della storia " for which his native city was famous from the Villani to Guicciardini. Early in the eighteenth century Sicily and Venice exhibited each some velleities of a collection of their local annals and chronicles, but the noble enterprise was happily left for the only Italian who had the will to the work and was qualified to plan it rightly and execute it quickly and perfectly.

Muratori lived in a wonderful age, a " saeculum mirabile " of heuristic scholarship. The folios of Bollandist hagiology were piling up on the floors of all the great libraries. The output of ecclesiastical literature, largely source materials, was aston-

ishing, — papal Bullaria, acts of councils, writings
of the Fathers, rules of monastic orders, lives and
letters of the Popes, acts of martyrs, primitive ecclesiastical discipline, ancient liturgies, the churches of
the Orient, ecclesiastical antiquities, Scripture antiquities, the history of dogma, Christian apologetics, the classics of asceticism. We live yet to a
great extent on the vast supplies hoarded by the
scholars of those extraordinary decades. This was
the age of outstanding ecclesiastical historians like
Natalis Alexander, Claude Fleury and Tillemont,
and of such extraordinary laymen as Baluze, Du-
cange and Henri Valois. When Apostolo Zeno, a
Venetian man of letters, left Italy in 1717 to accept
the office of " poeta Caesareo " at Vienna, he abandoned to Muratori his long-cherished design of a
collection of Latin medieval writers concerning Italy.
Muratori himself had once proposed a similar enterprise. He meant to collect (1703) all the " antiche
storie, si universali come particulari, che doman-
dianno scrittori nobili ed antichi delle cose romane,
e venendo sino al 1500. In questa gran raccolta di
storia dei tempi di mezzo avran luogo molti che non
han peranche veduta la luce e si conservano mano-
scritti in varie librarie con danno o almen senza
profitto delle buone lettere " (Carducci p. xxiv). In
other words, he would include all kinds of historical
documents, chronicles, annals, histories, documents,
and evidences of Italian life and thought from 500
to 1500. The humanist Latin historians of the " cin-
quecento " would not be included, and of the " quat-

trocento " only those hitherto unpublished, or the
least known. On the other hand he would include
vernacular writings, hitherto not considered in the
great national collections. He would revise and correct printed texts, add useful brief notes, and provide suitable prefaces or introductions. When later
the great work was finished (1738), he had taken
over about one hundred and sixteen earlier printed
texts, but had himself provided about two thousand
texts, diplomas, chronicles, histories, poems, statutes,
etc., hitherto unknown or inaccessible. This material
he had collected from many archives, family and
municipal, episcopal, monastic or capitular; also
from libraries, public and private. It was an enormous booty gathered partly by personal visits but
mostly by correspondence.

His credit is all the greater, when we remember
that no state, academy, or religious order stood by
him in all these arduous years, during which he
might have said with Cardinal Baronius " torcular
calcavi solus ": I have trodden the winepress alone.
Nay more, he met with frank hostility on the part
of the aristocratic republics of Genoa, Lucca, and
Venice, not to speak of the duplicity of Turin. Cardinal Albani refused him the entry to the archives
of Nonantola, in the very suburbs of Modena.
" You cannot imagine," he wrote (1722) to Sassi,
his Benedictine successor in the Ambrosiana, " how
many obstacles I met and meet constantly, in the
collection of these historical materials, being obliged
to deal with suspicious, ignorant and envious
people."

His admission of Italian documents was a novelty; elsewhere vernacular documents had been excluded, partly because of their lack of form, and partly because of their rather popular content. Muratori had dwelt so long and affectionately among these old Italian materials that he could say: " Quella stessa semplicità e popolar forma del descrivere che che succede, ha il suo pregio. Non vi scopri arte e colori da infoscare la verità, e vi accorrono minuzie che ingegni maggiori avrebbero saltate e però c'interessa conoscere." On the other hand, he cut out mercilessly from the larger chronicles the endless pages that began with the Christian era, even with Adam, and were taken mostly from Eusebius. Some critics blame him for suppressing this material, Latin and Italian, because of the many "paillettes d'or" which it contained. However Muratori was a critic of his own day, knowledge and interests, and not of ours.

The great work was printed at Milan in twenty-four folio volumes, or twenty-eight tomes, from 1721 to 1738, within the precincts of the royal palace, the old medieval burg of Visconti and Sforza.[2] A twenty-fifth additional folio was printed

[2] *Rerum Italicarum Scriptores ab Anno Aerae Christianae Quingentesimo ad Millesimumquingentesimum, Quorum Potissima Pars Nunc Primum in Lucem Prodit ex Ambrosianae, Estensis, Aliarumque Insignium Bibliothecarum Codicibus. Ludovicus Antonius Muratorius Serenissimi Ducis Mutinae Bibliothecae Praefectus Collegit, ordinavit, & Praefationibus auxit, Nonnullos Ipse, Alios vero Mediolanenses Palatini Socii Ad MStorum Codicum fidem exactos, summoque labore, ac diligentia castigatos, variis Lectionibus, & Notis tam editis veterum Eruditorum, quam novissimis auxere. Additis Ad plenius Operis, & universae Italicae Historiae ornamentum, novis Tabulis Geographicis, & variis Lango-*

in 1751, a year after Muratori's death. Of the entire work one thousand copies were struck off. This costly enterprise was financed by several Milanese gentlemen, known as the "Società Palatina." Prominent among them were the Marchese Trivulzio and the Conte Archinto, heads of prominent families of Milan. The publisher was Filippo Argelati, a bookseller of Bologna, friend and admirer of Muratori, and deeply interested in the financial success of the enterprise. Muratori enjoyed the good-will of the imperial authority, which protected the folios from any unwelcome censure, civil or ecclesiastical. By agreement with Rome, they appeared as printed "Superiorum facultate," without further indication of civil or ecclesiastical authority, not however without some rumblings of dissatisfaction from his ecclesiastical opponents in the Comacchio-Ferrara controversies. It was the first large comprehensive work of historical learning produced in Italy by Italians, amid adverse and pitiful conditions of Italian freedom. No pains were spared in the way of type, paper, and binding, so that, on its appearance, it surpassed any of the previous historical collections brought out in Germany or France. "L'Italia, già signora del mondo, caduta sotto peso della propria grandezza, oppressa da'

---

bardorum Regum, Imperatorum, aliorumque Principum Diplo-matibus, quae ab ipsis autographis describere licuit, vel nunc primum vulgatis, vel emendatis, necnon antiquo Characterum specimine, & Figuris Æneis. Cum Indice Locupletissimo. Medio-lani, MDCCXXXIII. Ex Typographia Societatis Palatinae in Regia Curia. Superiorum Facultate. 24 tomi in 28 voll.

barbari, lacerata da interne rabbiose fazioni, avvolta
fra le tenebre dell' ignoranza, ma dominatrice delle
coscienze, ribollente di nuova libertà, e studiosa di
uscire per nuove arti dalle proprie rovine, era uno
de' maggiori spettacoli della storia, e meritava le
indagini della storia, onde di servie di ammaestra-
mento e d' immenso diletto." [3]

The splendid folios met with universal approval
as they issued from the press, and in due time the
entire original edition was disposed of. Let the judgment of Montfaucon stand for the approval of the
best European scholarship. Writing to Muratori he
says: "The *Rerum Italicarum Scriptores* has met
with general approbation, and has made you famous
through all future ages." Scipione Maffei declared
him the "chief glory of Italy" (primo onore d'
Italia). This was also the opinion of Benedict XIV,
who greatly esteemed Muratori, consulted and encouraged him, and protected him against attacks
from influential quarters. Berti, the Augustinian
theologian, said of him that if Italy had never produced another scholar, Muratori alone would have
sufficed for her glory. Ugo Foscolo considered that
Muratori deserved a statue in every one of the
"cento città d' Italia." The respect, nay, the veneration of modern Italy is eloquently expressed by
two of its most distinguished spokesmen, Cesare
Balbo [4] and Allessandro Manzoni. The former de-

[3] Reina, *Classici Italiani,* Milan, 1818, *Annali d' Italia,* preface,
p. xxxvii.
[4] "Egli solo fece più per questa, che non abbia fatto per l'altre
niuna società letteraria, niuna congregazione di monaci studiosi.

clares him the best all-around historian of Italy, and
the latter asserts that the name of Muratori is henceforth to be met on every page of the long medieval
history of the peninsula.[5] In his scholarly preface to
the new edition of the *Scriptores* Carducci says that
only the potent voice of the Ezechiel of Vignola
could call together, clothe, and revivify the dry bones
of the medieval history of Italy.[6]

A new edition of the *Rerum Italicarum Scriptores*
was begun in 1900, at Città di Castello, but is now
published by Nicola Zanichelli, at Bologna: *Rac-*

Adempiè a tutti e tre gli offici che fanno avanzare la storia d'una
nazione, fu gran raccoglitore di monumenti nell' opera *Rerum
Italicarum;* fu gran rischiaratore dei punti storici difficili nelle
Dissertazioni, distese in latino ad uso più studiosi, abbreviate in
italiano ad uso de' più volgari; e negli *Annali* fu scrittore del più
gran corpo che abbiamo di nostra storia, scrittore sempre conscien-
zioso, non mai esagerato in niuna parte, non mai servile, sovente
ardito e forte, e talora elegante ed anche grande." — *Sommario,*
p. 318 (Turin, 1852).

[5] " L'immortale Muratori impiegò lunghe e tutt'altro che ma-
teriali fatiche a raccogliere e a vagliare notizie di quell'epoca:
cercatore indefesso, discernitore guardingo, editore liberalissimo
di memorie d'ogni genere; annalista sempre diligente e spesso
felice nel trovare i fatti che hanno un carattere storico, nel riget-
tare le favole che al suo tempo erano credute storia; raccoglitore
attento dei tratti sparsi nei documenti del medio evo e che possono
servire a dare una idea dei costumi e delle istituzioni che vigevano
in esso, egli risolvette tante questioni, tante più assai ne pose, ne
sfrattò tante inutili e sciocche, e fece la strada a tante altre, che il
suo nome, come le sue scoperte, si trova e debbe trovarsi ad ogni
passo negli scritti posteriori che trattano di questa materia." —
Disc. stor. long., cap. II.

[6] " Cosí la grande collezione *Rerum italicarum* tocca l'estremo
termine propostosi, e lo tocca con la storia di una città che a
punto raggiungeva ella in quel termine la cima della sua gloria.
Gli elementi storici della nazione italiana erano stati fino a quel
termine per un millenio dispersi come le aride ossa nel campo
dinanzi alla visione del profeta: occorreva la voce dell' Ezechiele
di Vignola acciò si ricongiungessero, si rincarnassero, rivivessero."
— Preface, p. lxviii.

*colta degli Storici Italiani dal 500 al 1500 ordinata
da L. Muratori, nuova edizione riveduta, ampliata, e
corretta con la direzione di Giosue Carducci e Vittorio Fiorini.* (Bologna, 1900–1926.)

In this edition the text of the *Scriptores* has undergone considerable revision, amounting in the case of some portions to a new edition. Closely related is the *Archivio Muratoriano,* a periodical devoted to the scientific interests of the new edition and now at its twenty-second " fascicule." Many of the best historical scholars of Italy are contributors to the new edition. Pius XI himself had intended at one time to contribute some fourteenth century texts, but was prevented by the events of the Great War.

III

What an incomparable panorama of medieval history is offered in this long shelf of noble folios! In their living pages alone can we catch any clear and sustained vision of the decadent Roman and his unspeakable conquerors, the Goth, the Frank, and the Lombard. Here alone can we follow the glorious rise of Venice from the nets of her fishermen and the huts of her refugees; the growth of Florence from the soft green hills of Fiesole, of Naples and Ravenna and Amalfi from the decay of Greek rule in the peninsula. Here are mirrored all the picturesque vicissitudes of Italian feudalism from Charlemagne to the Ottos and the Henrys. Here are all the slender threads and filaments of social life that

connect ancient Mediolanum with medieval Milano,
Senae with Siena, Padua with Padova, Ticinum with
Pavia, and so on. Here above all is the unbroken
Catholic life that supports and infuses all the
thought and effort of mediaeval Italy, from Saint
Benedict to Saint Francis and beyond; — the great
abbeys like Novalese, Nonantola, Bobbio, Monte
Vergine, Cava, Farfa, above all, Monte Cassino,
whose splendid Chronicle of six centuries Carducci
calls "the best historical work of the middle ages."
Within the shadows of these venerable walls the
common people began to live in their own right and
to act in their own name, soon to have their own
spokesmen in the earliest vernacular chronicles.
Here, too, is all the romance of the Southern Normans, that long-wavering battle-line between the
Church and the Empire, from Gregory VII to
Conradino. Here, too, are the maritime republics.
Genoa, Pisa, Venice, that political, social, and economic wonder of all time, with their stiff cumber-
some annals that will later become highly personal
narrative, like Dino Compagni and Gino Capponi,
or philosophical record of perfect form, like Macchiavelli and Guicciardini. The *Scriptores* are also
the greatest treasury of medieval Latin and of the
popular Italian speech into which one day this Latin
faded off.

Much of the medieval life of Italy, political, religious, social, common-human, is to be found only
in the *Scriptores* and in the wonderfully rich and
curious appendix and commentary that Muratori

soon added to these many folios. I mean the *Antiquitates Italicae Medii Aevi*. This great work, in six folio volumes, followed close on the completion of the *Scriptores,* appearing at Milan, from 1738 to 1743.[7] In seventy meaty dissertations, he discussed and illustrated the habits and customs, religion and government, laws and studies, letters and arts, markets, language, warfare, and coinage, government and treaties, vassals, freemen and serfs, Jews and lepers, of the peninsula from 500 to 1500 A.D., with a wealth of original materials, charters, privileges, coins, wills, and curious documents of many kinds, all of which were made known for the first time by this indefatigable magician of the past. Moved by patriotic considerations, he began an Italian version of this delightful encyclopedia of medieval Italian life, but died before finishing the last dissertation, which was added later by a friendly hand. In this shape, it was printed at Venice (1751). Of this unique medley of information concerning medieval Italy suffice it to say that it has greatly influenced all modern Italian historical thought, being indeed a kind of huge mirror in which the peninsular soul

[7] *Antiquitates Italicae Mediiaevi, Sive dissertationes De Moribus, Ritibus, Religione, Regimine, Magistratibus, Legibus, Studiis Literarum, Artibus, Lingua, Militia, Nummis, Principibus, Libertate, Serviitute, Foederibus, aliisque faciem & mores Italici Populi referentibus post declinationem Rom. Imp. ad annum usque MD. Omnia Illustrantur, et Confirmantur Ingenti Copia Diplomantum et Chartarum Veterum, Nunc, Primum ex Archivis Italiae depromtarum, Additis Etiam Nummis, Chronicis, Aliisque Monumentis Numquam Antea Editis. Auctore Ludovico Antonio Muratorio Serenissimi Ducis Mutinae Bibliothecae Praefecto Palatinis Mediol. Sociis Editionem Curantibus. Mediolano, MDCCXXXVIII. Ex Typographia Societatis Palatinae in Regia Curias. Superiorum Facultate.*

could recognize itself, as it were in the making.
Italian literature of the last century, so far as it offers a medieval content, is deeply indebted to this
work which has no counterpart in any language.
Finally, as though to complete a vast trilogy of this
historical life of Italy in Christian times, he undertook and finished, in a single year, it is said (1740),
his famous *Annali d' Italia* in twelve quarto volumes, reaching to the year 1500, afterward continued by himself to 1749, and by other hands, at
various times, to 1861. It is yet unsurpassed in several respects as a history of Italy. Carducci says
(p. lxiv) of these three works that never was the
history of any people presented in a manner at once
so rapid, perfect and compact.

Amid these major occupations he was tirelessly
active in other ways. For a brief hour the New
World attracted his attention and he halted the
progress of the *Scriptores* long enough to compose
his *Cristianesimo felice nelle missioni dei Padri della
Compagnia di Gesù nel Paraguay* (Venice, 1743),
based on letters to him from Paraguay by the Jesuit
Gaetano Cattaneo (1729–30), for which idyllic picture of simplicity and innocence of life he was
gratefully praised by the authorities of the Society.
On the strength of it Benedict XIV requested him
to undertake a general history of Catholic missions,
but he declined. He never quite lost his original interest in early ecclesiastical history, and toward
the end of his life produced a work of much importance, his *Liturgia Romana Vetus* (Venice, 1748)

in two folio volumes, containing the text of three ancient Sacramentaries, or mass-books, known as the Gelasianum, the Leonianum, and the Gregorianum, with a lengthy dissertation comparing the early medieval worship of the Roman Church with other Catholic liturgies, East and West. It is yet a very useful work, despite all that modern research and criticism have contributed to our knowledge of the religious services of early Christian Rome.

He was a lifelong student of Greek and Latin epigraphy, and his correspondence is filled with requests to his friends for copies of inscriptions, or solutions of epigraphic difficulties. He was particularly anxious to find hitherto unknown inscriptions, especially those omitted in extant collections. In his *Novus Thesaurus veterum Inscriptionum* published at Milan (1739–42) in six folio volumes, he brought up to date the collections of Spon, Gruter and others, and added notably to the justly famous collection of the Roman ecclesiastic, Fabretti.

A complete edition of Muratori's works, Latin and Italian, was published at Venice (1790–1810) in forty-eight octavo volumes, exclusive of the *Scriptores*. In his lifetime he had printed ninety-three volumes, forty-six in folio, thirty-four in quarto, and thirteen in octavo, a stupendous production, probably never equalled, particularly in view of his frail health and the incredible amount of his correspondence.[8] In the complete edition by Marchese

[8] Various additions to the monumental work of the *Scriptores* were printed before 1800. Thus Tartini published two folio vol-

Matteo Camporì (Modena, 1911–1922, fourteen large octavo volumes) over six thousand letters are printed, not a few of them learned treatises. One of them, written (1720) to Count Artico di Porcia (Friuli), is an account of his own literary career, replete with wise and beneficent counsel.

Muratori died at Modena, January 23, 1750, in his seventy-eighth year. He had long been ailing, and toward the end was affected with grievous eye-trouble. During his life he suffered much from headaches and was never robust. He had been always a pious and exemplary priest, and had never ceased to edify all who came in contact with him. His calm and recollected exterior was mirrored in his works, especially the controversial writings, never disfigured by violence. His daily life, described in considerable detail by Don Soli-Muratori, his nephew and heir, exhibits a deeply religious man, a blameless and zealous priest, and a laborious scholar, to whom every hour of time was precious. He survived by six years his famous contemporary, Gian Battista Vico (1668–1744) who spent at Naples an equally long life in the production of that epoch-making work, the *Scienza Nuova*, destined to revolutionize all previous philosophy of history. Meanwhile Muratori's successor in the granducal library, the Jesuit Tiraboschi (1731–1794), was preparing himself at Milan for his monumental history of

umes of allied historical materials at Florence in 1748, 1765; the Carmelite Mittarelli, one folio volume, at Venice in 1771. The new Bologna edition has so far nine Italian chronicles under the caption *Accessiones Novissimae*.

Italian literature, a natural and worthy sequel to the *Rerum Italicarum Scriptores,* and a fitting crown to the services rendered by the Modena library and archives to history and letters during the eighteenth century.

It is in one of his letters (November 25, 1718) that occurs the famous couplet of this indefatigable writer to the effect that the scholar's only true recreation is a change of occupation:

> *Non la quiete, ma il mutar fatica*
> *Alla fatica sia sol ristoro*

IV

In the annals of Italian charity Muratori is an outstanding figure. He was a lifelong servant of the poor and the friendless, particularly of youth of both sexes, of homeless and workless adults, and of prisoners. To the latter he was particularly devoted, acted as their spokesman and intermediary, and requested as a favor from the Grand Duke that he be constituted their chaplain without remuneration. He visited the poor in their homes, and provided for them heat, food, clothing, and all necessaries. In his well-known work *Regolata Divozione* (Venice, 1747) he pleaded strongly, not only for reason and moderation in the matters of feasts, images, processions, etc., but also for a considerable reduction of the holydays of obligation, whose excessive number affected the employment of the poor. Reina says of this work that "pochi libri contengono in

se tante verità quanto quel aureo libro degno de'
primi Padri della Chiesa e ripieno della più pura
filosofia pratica della religione cristiana." He
brought about in Modena a strict regulation of public begging, and caused worthy beggars to wear a
device of authorization. He advocated workhouses
for the poor, founded an association for the instruction of abandoned children, and established a public
hospital of two hundred beds that is yet in operation. In 1720 he established in Modena a citizens'
association for a regular collection of the funds necessary for the charges of municipal charities, known
as the " Compagnia di Carità " and during his lifetime he bestowed upon it large sums of money, the
earnings of his active and popular pen. In 1716, as
said above, he had become provost or parish priest
of one of the city churches, Santa Maria in Pomposa, and made it the centre of all his charitable
activities. Once a year he had a charity sermon
preached in that church, to which all Modena was
invited. He had the city divided into districts for
charitable service, and inspectors placed in charge
of each district. Finally, he published in 1723 his
famous work on Christian Charity and the love of
one's neighbor, *Della Carità Cristiana in quanto e
amore del prossimo,* hailed by all Europe as the
most notable contribution to the history and study
and practice of charity that had yet appeared. It
was at once translated into German, French and
English, and won for him the highest recognition,
ecclesiastical and secular. As a token of approval,

Emperor Charles VI bestowed upon him a rich col-
lar of gold, the value of which Muratori donated
for the use of the poor. In this work he treats at
some length of charity as a virtue, but it is mostly
in the light of good works that he discusses its nature and uses, as the practical love for our neighbor
in Christ Jesus. In its thirty-six chapters, long since
become a classic of the literature of charity, he exhibits an intimate sense of the sufferings of the poor
and a cordial sympathy that takes shape in useful
counsel and feasible suggestions. Scarcely any modern agency of charity is forgotten, — hospitals, or-
phan asylums, pawn-shops, foundling asylums; ref-
uges for the insane and the half-witted, for fallen
women; the care of prisoners, of the blind, the deaf-
mutes, and the crippled. Almsgiving is a strict duty,
a divine ordinance, and concerns particularly those
who can give. He urges sharply the personal visita-
tion of the poor, notably of the modest and retiring
poor, recommends employment and supervision,
and would forbid all begging by children, especially
by young girls. It is truly a wonderful book to come
from the hand of a man who for fifty years spent
his days habitually in a vast library amid old books
and historical trumpery of many kinds, coins, seals,
inscriptions, medals, and piles of old manuscripts
often written, as he picturesquely says, " in carat-
teri per cosi dire diabolici." He was indeed a worthy
forerunner of those two holy priests of Italy, the
foremost modern apostles of charity, Blessed Cot-
tolengo and Don Bosco. In 1733 he resigned his

parish and two small benefices, whose revenue he had used for public uses. He had been a model pastor, and gave much time to the confessional, to catechism, and to preaching, though his weak voice and blood-pressure prevented any great exertion in the pulpit. He rebuilt the parish church, equipped the sanctuary, and attended to every parochial duty, directly or through his vicar. He corrected the wayward and reconciled litigants. He was the father of his oppressed and harassed people during the wretched operations of a war that long eddied about Modena, and whose movements he graphically depicts in his correspondence.

BIBLIOGRAPHY

A. BIOGRAPHY

The best life of Muratori is that by his nephew Don G. F. Soli-Muratori, *Vita del proposto L. A. Muratori* (Venice, 1736). It is the source of most of the short biographical sketches which have appeared since Muratori's death (1750), especially those of Tiraboschi, Schedoni, Fabroni, Tipaldo and others. Reina, *Life of Muratori*, written as a preface to his edition of the *Annali d'Italia* in the *Scrittori Classici Italiani* (Milan, 1818), is an excellent character-sketch of the man and his work. Carducci's preface to the first fascicule of the new edition of the *Scriptores* (1900) is the best account of Muratori's place in modern historiography. Muratori's enormous correspondence, now accessible in the edition of Camporì, *Epistolario di L. A. Muratori* (Modena, 1911–1922), offers in fourteen volumes over six thousand letters, a

marvelous panorama of Italian life in the first half of
the eighteenth century, and a self-revelation of unique
psychological value.

B. GENERAL WORKS ON MURATORI
AND HIS WRITINGS

CAPOLLA, C., *Leibniz e Muratori* (Milan, 1893).

BALZANI, U., *Le Cronache Italiane del Medio Evo*
(Milan, 1884).

BELVIGLIERE, *La Vita, le Opere, ed i Tempi di L. A.
Muratori* (Florence, 1872).

FUETER, *Historiographie Moderne,* pp. 395–397 (Paris,
1914).

GAY, *L. A. Muratori, padre della Storia italiana* (Asti,
1887).

MERKEL, C., *Gli Studi intorno alle Cronache del Medi-
oevo* (Turin, 1894).

SCHEDONI, *Elogio di L. A. Muratori* (Modena, 1818).

JOHANN ADAM MOEHLER (1796–1838)

REV. LEO F. MILLER, D.D.
Pontifical College Josephinum, Columbus, O.

1. LIFE

THE life of Johann Adam Moehler, the most promising Catholic scholar of Germany in his time, and a leader of the reaction against liberalism, was cut short in his forty-second year. Moehler was born March 6, 1796, of a well-to-do family in the village of Igersheim in Wuertemberg. Recognizing the boy's gifts, his father gave him the best opportunities for education, sending him first to the Catholic *Gymnasium* at Mergentheim near his home. Having completed his course with distinction, he continued the study of the classics in the lyceum at Ellwangen, 1814–1815. To prepare himself for holy orders, he then removed to Tuebingen where he attended the lectures of Drey, Feilmoser, Herbst, and Hirscher, who ranked with the foremost Catholic theologians of Germany in this period. According to the custom of the time Moehler spent the last year of his theological course in residence at the Wilhelmsstift, the Catholic seminary at Tuebingen. On the 18th of September, 1819, he was ordained to the priesthood.

The second part of Moehler's life was the uneventful but highly fruitful career of a scholar.

Shortly after his ordination he was appointed vicar of Weilderstadt and Riedlingen, where he remained for one year, fulfilling the duties of his sacred office with scrupulous care. But the love for study grew upon him, and he welcomed his transfer to the position of tutor in the seminary at Tuebingen in the fall of 1820. In the two years during which he was connected with the Wilhelmsstift in this capacity, he devoted all his leisure hours to the study of ancient classical literature. He specialized in early Greek philosophy and history, thus laying the foundation of his extensive patristic knowledge, which in the years to come enabled him to break the spell of the Illumination and to lead himself and others nearer to the ideals of the ages of faith. Through his long and thorough study of the classics he also acquired those eminent qualities of literary style which played no small part in making his influence dominate those who heard his lectures and eagerly read his writings.

September 8, 1822, Moehler was appointed *Privatdozent* for Church history and kindred branches in the Catholic faculty of theology at the university of Tuebingen, where he remained until 1835. Before taking up his duties at the university, he was offered a year's leave of absence in order to acquaint himself more thoroughly with the principles of historical research and the methods of university work. With this end in view Moehler spent the allotted time principally at the universities of Berlin, Goettingen, and Vienna. The sequel proved that it was time well spent. For the lectures which he attended, the scholars with whom he associated, and the libraries to which he was given free access broadened his mind, deepened his knowledge, gave him the true historical spirit, and filled him with enthusiasm for great undertakings. In Berlin he associated with Neander, whose stimulating conversation and kindly encouragement exerted a powerful influence upon his future work. In a letter written during his stay in the capital of Prussia, Moehler extols Neander's insistence upon the study of sources, his calm judgment, his deep religious sense, his moral earnestness, and his clear and concise manner of presenting the matter of his lectures. In the fall of 1823 Moehler took up his duties at the university of Tuebingen. His course consisted of seven lectures weekly on Church History and two to three lectures on Patrology. From 1823 to 1825 he also substituted in Canon Law, and in 1830 and 1831 he lectured on Symbolics. He became a frequent and valued contributer to the *Theologische Quartalschrift*. In 1825 he published his first book, entitled *Die Einheit der Kirche, oder das Prinzip des Katholizismus*.

Immediate and tangible recognition came to him in the form of promotion to an assistant professorship March 16, 1826, and he was no longer required to lecture on Canon Law. In 1827 he published the first of his larger historical works, *Athanasius der Grosse und die Kirche seiner Zeit, besonders im Kampfe mit dem Arianismus*. Moehler's ability was recognized also away from home, the university of Breslau offering him a full professorship in 1828. Loyalty to his Alma Mater prevented him from accepting the tender and was rewarded by the honorary doctorate in theology (December 23, 1828) and by promotion to full professorship at Tuebingen on the last day of the same year. Moehler was now well established in the scientific world, and the ten remaining years of his short life were devoted to Church history and Symbolics. In preparing his work on Athanasius, he remarked the similarity of the rationalistic tendencies in the fourth and early nineteenth centuries and their baneful effects. The results of his investigation into the causes of the liberalism of his own time were published in his *Symbolik* (1832), which is his principal title to literary and theological fame. This book stirred the religious mind of Germany to the depths and was quickly translated into English, French, and Italian. It provoked a sharp rejoinder in 1833 from the pen of Ferdinand Christian Baur, the leader of the later Protestant school of Tuebingen, whose chief aim was to establish a higher synthesis of Christianity and rationalistic philosophy according to the dialectical formulas of Hegel. Nothing daunted, Moehler replied in 1834 by his *Neue Untersuchungen,* which a second time established the Catholic position in unassailable security.

Though his controversial gifts were of a high order, Moehler's nature was irenical. The pettiness of certain ones of his Protestant colleagues made his position at the university difficult, restricted his influence, dimmed his prospects, and embittered his life. Accordingly he accepted a professorship at the university of Munich April 30, 1835. Nominally he was to teach New Testament exegesis, but in fact he was to take over Doellinger's course in Church History, since the latter was becoming estranged from the faith. In the same year the universities of Bonn and Muenster unsuccessfully attempted to add the fame and luster of Moehler's scholarship to their own, and Bonn made another equally fruitless endeavor in 1837. Moehler was far from well when he arrived in Munich. During the short period of his activity in his new position he worked with his usual consuming energy. Owing to the decline of his health, the king relieved him of the work he loved so much, making him dean of the cathedral chapter of Wuerzburg in the hope of thus prolonging a noble life. Providence had decreed otherwise, for on Holy Thursday, April 12, 1838, the illustrious scholar returned his soul into the hands of his Creator. His tomb in Munich is surmounted by his likeness in marble and graced by the inscription: Defensor Fidei, Literarum Decus, Ecclesiae Solamen.

2. THEOLOGICAL VIEWS

To appreciate Moehler's position as a historian and to understand the encomiums which German scholars have not ceased to lavish upon him, it is necessary to outline the development of his theological views; for Moehler the historian of the Church is inseparable from Moehler the theologian. Moehler's historical judgment is conditioned by his doctrinal views of the Church, her institutions, and the exercise of her powers.

Moehler's career is that of a mind thoroughly orthodox in intention from the outset, but not free from the liberalism which pervaded his intellectual environment. His initial rightmindedness and his sympathy for the Church and her ideals, joined with years of careful and unremitting study in the Fathers, enabled Moehler gradually to free himself from the incubus of the Illumination and to arrive at a better understanding of the Church, her institutions, and her discipline, in strange contrast to Doellinger, who gradually strayed from liberalism to schism and heresy.

Moehler's writings are of unequal value for tracing the course of his theological views, but they remain the primary sources for establishing his intellectual development. Hence they constitute the basis of any inquiry into the subject. The *Kirchengeschichte von J. A. Moehler,* which Father Pius Boniface Gams, O. S. B., published in three volumes at Regensburg in 1867–1868, thirty years after the author's death, is really constructed of students' notes made between 1825 and 1838, but of which the chronology is uncertain. The only parts of Moehler's manuscript which have been made accessible are the sections published by Friedrich in 1894 as supplements to the *Kirchengeschichte,* but their chronology also is uncertain. Hence this work must be used with considerable caution in determining Moehler's development. The same reservations must be made with regard to the *Patrologie aus den hinterlassenen Handschriften mit Ergaenzungen,* edited by Moehler's friend Reithmayr in 1840, and the *Kommentar zum Brief an die Roemer* edited by the same scholar in 1845. In both of these works as published, the original is not distinguishable from the editor's additions. The principal sources remaining are the manuscript of Moehler's lectures on Canon Law, numerous articles and reviews in the *Theologische Quartalschrift, Die Einheit der Kirche, Athanasius der Grosse, Symbolik,* and *Neue Untersuchungen.* On these the following sketch of Moehler's development is based.

I. THE CONSTITUTION OF THE CHURCH

In a review of Walter's *Lehrbuch des Kirchenrechts,* published in the *Theologische Quartalschrift* in 1823, Moehler openly declares for episcopalism and denies that the pope in virtue of his office has the power of convoking ecumenical councils, presiding over them, and confirming them. Not the pope, but the teaching Church as a whole is infallible. In another review, published in the same year, Moehler asserts that the pope's primacy of jurisdiction is based on the divinely instituted center of unity in the Church. Similar incompatible statements are found in *Die Einheit der Kirche,* of which Moehler in later years said: " I do not like to be reminded of this book. It is a work of my enthusiastic youth, in which I sincerely endeavored to form a correct view of God, the Church, and the world. But the book contains many statements which I no longer maintain. Many things in it are not sufficiently digested nor clearly presented."

Moehler further maintained that the episcopate is not an order, but merely an extension of the priestly power, and only mediately of divine institution. This extension was made to maintain the unity of the Church, where several presbyters had been appointed to the same local church.

Moehler also taught that the texts of Holy Scripture taken singly do not prove the primacy, not even Matthew 16, 18, nor John 21, 15–17, for the Fathers interpret them in various senses. The primacy is proven by the position of St. Peter as recounted by the New Testament as a whole. According to Moehler, therefore, the primacy is an inference from Scripture rather than a statement contained in it.

Moehler adduces an argument from tradition to prove the primacy of the bishops of Rome as the successors of Peter. Cyprian and Irenaeus, he says, speak of the primacy without determining its nature. Rome was not the center of the Church in the first three centuries. With the increase of heresy and of the selfishness of bishops, which caused the spiritual unity of the Church to wane, a visible center became necessary to preserve the unity of faith. The wide diffusion of the Church also made it increasingly difficult for the individual to recognize the agreement of his faith with that of the universal teaching Church; hence the necessity of concentrating the supreme power in a visible center. Moehler, therefore, claims a vague foundation in divine right for the primacy of Rome, but dates its exercise from the time of Cyprian and assigns the need of unity as its motive.

Moehler mentions a number of reasons in favor of the separability of the primacy from the Roman See by the consent of the universal Church, but does not commit himself on their value.

The primacy of the bishops of Rome is a primacy of jurisdiction in the sense that the pope is to maintain and execute the decrees of the body of bishops, who are the supreme governing power in the Church. Moehler gives many proofs drawn from the Acts of the Apostles, the history and practise of the Church, and the ecumenical councils to show that the pope is subordinate to the body of bishops. He is also a pronounced anti-infallibilist.

By divine right all bishops and priests are rightful members of an ecumenical council. The great number of priests and the need of their constant presence in their parishes makes it impossible to convoke them for a council; hence the bishops alone are called to it. For the validity of an ecumenical council a relatively large number of bishops from all parts of the Church must be present at it, and its decisions must be accepted by the entire teaching

Church. The pope is only the equal of his brother bishops in the council. A council does not become valid nor ecumenical by being confirmed by him. The purpose of councils is to bring about unity in the Church.

The pope has essential and accidental rights. His essential rights are the supervision of the universal Church; the execution of doctrinal and disciplinary decrees, including the right of devolution and the protection of bishops; and the promulgation of provisional doctrinal decrees, which become legal in those churches in which they are promulgated and accepted. Accidental rights which accrued to the popes in the course of history are: preconizing bishops; authorizing their transfer to other sees; appointing coadjutors; granting exemptions and dispensations; and conferring benefices.

All these details are found in Moehler's lectures on Canon Law, which were delivered 1823–1825. They are far removed from the errors of the ecclesiastical democracy propounded by De Dominis, Richer, Febronius, and others. But they are plainly Gallican, and embody other personal views of Gerson, D'Ailly, and their contemporaries. Moehler derived them from German theologians of his own time, such as Michl, Sauter, Drey, and Hirscher. He maintained them also in his Church History as edited by Gams and Friedrich. Here he says, stressing the necessity of the papacy for the unity of the Church: " The papacy is the product of ignorance and barbarism, but ignorance and barbarism are

not the product of the papacy. . . . Not the physicians brought the malady; the malady made the
physicians necessary."

Moehler's progress in the right direction away
from Gallicanism began in the next following years.
In his book on Athanasius he does not restrict himself to the testimony of the first three centuries. He
quotes Sozomenes saying that no general laws of the
Church may be made without the consent of the
bishop of Rome. Speaking of the council of Sardica,
he remarks that in order to avoid the disunity
caused by Arianism the local churches must remain
united with the pope, who has the rank of Peter.
Moehler began to realize that the center of unity,
as which he recognized the papacy, cannot be subordinate to the parts which it is to unite. Hence also
the favorable review which he wrote of the sixth
edition of Walter's treatise on Canon Law in 1829,
the first edition of which he had criticised. But here
again he erred in praising the author's avoidance of
both episcopalism and papalism.

In *Fragmente aus und ueber Pseudoisidor*, published in 1829 and 1832, Moehler seeks the origin
of the false decretals in France and admits the good
intentions of their author.

In the first edition of the *Symbolik* (1832), § 37,
he maintains that only a united episcopate gathered
about the pope can preserve the life of the Church.
In the fourth edition of the same work (1835) he
abandons his Gallicanism in § 43 where he says
that the harsh theory subordinating the pope to a

general council has disappeared. Though he does not prove this important thesis, the support he gives to it shows that he had now abandoned his former views of the equality of all bishops, including the bishop of Rome, of the validity of councils without the pope, of the distinction between essential and accidental rights of the pope, and of the separability of the papacy from the Roman See by the consent of the whole teaching Church. But he did not reach the position of the constitution *De Ecclesia* of the Vatican council, which subordinates the body of bishops to the pope.

II. CHURCH REFORM

The principle that all forms of worship, piety, and clerical discipline must be filled with true ecclesiastical spirit pervades all Moehler's writings. But just as he was obliged to correct the ideal of the Church which he had formed in his youth, so he was constrained to abandon also many of his ideas of liturgical and disciplinary reform. In his first two years at the university he advocated communion under both species for the laity, a vernacular liturgy, abolition of the so-called solitary masses, and of mass stipends. He always stood for the best possible education of the clergy. He was relentlessly opposed to the request for the abolition of the celibacy of the clergy, which was made to the government of Baden. " Celibacy," he wrote in 1828, " is a living protest against the attempt to lose the

Church in the state. . . . It will prevent worldly-mindedness in the church, and frustrate any possible attempt by powerful men in the Church to subordinate the state to the Church." Another time he wrote, " A clergy without spirituality is a born cripple." In 1838 he had given up the idea of a vernacular liturgy. In the later editions of the *Symbolik*, § 34, he desired that communion under both species be made optional for the laity. From 1830 he also modified his views on ecclesiastical discipline: the general laws of the Church should be made by the pope, but only with the consent and sanction of the local bishops. He remained opposed to the granting of quinquennial faculties to bishops by the Holy See and to the establishment of permanent papal nunciatures.

III. CHURCH AND STATE

In his earliest discussion of this subject Moehler placed the idea of the Church above that of the state, but in practice he wanted Church and state coördinated. " If the Church dominates the state as it did in the Middle Ages, it loses its distinctive character, that is, as soon as the Church no longer acts as a Church, it begins to dominate the state; for liberty has then become coercion, and spirit has become mechanism." The Church renders moral support to the state, making civic loyalty an obligation of conscience. The state must protect the Church in externals, because the sovereign has the duty of preventing all harm to the state. By reason of its right of supervision the state has the general power of insisting upon the abolition of antiquated discipline and custom, e.g., processions, pilgrimages, and superfluous holydays. The state may further insist that laws and ordinances of popes and bishops be submitted to the government for approval before promulgation. In particular, according to Moehler's view, the state has the right to supervise the education of the clergy, to fix their number, to control the rules of religious orders, to control the connection of religious with foreign superiors, to accept appeals, to supervise the administration of church property, to amortize such property, and to fix the limits of dioceses and parishes.

Moehler opposed all but state universities. He says that " at the present time a university which is not in its essentials incorporated into the state would be an anomaly and an element of antiquated education."

At the same time Moehler advocated a relative independence and liberty of the Church, though it is hard to see wherein it consists after all the concessions he had made. Writing of St. Anselm as a champion of the Church, he says, " Christ redeemed the Church and made her free through his blood; she cannot be a servant of the state."

In all these theories Moehler failed to see that accidental advantages accruing to the Church from a friendly government can never be constituted into a principle, and that occasional weakness and error of subordinate individuals in the government of the Church can never diminish or extinguish her divine rights. It is certain that in later years Moehler veered to the right in his views on the relation of Church and state, but we have no written record of these later opinions. In the preface to his edition of Moehler's *Gesammelte Schriften und Aufsaetze*, Doellinger says that in speaking to his friends, Moehler repudiated many of his earlier statements, and that he would have given public utterance to his changed attitude if his life had been spared to enable him to carry out his literary plans.

IV. FAITH AND REASON

Moehler's early views on this important subject may be characterized as a mild form of traditionalism and summarized in these propositions: (1) true knowledge of God is founded on natural faith (*Vernunftglaube*). Following his teacher, Sebastian Drey, Moehler requires a kind of natural faith for all true knowledge of God, without saying, however, whether this faith is to be acquired through natural or through supernatural revelation. He bases his view on the early Christian apologists, especially on Clement of Alexandria. He appears to have maintained this view to the end, as it is still found in his letter to Bautain, written in 1834. (2) This natural faith is impossible without positive revelation and illuminating and sanctifying grace. Positive revelation is the necessary excitant of natural faith, but not the ultimate ground of its certainty. Echoes of this view are found in the paper on St. Anselm (1827–1828), and in § 1 of the first four editions of the *Symbolik*. In the fifth edition they are omitted. (3) The evidence of the divine origin of revelation is found in criteria immanent in itself, not in external proofs. The testimony of the Holy Ghost in the soul of each individual man proves both the fact and the content of revelation to be supernatural. Moehler later saw how untenable this proposition is, and how uncertain and fleeting the testimony of mystical experience. He then propounded the usual external criteria of revelation and stressed the necessity of grace for the act of faith and the necessity of faith for the full and true understanding of the content of revelation.

V. NATURE AND GRACE

In his earlier years Moehler had a certain sympathy for the mystical inwardness, the desire for spiritual perfection, and even the ethical rigor of the Jansenists. Though he acknowledged that the faith was preserved in his native country largely through the work of the Jesuits, he had an antipathy to what he considered their superficial intellectualism in theology, their probabilism, and their overstressing of the external elements of religion. These preferences and aversions were conditioned by his doctrinal views on nature and grace.

In 1826 he wrote that he could not read the bull

Unigenitus without horror. In the sections of his Church History, as published by Friedrich, he says that Jansenism could not be allowed to win, but that it was much better than the degeneration of Jesuitism. He still held this view after 1830.

In the *Symbolik* Moehler finds the root of the difference between Catholicism and Protestantism in their different conception of Christian anthropology. According to the former original sin did not substantially alter man's nature, according to the latter it did. First Moehler considered the gifts of the state of original justice, apart from sanctifying grace, as natural, but in later editions of the *Symbolik* he recognized that this state is supernatural (§ 1). He had been led to adopt the view that the original harmony of all elements and faculties of man is a natural endowment, because he was convinced that man as created by God could not be defective in his relations with God, nor have elements disturbing the use of his free will. Hence his opposition to Bellarmin's teaching that original sin deprived man only of supernatural gifts.

Moehler could not accept the probabilism of the Jesuits. In the first edition of *Neue Untersuchungen* (1834), p. 293, he says: " Those who desire to oppose Protestantism with success must have something in common with Protestants. . . . In order to reconcile men with the severity of Catholic ethics, the Jesuits gradually adopted the view that it was necessary also to stress everywhere the frailty of human nature, as Protestants did; they considered it necessary to moderate the requirements of Catholic ethics for people as they are in order to quiet and console them. Since they could not alter Catholic dogma, they endeavored by indulgent and lax treatment of individual cases to effect what Protestants granted in principle by the doctrine that faith alone is required for salvation." It is needless to say that Moehler completely misunderstood probabilism. We have no means of establishing whether Moehler was a probabiliorist or equiprobabilist, nor whether he considered that these doctrines also may contain false qualifications of a course of action.

VI. THE SACRAMENTS

In his lectures on Canon Law, 1823–1825, Moehler maintained that in virtue of his ordination every priest can validly confer sacramental absolution even from reserved cases. The approbation of the ordinary is required only for the licit exercise of this power. In a review published in 1823 Moehler considers indulgences merely as an ecclesiastical institution remitting canonical penance. The custom of conferring them remained even after this penance had been abolished, because a new penance was imagined and then remitted by applying the merits of the reputed treasury of the merits and satisfactions of Christ and the saints. He considered the Portiuncula indulgence particularly undesirable.

It is not known whether Moehler maintained his errors on the priest's power of absolution in his

later years. In his Church History and *Symbolik*
he modified his views on the nature of indulgences
and the treasury of merits and satisfactions to the
extent of declaring them well founded scholastic
doctrine. Apparently he never realized that they
are generally considered in the Church as *doctrina
fidei proxima*.

Moehler granted both to Church and state the
right of establishing diriment impediments of mat-
rimony, since marriage is both a contract and a
sacrament. According to his view the state originally
exercised this right with regard to unbelievers and
did not lose it when they became Christians. The
Church also exercised this right independently of
the state, and gradually the state accepted the ecclesiastical code as its own civil code. In the lectures
on Canon Law he modified these opinions to the
extent of saying that civil impediments are void
when they are opposed to the nature of Christian
marriage. In the last year of his life Moehler opposed the Prussian practice of forcing a certain religion upon the offspring of mixed marriages, though
conceding to the state the right of subsidiary legis-
lation in this matter when parents neglected the
religious instruction of their children.

3. The Historian

Coming now to the final question, we inquire,
what are the achievements of Moehler the historian,
and how did he attain to them?

The Catholic faculty of theology at Tuebingen was founded toward the close of 1817. The first incumbent of the Chair of Church History, who also taught Canon Law, Georg Leonhard von Dresch, Dr. iur. utr., was a Catholic layman who had been professor of history and the philosophy of law at Tuebingen since 1811. Lacking interest in Church history, he resigned this course in 1818 and was temporarily succeeded in it by J. G. Herbst, professor of Old Testament exegesis. When Dresch accepted a position at Landshut in 1822, Moehler was appointed to the chair of Church history in Tuebingen. Though he had not previously specialized in Church history, his ability, which bordered on real genius, combined with indefatigable industry and stimulated in the highest degree by the inspiring example and the scientific bent of his colleagues and by the literary travels he had undertaken at the request of the university, soon made Moehler one of the beacon lights of science in his Alma Mater.

Moehler's course in Patrology considered both the literary and the theological aspects of patristic literature. The " *patristische Uebungen* " of 1825, in which he trained his students in the study of sources, were the beginning of the modern seminar. According to the lecture lists of the university Moehler's seminar course dealt with the *Stromata* of Clement of Alexandria in 1823–1824; with St. John Chrysostom's *De Sacerdotio* in 1824; with explanations of the Epistle to the Romans by St. Augustine, St.

Chrysostom, and Theodoretus in 1825; with St. Athanasius' *De Incarnatione* and *Contra Arianos* in 1825–1826; with the *Commonitorium* of Vincent of Lerins in 1826; and with the letters of the Apostolic Fathers in 1826–1827. In 1832–1833 Moehler added a general course in Christian literature to his course in Patrology. The great influence of his lectures on Patrology was due to the fact that Moehler combined a penetrating analysis and sympathetic appreciation of his subject with the magnetic gifts of a harmonious personality, infusing into his work a contagious enthusiasm which kindled similar fires of a lifetime in the minds of his students. In a letter written in 1823 to his uncle in Rottenburg, he avows that his endeavor to reach the spirit and sentiment of the Fathers rather than their ideas alone was due to the stimulus he had received in Berlin from Neander.

Die Einheit der Kirche (1825) is the pioneer Catholic monograph on the history of dogma in Germany. An atmosphere of deep feeling pervades this work, which is an attempt to expound the organization of the Church and its functions as directed by the Holy Ghost. It sets forth the spiritual unity of the faithful in belief, morals, and worship, and the visible unity effected by the hierarchy of the Church. By stressing the spiritual life and the sanctifying power of the Church, this work of Moehler brought before the minds of Catholics tainted with rationalism the true nature and purpose of the Church, infusing new courage into the de-

pressed, sustaining faltering belief, and winning recognition for the ideals of Catholicism even from its
enemies. Though it would be difficult to trace the
effects of this book upon theological science in concrete detail, there is no doubt that it constitutes the
driving impulse which led a whole generation of
German scholars to a fruitful study of the history
of dogma. In his later years Moehler was well aware
of its defects. Despite its positive character, it is
under the spell of Hegelian ideas, evolving the existence and nature of the Church from its abstract
concept, rather than from the empirical facts of
revelation and from the supernatural marks of the
Church in all epochs of history. Other errors on
the constitution of the Church and the primacy
have been mentioned in the section on Moehler's
theological views. In recent years a regrettable attempt was made by E. Vermeil to show that Moehler
is the father of modernism in Germany. He was not
one to foster modernistic opinions, for he maintained
the divine institution of the Church, of the primacy,
and of the episcopate; furthermore he asserts the revealed character of the dogmas of the Church, and
denies the objective perfectibility of revelation. His
shortcoming lies in the fact that his ideas on these
subjects were vague and imperfect rather than subjectivistic, and that he did not touch upon them in
this book.

They attain prominence in *Athanasius der Grosse*
(1827), which stands in the vanguard of a new form
of historical writing, the historical monograph as

distinguished from biography. Moehler gives prominence to the general position of Athanasius in the history of the Church and in the development of her doctrine. The permanent value of this book lies in its brilliant analysis of the writings of Athanasius and its careful study of his doctrine on the Trinity and on the Logos. The study of Athanasius removed many of Moehler's Gallican views. He now considers the Church as " the living, objectivated Gospel"; he realizes that the primacy of the bishop of Rome was the only safeguard against " schism, arbitrary power, and destruction " in the Church. Like others among his contemporaries he limited the primacy of the pope to the supreme executive power. The monograph on St. Anselm of Canterbury, which was published as a series of articles in the *Theologische Quartalschrift* in 1827–1828, glows with the same enthusiasm for the Church, whose liberties St. Anselm was defending against William II and Henry I. Though failing to do justice to St. Anselm as the Father of Scholasticism, this monograph has the imperishable merit of having shown the necessity of a renewal of theological science by returning to the much decried schoolmen. It is a matter of history that the revival of scholasticism in Germany proceeded from three sources: the seminary at Mainz, Moehler and his pupil Kuhn in Tuebingen, and the philosophical current of romanticism (Baader, Deutinger, Rosenkrantz, Windischmann, etc.).

Fragmente aus und ueber Pseudoisidor is an in-

vestigation into the purpose and the origin of the
Pseudo-Isidorian decretals. Moehler's solution of
the problem is that these decretals are a pious fraud
contrived between 836 and 840 in order to effect
the reform of the Church in the western part of the
Frankish empire, which had been disrupted by the
civil wars under Louis the Debonnaire and his sons.
Later historians have judged more severely of
Pseudo-Isidore, but the substance of Moehler's investigation has been accepted.

Moehler's *Symbolik* has not the reading public
to-day which eagerly devoured its contents in the
thirties. This is not because it has lost its apologetic value, but because the battleground between
Catholicism and Protestantism has shifted from the
field of positive faith in revelation to that of the
historical foundations of Christianity. The origins
of the *Symbolik* are found in the new subjects to
which Moehler turned his attention. From ancient
Christianity he turned to the final phase of the
Middle Ages and to the Reformation. The latter he
characterized as a revolutionary movement, which
interrupted the course of regular and legitimate reform and destroyed the germ of much that was
good.

The attack of Protestant scholarship on Catholicism in Germany was the immediate cause determining Moehler to write the *Symbolik*. The comparative evaluation of the doctrines of the ancient
faith and of the new churches founded by those
who seceded from it in the sixteenth century had

been attempted before Moehler. Bellarmin's *Controversies,* published at Ingolstadt, 1586–1593, Becanus' *Manuale Controversiarum,* first published in 1623, and various writings of Bossuet were Moehler's earliest predecessors. His immediate forerunners in Comparative Symbolics are two Protestant works: Planck's *Abriss einer Historischen und vergleichenden Darstellung unserer verschiedenen christlichen Kirchenparteien* (Goettingen, 1796), and especially Marheineke's *Christliche Symbolik* (1810–1813) and *Institutiones Symbolicae* (1812). In the *Theologische Quartalschrift,* 1828, p. 346, Moehler regrets the lack of a German counterpart of Milner's *End of Controversy.* Sebastian Drey, whose lectures Moehler had attended in Tuebingen during his student days, had already propounded in briefer form some of the ideas which Moehler developed with so much brilliance in the *Symbolik.* Drey had called attention especially to the true mean between the divine and the human, the natural and supernatural, the subjective and the objective, and between mysticism and intellectualism, which is found in the Catholic faith as distinguished from the extremes of hyperspiritualism and rationalism found in Protestantism.

Moehler's method in the *Symbolik* is both historical and systematic. His power of synthesis, grouping many varied details under principles which are unified among themselves, is here at its height. The historical basis which forms the groundwork of his systematic construction is everywhere prominent.

It stamps the *Symbolik* with a character of objectivity and imparts to it a power of conviction which are unsurpassed. The serene calm with which Moehler discusses the dogmatic differences between Catholics and Protestants reaches the high level of scholasticism; and by everywhere applying the principle of historical induction, he puts the master weapon of modern science into the defence of the faith. Not since Bellarmin and Bossuet did the Church have a champion who pressed the attack with such vigor upon the principles and consequences of the doctrines of the Reformers.

The purpose of the *Symbolik* is irenical, for Moehler was deeply convinced that the cleavage in religion which the Reformation had caused in Germany had harmed the country in many ways. He believed also that the cause of religious peace, if not reunion, would be served best by showing and refuting in their connection the principles which caused this opposition to the ancient faith. Because he always grants the good faith and the deep religious spirit of his opponents, his own sincerity is the more apparent. It is hardly too much to say that the *Symbolik* is the best theological criticism of the doctrinal and philosophical principles of the Reformers which was produced by Catholic scholarship in Germany.

Two thirds of the *Symbolik* is given over to the discussion of the doctrines of the Lutheran and the Reformed churches. The remainder is devoted principally to the teaching of the Methodists, Baptists,

Friends, and Swedenborgians. Moehler's plan is to present the opposition between Catholic and Protestant doctrine first by comparing their teaching on the original state of man, his fall, and its disastrous consequences for mankind. Then he enters into the discussion of the doctrine of justification, which is the heart of the controversy. From this he proceeds to expound the influence of the two religious faiths upon the interior life of their adherents. He concludes by a study of their teaching on the Church.

Moehler takes the material for his work from the symbolic documents of the Catholic and Protestant churches. He constantly recurs to the writings of the Reformers in order to determine the meaning of Protestant symbolic documents. In determining the teaching of the Reformers, he proceeds with great circumspection. In the case of Luther, Moehler is well aware of Luther's fickleness, his impressionability, and his exaggerations. Hence he lays down the principle that Luther's teaching must be determined by the general trend of his writings rather than by isolated statements. The decrees and canons of the Council of Trent are the standard by which Moehler judges the doctrines of the Reformers.

Liturgies, prayers, and hymns are not used as symbolic sources, because their terms often lack theological precision. The writings of individual Catholic theologians are not given the same value in explaining Catholic doctrine as is accorded to those of the Reformers in the interpretation of Protestant symbolic documents; for Catholic theological writings are private attempts of individual scholars to expound the faith which they presuppose but do not determine, whereas the writings of the Reformers are the constitutive sources of Protestantism. Followers of the Reformers had often forgotten this, because their doctrinal systems are founded on individual opinions elevated to the rank of universal truths. The Reformers took over into their doctrinal systems certain parts of the ancient faith, because these items agreed with their personal views.

Furthermore, according to the *Symbolik* the Reformation owed its rise and progress partly to its attacks on abuses in the Church, and partly to its opposition to certain theological theories which had found favor in some Catholic schools of theology. In this connection Moehler remarks that the Church always combated the abuses which arose, and that she cannot be held responsible for private opinions fostered by individuals among her members. The Reformers confused these abuses and opinions with the precepts and doctrines of the Church; here again they confused the particular with the universal.

The effects of Moehler's *Symbolik* were far-reaching though they are not easily determined in detail. The sale of five editions of this work in six years is evidence of its wide diffusion in Germany. The first edition was translated into English almost immediately upon publication by James Burton Robertson (London, Dolman, 1832). Lachat's

French version is rather a paraphrase than a translation (3rd edition, Brussels, Fonteyn, 1853). There is also an Italian translation. In Germany primarily the *Symbolik* did much to remove prejudice, to strengthen the convictions of Catholics and their confidence in the Church, to destroy indifferentism, and to win for Catholic scholarship its rightful place in the world of science. A number of distinguished converts found their way into the Church through the study of its enlightening pages. Among them are numbered Hurter the historian, Hammerstein the apologist, Bickell the philologist, and the Duke Victor de Broglie. Newman may have come under the influence of the *Symbolik* though there is no direct proof of the fact.

For Moehler himself the *Symbolik* had other effects, which were far from comforting. While Marheineke and Nitzsch replied to it with a dignified defence of the Protestant position, Baur's polemical diatribe is disfigured by unwarranted personal attacks, which stirred up the notorious *furor theologicus*, but did not further the scientific study of the questions under discussion. Hence it has long been consigned to well-merited oblivion by all parties. In 1835 the king of Wuertemberg commanded a report on the *Symbolik* by a prominent Protestant churchman. In consequence of the opinion rendered by this divine, he forbade Moehler to write on certain subjects as long as the latter remained in Tuebingen. When Altenstein, the Prussian minister of worship, offered Moehler a professorship in Bonn, it was also on condition that he remain silent on topics which were likely to arouse controversy. Moehler preferred his liberty to what he termed a well-furnished prison for his faith and accepted a position in Munich.

The works of Moehler's last years are preliminary studies for a general history of the Church, which he intended to be his *opus magnum*. In 1831 he published the *Versuch ueber den Ursprung des Gnostizismus* in the commemorative volume of the university of Tuebingen for the golden jubilee of G. J. Planck, professor of Evangelical theology in Goettingen. This coöperation with the Protestant section of the university was a truly Christian reply to the hostile attitude of his brethren of the cloth among the Evangelicals. In this essay Moehler sets up the theory that gnosticism originated from a morbid Christian contempt for the world and a pathological Christian asceticism. Moehler's old adversary Baur and his respected friend Neander of Berlin had no difficulty in showing that gnosticism is a pagan creation. Further research has shown that it is a syncretistic product of an expiring paganism, and that it owes its origin to the undisciplined speculation of the hellenistic intellect.

In 1830 Moehler published a series of articles in the *Theologische Quartalschrift,* entitled *Ueber das Verhaeltniss des Islams zum Evangelium.* Lacking original sources, he shared the views of his contemporaries, who overestimated the civilizing influence of Mohammedanism and the willingness of its ad-

herents to embrace Christianity. In 1834 he published *Bruchstuecke aus der Geschichte der Aufhe-
bung der Sklaverei,* which appears to be the first
detailed study of this important subject based on
original sources; but it is antiquated to-day. The
delightful sketch *Geschichte des Moenchtums in der
Zeit seiner Entstehung und ersten Ausbildung* appeared in 1836 and 1837. The asceticism and mysticism of the monks had a fascination for Moehler
from his youth. He had planned to write the history
of the civilizing influence of the Benedictines, of
whom he had previously written with sympathy in
his *Athanasius* and *Anselm of Canterbury.* The
promise which he did not live to fulfill was realized
in Montalembert's *Monks of the West.*

Moehler's *Kirchengeschichte* shows us rather his
capacity than his achievements, since it is a mosaic
of students' notes extending over a period of thirteen years and unified by Gams. The true Moehler
is apparent in its brilliant narrative, its striking description, its penetrating analysis, its telling characterization of large spans of history, and its appreciation of the religious and cultural influence of
leading personalities. In the *Patrologie oder christliche Literaergeschichte* Moehler's work is indistinguishable from that of his friend and editor,
Reithmayr. In its published form it is merely a
chronological series of finished biographies with an
elaborate general introduction. Besides the biography each subject contains an analysis of the writer's works and a summary of his doctrinal views.

The lack of pragmatic exposition and systematic grouping is explained by the unfinished character of the work. Moehler was the first Catholic scholar in Germany to put patrology on a scientific basis. His Patrology is a combination of the literary and theological history of the Fathers and later Christian writers. His division of patrology thus conceived (and also of Church history) into a Greek-Roman (1–8 century), a Germanic (8–15 century), and a Roman-Greek-Germanic period was rejected, partly because it is too vague and extensive, and partly because it fails to recognize the fundamental importance and the unique character of ancient Christian literature.

Moehler's conception of the task of the historian of the Church included not only the study of Church history proper, but also the history of dogma, of religion in general, of canon law, exegesis, and apologetics. He placed these historical sciences on a par with systematic theology.

Moehler and Doellinger are the founders of the Catholic school of history in Germany. They were contemporaries and friends. Moehler flashed across the sky of the nineteenth century like a blazing meteor, and his memory is held in benediction; to Doellinger was granted length of years beyond the usual span of human life, but he declined in faith and scholarship. How great Moehler's achievements would have become had Providence granted him the ninety-one years accorded to Doellinger! Doellinger was superior to his friend in the keenness of his intellect, the depth of his criticism, and the power of historical combination; but Moehler towered above the Munich historian by the noble qualities of his heart, his mature judgment, his objective attitude toward the problems of history, and the enthusiasm of his mind. Doellinger was a realist in history; Moehler was an idealist. It is from Moehler that Catholic historical scholarship in Germany takes its rise. The Catholic school of Tuebingen stands on his shoulders, and all who have profited by Germany's Catholic historical scholarship are his debtors.

Moehler's theory of the method of historical studies cannot be fixed in a formula. He was largely self-taught and possessed the method and the mind of a discoverer. The ideal historian, he says, possesses the rare but characteristic gift of abstracting from present conditions and of placing himself sympathetically and forgetful of himself into the period of which he is writing. He does not project his ideas into the facts, for by doing so he would subjectivize the facts and observe them through a medium constructed by himself. Historical study becomes a science when it attains a thorough knowledge of the connection and interaction of a group of facts.

It was one of Moehler's deepest convictions that the study of sources is the first requisite of historical scholarship. The best, and indeed the only method of procedure, he says, is to see and search for oneself. The second quality of the historian is veracity. The best defence of a good cause, he says again, is the honest study and truthful presentation of it. Another quality of the historian of the Church is the Catholic sense. Moehler rejects *Voraussetzungslosigkeit* as the foolish delusion of rationalism. One who writes the history of the Church must take his stand within the Church and work himself into her spirit. How can one understand the Church, he asks, if one possesses only fragments of the truth and views the Church with the eyes of an enemy? Failing to see the supernatural guidance and workings of the Church, the historian will fail also to present its human aspect correctly, and perhaps record it as a chronicle of scandal. Without faith the historian of the Church is like a man without a soul.

Furthermore Moehler insists on the genetic presentation of history. To be satisfactory, history must be written according to the genetic method, not viewing facts as accidents, but presenting them as events in their origin and genesis, their mutual influence and dependence. In the spirit of this principle Moehler endeavored to present the historical continuity of the Church, the organic development of her doctrines from the objective data of revelation, and her expansion in virtue of her divine endowments.

Moehler was much impressed by the influence of great ideas upon the course of history. Not only was he well acquainted with the contemporary German and French literature on the subject, but he was also in contact, since his literary travels of 1822, with the principal exponents of this method of historiography. Planck and Neander were writing history according to the idealistic method, and Moehler fell under their spell. After hearing Neander, the star of Planck, whom he had praised with youthful enthusiasm in his letters, began to pale before the greater luminary of Berlin. Moehler's conception of the philosophy of history as the working out of the architectonic ideas which dominate the course of events, was drawn immediately from Neander's pioneer monographs of St. Bernard (1813), St. John Chrysostom (1821–1822), and Tertullian (1825), which he reviewed at length in the *Theologische Quartalschrift*.

Ultimately this conception of history was derived from Hegel. Moehler purged it of its subjectivism and of most of its apriorism, though he occasionally involved himself in artificial constructions of history. Whatever his faults, he was the first to apply this fruitful method to the writing of Catholic history. Generally speaking, his method is correct, because there *is* a guiding Providence which directs the course of the world to the end for which it was created. Adopting the words of Johannes von Mueller, Moehler says, " Christ is the point of departure and the last end, and consequently also the center of all history." Moehler was so convinced of the correctness of this philosophy of history that he said in the preface to the first edition of his first publication, " It is so impossible to attempt a historical construction without any connection with a higher idea which contains and permeates all history, that I would rather abandon all history than surrender the conviction of its progressive development from within." Yet his conception of history was not subjectivistic, for he says further, " We want ideas drawn from tradition, not tradition fashioned according to an idea." To his mind history is the plan of God with mankind, an eternal plan developing in time. By this plan God prepares for Himself in mankind through the mediation of Christ the honor and glory due Him, and resulting from the freely given homage of men. The dominating purpose of Moehler's history is to portray the Church as the spiritual power directing all things and permeating all the activities of mankind. The Church is the divinely constituted mother and guide of all the faithful, whose temporal vicissitudes manifest the operation of God's Providence.

Moehler's career was a series of great beginnings. They were the great and forward, though sometimes faltering steps of a pioneer, as the sequel showed. The future of Church history is bound up with the inductive and philosophical study of the subject in which he pointed the way.

BIBLIOGRAPHY

A. BIOGRAPHY

WOERNER, *J. A. Moehler, ein Lebensbild.* Edited by P. B. Gams, O.S.B., 1886.

FRIEDRICH, *J. A. Moehler der Symboliker. Ein Beitrag zu seinem Leben und seiner Lehre aus seinen eigenen und anderen ungedruckten Papieren* (Munich, 1894).

KNOEPFLER, *J. A. Moehler. Ein Gedenkblatt zu dessen hundertstem Geburtstag* (Munich, 1896).

A. v. SCHMID, *Der Geistige Entwicklungsgang J. A. Moehlers,* in the *Historisches Jahrbuch,* Vol. 18 (1897), pp. 322–356, 572–599.

GOYAU, *Moehler. (La Pensée Chrétienne)* (Paris, 1905).

LOESCH, *Moehlers Lehre von der Entwicklung des Dogmas* in the *Theologische Quartalschrift,* Vol. 99 (1917–1918), pp. 28–59, 129–152.

BIHLMEYER, *Moehler als Kirchenhistoriker,* in the *Theologische Quartalschrift,* Vol. 100 (1919), pp. 134–198.

B. GENERAL WORKS ON MOEHLER
AND HIS WRITINGS

Besides the above biographical sketches, all of which contain commentaries on Moehler's historical writings, the following may be added:

GOOCH, *History and Historians in the Nineteenth Century* (London, 1920).

EDMOND VERMEIL, *Jean-Adam Möhler et l'école catholique de Tubingue (1815–1840). Étude sur la théologie romantique en Wurtemberg et les origines germaniques du modernisme* (Paris, 1913).

A. FONCK, *Möhler et l'école catholique de Tubingue* in the *Revue des Sciences Religieuses,* VI, 2 (April, 1926), pp. 250–266.

LINGARD (1771–1851)

Rev. Edwin J. Ryan, S.T.D.
Catholic University of America

IN speaking of Lingard one is confronted with a problem which while it implies a tribute to his greatness constitutes none the less a real difficulty. I refer to the danger of seeming to exaggerate his claims. For the more we consider the man's work, especially when account is taken of the circumstances in which it was accomplished, the more intense becomes our admiration and the more compelling the impulse to voice that admiration and to increase in others that sentiment of gratitude which all students must feel. At the same time I should not care to appear in the rôle of a mere enthusiast chanting a paean of praise "like a tale of little meaning though the words are strong"; hence I shall endeavour to confine my effort to pointing out those of his claims which I am confident are acknowledged by everyone who has studied his *History,* and especially by those who have utilized it as a basis for their instruction of others. So, if in the end I shall have said too little rather than too much I trust my reader will impute it not to deficient appreciation but to a prudent solicitude not to injure his fame by over-praise.

First let us consider the time in which he produced his great work, viz., the second and the third

decades of the nineteenth century. The Catholic
body in England had then but recently emerged
from its seclusion and the emergence was far from
complete. Relief had been granted in grudging bits
during the last quarter of the century preceding
but entire emancipation was still in the future and
English Catholics were still a race apart, taking
little share in the national life and many of them
content to be regarded by the ruling Protestant
majority as harmless. That they possessed any intellectual force, any scholars who might compare
with the graduates of the two Universities, was not
suspected. The genuine learning that had flourished
among the English Catholics on the Continent from
the days of Elizabeth to the French Revolution
was a sealed book to most Englishmen; which clari-
fies the commonplace of History that contempt had
something to do with bringing on the partial relief
of the eighteenth century. Even those Catholics
who like Milner wrote *for* and *to* Protestants secured but a fraction of the audience they ought to
have enjoyed. Hence an English Catholic who
would set out to re-write the whole history of his
country and expect a hearing might well have appeared to many of his co-religionists, and those far
from the least worthy, as embarked upon an enterprise which if it should attract attention at all would
but irritate the adversary and thereby delay those
further measures of justice so eagerly yearned for.

This brings us to the consideration of the internal condition of the Catholic body; and to indi-

cate the spirit that animated at least a portion
thereof probably no more graphic method will be
found than to mention the Cisalpine Club. To the
student of English Catholic history this name will
suffice to conjure up the bitter and at times scan-
dalous state of mind of many prominent Catholics
of Lingard's day — their inharmonious relations
with the hierarchy, their tampering with the spiritual allegiance of the clergy, their faulty methods
of attempting a compromise with the government,
and (which is not the least of their failings) their
excessive fear of arousing antagonism by any manly
assertion of their rights or any open presentation
of Catholic teaching. In 1819, the year when the
first volume of Lingard's *History of England* appeared, the probably unsympathetic attitude of
such Catholics was a danger to be reckoned with;
for, coming as it did from within, it was even more
likely to wreck the enterprise than the bitter antagonism of open and avowed enemies. Lest this be
deemed an exaggeration I cite the significant fact
that of the two Catholic publishers to whom the
work was offered one would not give more than
£300 and the other refused to touch it at all.

That despite these considerations Lingard went
ahead and succeeded is a testimony not to the man's
courage only but to his keen insight as well. For it
can not be said that he was unaware of the difficulties in his path and that therefore his success was
but a happy accident of ignorance. On the contrary, Lingard knew well the state of affairs, for

he is among that band of historians who have not only written history but helped to make it. From his return to his native land in 1793 to the appearance of his *History* and even on to his death in 1851, far from being a scholarly recluse, he was an active participant in ecclesiastical affairs, consulted by bishops and on at least one occasion refusing a mitre for himself. Knowing then as he did the mind of contemporary Catholics, he displayed something akin to statesmanship when he calmly proceeded to correct the Protestant tradition of history and to set before the English people, Catholic and Protestant, the true story. The poet teaches us that "the better part of valour is discretion." But what is "discretion"? Is it mere pusillanimous timidity? Or does it not lie oftentimes in a bold sallying forth into the lists in a chivalrous pursuit of the enemy? Discretion can assume many forms; and he is truly valorous who can discern which particular form is demanded by the circumstances he is summoned to meet. That Lingard gauged the situation so accurately and so aptly is not the least among the evidences of his fitness for his task.

Secondly, let us consider the spirit animating his *History*. I have already alluded to the scholarship that had flourished among the English Catholics on the Continent during the penal days. But from the untoward circumstances this learning had perforce assumed a controversial cast; the exiles could not afford to devote much attention to loftier purposes.

They had to fight; and while the employment of
the resources of learning in the attack on error is
in itself noble, it is not the rôle wherein intellectual
activity appears to best advantage. It can never be
more than a painful, if necessary, evil; and probably the chief drawback lies in the baneful influence it exercises on those very persons who even
from the loftiest motives so employ their gifts. For
controversy is sadly apt to beget narrowness of
mind and a dangerous readiness to sacrifice strict
accuracy to an immediate advantage over the adversary. Exaggeration of one's opponent's difficulties and the minimizing of one's own are but too
familiar phenomena in controversial writing, while
a tone of Christian charity and courtesy is not
exactly among its characteristics. I fear it must be
allowed that such shortcomings are not confined
to Protestants; at the risk of seeming ungenerous
to those doughty champions who in a dark era
waged war for Catholicism, we are constrained to
admit that they did not keep themselves entirely
unspotted from the stains of the arena.

Now, observe in how different a spirit Lingard approached the task of writing History. He had all the
zeal of the knight-errant and all the fearlessness; but
in addition to these and to that insight into conditions already touched upon, he had a whole-hearted
devotion to Truth and with it a realization that this
devotion, far from being a hindrance, could be
turned into an ally in winning the Protestant mind.
Years before he set out to chronicle the story of

England he wrote in reference to his *Antiquities
of the Anglo-Saxon Church:* " The great event of
the Reformation, while it gave a new impulse to the
powers, embittered with rancour the writings of the
learned. Controversy pervaded every department of
literature; and history, as well as the sister sciences,
was alternately pressed into the service of the con-
tending parties. . . . My object is truth." These
words would apply equally well to the *History of
England.* For despite the scrutiny to which the
work was subjected by non-Catholic critics no case
of prejudice or of wilful misrepresentation was
made out. The favourable critiques, like those in
the *Edinburgh Review,* the *Westminster Review*
and the *Monthly Review,* and the unfavourable,
such as that in *Blackwood's,* agree in recognizing
the author's purpose to present a true picture and
his sincerity at least is unquestioned. And a few
months after the first three volumes appeared he
returns to this topic in a private letter: " Through
the work I made it a rule to tell the truth, whether
it made for us or against us." Thus he sounded a
new note in English historiography. Beside Lingard such writers as Hume and (to anticipate)
Macaulay, for all their brilliance, sink to the level
of partisan scribes. And if today such pseudo-
historians no longer obtain credence we owe that
largely to Lingard.

But we must record regretfully that this honesty
was not hailed universally; among the various reviews there was one loudly-discordant note sounded,

and that by one of his own household. Bishop Milner had long been known as a rather vehement defender of Catholics and his ardour had led him into precisely those errors which we spoke of a few pages back as of frequent occurrence among controversialists. To him History was but a weapon and he was not too particular as to how or to what extent he adapted the weapon to his purpose. Being therefore of a type quite different from Lingard he was disappointed on reading the *History* to find that it was not of that vehement kind which he so desiderated. He vented his wrath in the pages of the *Orthodox Journal,* declaring that the work was not " such as our calumniated and depressed condition calls for "; and later in conversation he called it " a bad book only calculated to confirm Protestants in their errors." It is not necessary to dwell on this incident in detail. Time has shown which of the two men had the more correct notion of History. It is difficult to imagine any Protestant " confirmed in his errors " by reading Lingard; on the contrary, his work has proved a veritable arsenal in the war on error, which it would never have become had it been written to suit the taste of Milner. For to his devotion to Truth Lingard added a prudence foreign to the mind of Milner. In his own words: " I have been careful to defend the catholics, but not so as to hurt the feelings of the protestants. Indeed my object has been to write such a work, if possible, as should be read by protestants: under the idea, that the more it is read by them, the less

Hume will be in vogue, and consequently the fewer prejudices against us will be imbibed from him." And again: " [I made it a rule] to avoid all appearance of controversy, that I might not repel protestant readers; and yet to furnish every necessary proof in our favour in the notes; so that if you compare my narrative to Hume's, for example, you will find that, with the aid of the notes, it is a complete refutation of him without appearing to be so. This I thought preferable. In my account of the Reformation I must say much to shock protestant prejudices; and my only chance of being read by them depends upon my having the reputation of a temperate writer." This led him to omit in the first edition matter included later, but there was nothing that amounted to falsification. He was following what he considered a dictate of common sense; and that his work did thereby gain readers among Protestants we shall presently see.

In the meantime we must consider another point. Love of truth will not by itself make an historian. He must know how to discover the truth. And in this connection we may say without exaggeration that Lingard is positively the first of modern English historians to go to the sources. I shall quote him again: " In the pursuit of Truth I have made it a religious duty to consult the original historians. Who would draw from the troubled stream when he may drink at the fountain head? " Today these words sound like a truism: in those days they were almost a revelation. For to his time no historian in

England had dreamed of going to any such trouble
as "a religious duty" or any other kind of duty.
The anti-Catholic tradition had been carefully elaborated and handed on in print from generation to
generation. The method was to begin with a pre-
conception of what the writer wanted to prove, cull
from printed books such statements as harmonized
with his prejudices, colour them with his own interpretation, and present them (if he could) in the
glamour of a polished style. History had degen-
erated into a mere literary *genre*, a handmaid of
creed or of party, a rostrum of philosophy, anything but the school of truth. It was Lingard who
changed all that by the process, simple with the
simplicity of genius, of testing every statement,
verifying every reference, going back, not to those
who wrote only what they were inclined to write or
were ordered to write, but to those who stood nearest the events and whose knowledge and character
gave assurance that they knew what they told and
told what they knew.

And for a man to hark back to sources was no
easy feat in those days. Every historiographer who
knows his craft does that now, but consider the
situation a hundred years ago. State archives, private collections and the like now available were
closed then or could be consulted only at considerable inconvenience, and many were not even known
to exist. This, coupled with the fact that Lingard,
like Creighton, did most of his labour in a remote
rural parish, leaves one marvelling at his success;

for despite the vast amount of original material since become available, no substantial alteration of any important part of his *History of England* has been found necessary. If I may be indulged in a personal reference: About fifteen years ago I had occasion to prepare a set of lectures on the English Reformation. I first made up my notes from Lingard and then proceeded to correct them in the light of what had been produced by later historians who had access to sources more copious than those at his disposal. I found that no real *correction* was necessary but that when my work was finished all I owed to the more recent writers was a greater fulness of detail, the narrative of Lingard standing firm and immovable.

And now after praising him I have to record one point wherein we must all dissent from him. In a letter written in 1850, about a year before he died, we find the following: " I have long had the notion — a very presumptuous one, probably — that the revolution in the protestant mind as to the doctrines of popery was owing to my History. Young and inquisitive minds in the Universities were induced to examine my authorities concerning their favourite religious opinions; and finding me correct began to doubt of their convictions. This is very presumptuous in me." I consider that in that last sentence he lapsed into error. In entertaining the notion that he had revolutionized the Protestant attitude he was far from presumptuous, for that was the opinion of most persons at the time. One of his friends,

Mr. Darcy Talbot, ascribed to Lingard's *History of England* many of the conversions that occurred about that time among students of Oxford and Cambridge. And where the work did not lead to conversion it at least contributed enormously to destroy prejudice. Ever since it appeared there has been an improved tone among educated Protestants.

Great indeed is our debt to him for his scholarly achievement. Still I venture to say that we owe him an even greater debt for the example he has left us of sterling courage in facing difficulties — limitation of opportunity, paucity of resources, opposition from within and from without. Herein he shines forth as possessing that strength of character without which the loftiest genius may be futile, and the possession of which renders his life a kind of exegesis of Goethe's immortal line: "In dem Begrentzen zeigt sich der Meister."

BIBLIOGRAPHY

A. BIOGRAPHY

The only adequate biography of Lingard is that by MARTIN HAILE and EDWIN BONNEY. *Life and Letters of John Lingard (1771–1851)*. London, 1911. A bibliography (*ibid.*, pp. 383–388) gives an authentic list of Lingard's published works.

B. GENERAL WORKS ON LINGARD

The *Cambridge History of English Literature* (Vol. XIV. pp. 54–59) gives an estimate of Lingard's historical work. Interesting details of the reception of his *History of England* will be found in GILLOW, *Biographical Dictionary of the English Catholics*, Vol. IV, pp. 254–278. Articles on his Works are in the *London Times*, for July 21–28, 1851; the *Dublin Review*, Vol. VIII, p. 334, XII, p. 312; *Brownson's Quarterly Review*, for January and July, 1855. Cf. also *The Making of Lingard's History*, in the *Ushaw Magazine*, Vol. XIX (1909). A recent estimate is GUILDAY, *John Lingard*, in *America* for Jan. 22, 1917.

HERGENROETHER (1824–1890)

Rev. Herman C. Fischer, Ph.D.
Pontifical College Josephinum, Columbus, O.

JOSEPH ADAM GUSTAV HERGENROE-
THER [1] was born at Wuerzburg, Bavaria, on
the 15th of September, 1824, the son of Dr.
John Jacob Hergenroether, professor of medicine at the University of Wuerzburg, and of Eva
Maria Horsch, daughter of the Medical Councillor
and Professor Philipp Joseph Horsch of the same
city, Joseph was one of fourteen children, seven of
whom died in early youth, while three of the remaining seven, Joseph, Philipp, and Franz, rose to posi-
tions of distinction in the Church.

In consequence of political events the elder Hergenroether found himself compelled to resign his
chair of medicine at the University and to take up

[1] We have no biography of Cardinal Hergenroether. His extremely valuable and interesting correspondence has not been
published as yet. This sketch of his life is based mainly on
Stamminger, *Zum Gedaechtnisse Cardinal Hergenroethers*
(Herder, 1892), and on the articles of Heinrich in *Der Katholik*
(1890, 2), pp. 480 sq. and of Hollweck in the *Historisch-po-
litisiche Blaetter* (1890), pp. 721 sq.

We have also consulted with profit the articles on *Hergenroether* in the *Catholic Encyclopedia* (Msgr. Kirsch) and in the
Allgemeine Deutsche Biographie (Lauchert). Above all, however,
we have tried to give an interpretation of his works, in as far
as they have been accessible to us. For the general historical
background the reader may consult Brueck, *Geschichte der
katholischen Kirche in Deutschland im neunzehnten Jahrhundert*,
Vols. 3 and 4, and Granderath, *Geschichte des vatikanischen
Konzils*, 3 vols.

the duties of a physician at Marktheidenfeld.[2] In the popular schools of that village Joseph received his elementary education. Under the solicitous instruction of his father and of the venerable pastor of Marktheidenfeld, Georg Christian Uhrig, young Hergenroether made such progress in Latin and the other branches commonly taught in the German Lateinschule, that he was enabled to finish his college course at the Gymnasium of Wuerzburg within four years and to leave there in 1842 with splendid testimonials. Here he laid the foundations of that solid and extensive philological knowledge which was to stand him in such good stead in later years. He now gave two years to the study of philosophy at the University of Wuerzburg, devoting part of his time, however, to the courses of the professor of dogmatic theology, Andreas Deppisch, and to those of the exegete, Valentin Reissman, in later years Bishop of Wuerzburg (1871–75).

During the sixteenth, seventeenth, and a part of the eighteenth century numerous German youths had wended their way to the Eternal City to prepare for the priesthood in the famous institution, founded by St. Ignatius, the Collegium Germanicum. But the philosophy and theology of the *Enlightenment* and the succeeding revolutionary movements had placed a barrier between Rome and Germany and severed to a great extent the intimate relations hitherto existing between the Roman See

[2] Cf. STEINER, *Der Episkopat der Gegenwart in Lebensbildern dargestellt: Cardinal Hergenroether* (Wuerzburg, Woerl, 1883).

and the German clergy. The *Enlightenment* had
cast a spiritual and religious blight over the whole
of Germany. Men like Moehler, Klee, and others,
to whom we owe the revival of Catholic Theology
in Germany, had to seek their way upwards
through their own exertions, so to say, without living guides; their teachers were the great dead of
the past centuries and their works. Hergenroether
was more fortunate. The readjustment of ecclesiastical conditions and the Concordats entered into by
the Holy See with the different German states in the
first half of the nineteenth century had reopened
the way to Rome to aspiring German ecclesiastics.
Georg Anton v. Stahl, Bishop of Wuerzburg, had
already sent Denzinger and Hettinger to the Collegium Germanicum, of which the bishop himself
had formerly been an inmate, and in 1844 Hergenroether, having finished his philosophical studies
and acceding to the wish of his bishop, followed
them there. The cosmopolitan character of the
Eternal City, its art, its glorious Past and its rich
and powerful Present made, as Hergenroether himself assures us, a deep and lasting impression on
his mind and heart. And these impressions were undoubtedly strengthened by the fact that the years
which Hergenroether spent in Rome were a time of
storm and stress in the life of the Church: the last
years of the firm, unyielding or, shall we say, obstinate Gregory XVI, so full of dark forebodings, and
the beginnings of the Pontificate of the mild Pius
IX, beginnings so full of hope and promise for

Church and State and of dangers in the eyes of many.[3]

At Rome Hergenroether spent four years (1844–1848) and followed the courses at the Collegium Romanum of such scholars as Perrone and Passaglia in dogmatic theology, Tomei in moral theology, Ballerini in Church history, Patrizi in exegesis and Oriental languages, and Marzio in canon law. The Revolution of 1848 forced him to discontinue his studies before the acquisition of his degree in theology. After his ordination to the priesthood on the 28th of March, 1848, by Canali, Patriarch of Jerusalem, he returned to Germany, entered the seminary at Wuerzburg and resumed his theological studies at the University during the summer of 1848 and the winter of 1849. For about a year after this he devoted himself with great zeal to pastoral work, as curate of Zellingen, but his bishop desiring that he become a professor he entered the University of Munich in the May of 1850. It was here that he and Ignaz v. Doellinger, even then a scholar of European fame and a star of the first magnitude at the University, met for the first time. "In the year 1850," says Hollweck, in an appreciation of Hergenroether in the *Historische-politische Blaetter*[4] "a young priest called on Doellinger and informed him of his intention of acquiring the degree of Doctor of Theology at the University of Munich. Doellinger asked drily:

---

[3] STAMMINGER, *l. c.*, p. 5 sq.
[4] Vol. 106 (1890), p. 721 sq.

'Where did you make your studies?' The answer
was: 'At Rome.' 'Very well,' said Doellinger with
a sneer, 'then you undoubtedly know some Latin?
But how would it be, if I should use Greek in the
Disputation?' 'If you wish, you may do so,' replied
the young priest. You may choose Hebrew or
Syriac, if you see fit. I will not fail to answer.'
Doellinger was impressed. When on the 18th of
July, 1850, after a splendid examination, Doellinger
as Dean of the Faculty of Theology, placed the
Doctor's biretta on the brow of the young priest,
he spoke the significant words: 'Coronasti nos.
Coronamus te.' Doellinger and Hergenroether —
this was the young Doctor's name — were to meet
again."

Hergenroether's first writings of some importance
were a treatise on *The Trinitarian teaching of St.
Gregory of Nazianz* (1850),[5] his dissertation for
the Doctorate, and a thesis, entitled: *De catholicae
Ecclesiae primordiis recentiorum Protestantium sys-
temata* (1851), in which he defended the historic
basis of the Church against the destructive criticism
of the School of Tuebingen, and which he submitted
to the Faculty of Theology of Munich, in order to
qualify as privatdocent or instructor at the University of that city. It was Doellinger himself, whose
keen insight had immediately appraised at its true
value the extraordinary ability of Hergenroether,
who prevailed upon him to remain at Munich as
instructor. From 1851–52 Hergenroether gave

[5] Regensburg, Manz (1850).

courses at Munich in patrology and the theological virtues, and conducted disputatoria on dogmatic and moral theology.

But his home city, Wuerzburg, to which he was much attached, was to receive him back. In Wuerzburg the Theology of the *Enlightenment* had possessed its keenest and most advanced representative in Franz Berg, professor of Church history at the University of that city, a man who seems to have had no faith in the supernatural whatever and yet was freely permitted to instill his radical ideas into the minds of the young aspirants for the priesthood during a period of twenty years (1789–1809).[6] One shudders when one considers into what hands the training of ecclesiastics was frequently delivered in that age. Berg's immediate successors in the chair of Church history at Wuerzburg, Joseph Leiniker and Franz Moritz, though not as important as he, were both suffering in a greater or lesser degree from the after effects of the great intellectual disease of the eighteenth century. Then followed John Baptist Schwab, the biographer of Berg, a brainy man and a scholar of note. But his critical, skeptical temper hindered Schwab from forming a firm opinion on the most important questions, or, at all events, if he ever formed an opinion, he lacked the power of giving it adequate and final expression. This, of course, was bound to lead in time to friction with the Church authorities. It is

6 On BERG compare the articles *Professor Berg in Wuerzburg* in the *Historisch-politische Blaetter*, Vol. 65 (1870), p. 54 sq. and 185 sq.

a remarkable fact that consequent upon an expert's opinion, given by Doellinger, Schwab was deposed from his professorship of Church history at Wuerzburg and Hergenroether called to take his place. On the 3d of November, 1852, Hergenroether was appointed professor extraordinary of Church history and canon law at the University of Wuerzburg; three years later (1855) he was promoted to the full possession of that chair. Speaking of these events Stamminger pertinently remarks: " The hand of Providence is sometimes so clearly active in human affairs, that we cannot help seeing it. This was the case here. The young scholar Hergenroether was to hear the Catholic Doellinger, before he was called to combat the apostate Doellinger. Doellinger himself, who was wont to compare science with the spear of Telephus, which healed the wounds which it made, could hardly foresee at that time that the privatdocent whom he had recommended would one day wrest the wounding spear from his hand and use it in order to heal." [7]

With real enthusiasm Hergenroether devoted himself to his duties as a teacher. At Wuerzburg he entered upon a different line of studies from that with which he had been occupied so far. Up till now he had given his attention mainly to dogmatic theology; from now on he was to teach Church history, canon law, and patrology. His extensive and profound knowledge of dogmatic theology was naturally of the greatest service to him in these

[7] *L. c.*, p. 7.

branches. It gave him that keen sensitiveness for
the correct solution in questions of canon law, that
solidity and accuracy in the exposition of heresies
or theological controversies which are so eminently
characteristic of his historical writings. In canon
law his strength lay in his exposition of the con-
stitutional law of the Church: the *potestas plenaria*
of the Roman Pontiff has never had a more brilliant defender. In patrology he fascinated his hear-
ers by his pertinent characterizations of the Fathers
and ancient Christian writers. His vast theological
erudition rested on a substructure of broad, general
culture; he read his sources in the original language.
The great revival in religious faith and life which
Germany was experiencing when Hergenroether was
appointed to his professorship, was also instrumen-
tal in stimulating his enthusiasm and idealism and
in giving wings to his ambition to do something
worth while for the Church of Christ.

From this time onward until his elevation to the
Cardinalate — a period of twenty-eight years —
Hergenroether devoted himself to his duties as a
teacher with remarkable conscientiousness and application. How different was the University of
Wuerzburg of 1855, of Hergenroether, Denziger,
and Hettinger, from that of Berg! Adorned by
these three great luminaries, the Alma Julia of
Wuerzburg became a centre radiating sound,
immaculate doctrine, and a nursery of priestly virtues and ecclesiastical spirit in numerous young
men.

Since we are here mainly concerned with Hergenroether, the historical writer, it will be impossible for us to give detailed attention to Hergenroether's activities in other fields, as for instance in the pulpit, as a speaker at the annual meetings of German Catholics, the so-called *Katholikentage,* which he frequently attended since 1863, and as a loyal friend and fosterer of Catholic societies in Germany.

If the words of Stamminger "bene dixit"—he was a great teacher — are true of Hergenroether, the words " bene scripsit " are still more adequate. He was indeed a great writer. The fertility of his literary activities is astounding. His earlier writings were mainly polemical in nature. From whatever side the battalions marched against the Church, Hergenroether was always to be found on the battlements, ready to meet the onslaught with his pen.

We have seen how, at the beginning of his teaching career, he gave his attention to the destructive tendencies of the Tuebingen School. The years 1848–1870 were remarkable for incessant attacks on the part of political liberalism on the Temporal Power of the Pope. Numerous accusations were brought against the administration of the Papal States, while there was no end of the intrigues against the Papal Government and of the obstacles thrown in its way by its enemies. Hergenroether reduced these accusations to their proper value and exposed these intrigues and maneuvres in his work on *The Papal States Since the French Revolution.*[8] The ideas contained in this work had first been elaborated in a series of articles in the *Historisch-politische Blaetter,* and even in this earlier form had created a sensation in France and Italy. Deplorable was the attitude taken by certain Catholic theologians, notably by Doellinger, on this question of the Temporal Power of the Pope. It was undoubtedly an act of disloyalty for Catholics to encourage the enemies of the Holy See by petty criticism and faultfinding at a time when attacks were coming from all sides. When in April and May, 1861, Doellinger in his famous lectures at the Odeum in Munich, later in the same year enlarged upon in his book *Church and Churches, Papacy and The Papal States,*[10] made a veiled attack on the Temporal Power of the Pope, Hergenroether came back at him in a series of articles in the *Katholik.*[11] It is extremely interesting to make a comparative study of Doellinger's *Papacy and The Papal States,* and Hergenroether's articles in the *Katholik,* and control the statements of the first by the answers of the other. The attentive reader of Doellinger's *Papacy and The Papal States* cannot help feeling an undercurrent of bitterness against the Papacy running through the whole exposition, a bitterness,

---

[8] *Der Kirchenstaat seit der franzoesischen Revolution* (Herder, Freiburg, 1860).

[9] Vol. 43, pp. 859, 971; Vol. 44, pp. 34, 97, 305, 365, 533, 663, 756, 804, 877.

[10] *Kirche und Kirchen, Papsttum und Kirchenstaat* (Munich, 1861).

[11] (1861) Vol. 1, p. 513 sqq.

which, nine years later, was to develop into open rebellion. Doellinger sees everything through colored glasses: he seems to dwell with particular delight on the weaknesses and abuses of the Papal Government of the Roman States; there is hardly anything mentioned which would serve to relieve the gloom which settles down upon the mind while reading this book; there is nothing said as to the causes which might explain conditions, while at the same time exculpate the Holy See to a great extent; nor are the numerous benefits conferred upon the Roman territories by the Holy See in the course of centuries placed into the proper relief. We miss, therefore, in Doellinger that adjustment of light and shadow, which we should find in every historical picture; we are only too often face to face with exaggerations, and, while generally speaking, we may admit the accuracy of Doellinger's data, we find him at times accepting mere rumors and the gossip of irresponsible journalists in lieu of serious documentation. We have here in germ the outstanding faults which at a later period characterized *Janus,* the *Roman Letters from the Council,* and the mass of Old Catholic literature. In fact, we find here traces of that peculiar conception of Church history prevalent among the historiographers and professors of the eighteenth century, who in their writings and lectures reduced the history of the Church to a mere *chronique scandaleuse* and made of the Church itself a monstrous caricature.

Hergenroether, on the other hand, admitting the

substantial accuracy of many of Doellinger's facts, tends to show, and, we believe, successfully, that some of the facts alleged had been given an undue importance, that the Holy See in many instances could not be held responsible for conditions, since it had been consistently thwarted by sinister influences from within and without in its most beneficent purposes, while he at the same time places the manifold blessings which had come to the population of the Roman territories under the benign rule of the Pope-Kings into their proper perspective.

When in 1864 Pius IX was faithlessly betrayed in the September Convention by Napoleon III and Victor Emmanuel II, and again on the occasion of the spoliation of 1870, Hergenroether raised his voice in behalf of the indefectible rights of the Holy See.[12]

A peaceful interlude in these controversies was Hergenroether's patristic study *Hippolytus or Novatian?* (1863), in which he successfully defended the opinion prevalent among German scholars against Armellini and others, that Hippolytus was the author of the *Philosophoumena*.[13] The stand he took on this question shows how unfounded was the slur, often cast upon him, that he was utterly dependent on the Jesuit schools for his scientific opinions. In his difference of opinion with Dr. Doel-

[12] *Die franzoesisch-sardinische Uebereinkunft vom 15 Sept. 1864* (Frankfurt a. M., 1865), and *Denkschrift ueber die an dem Papste vollbrachte Gewalttat* (Mainz, 1871).
[13] *Oesterreich. Vierteljahresschrift fuer katholische Theologie,* 1863, Heft 3. Separately printed (Vienna, Braumueller, 1863).

linger,[14] as to whether Hippolytus was also the author of the *Smaller Labyrinth,* in which discussion he took the negative, it may be said, in the light of what we know today, that Doellinger had the better of the argument.[15]

As early as 1854 Hergenroether had turned his attention to the life of Photius and the origins of the Greek Schism. Some of the results of his researches in the principal libraries of Europe for manuscript copies of the works of Photius were incorporated in a publication entitled *Photii Constantinopolitani Liber de Spiritus Sancti Mystagogia.*[16] This was the first critical edition of this work of Photius on the Holy Ghost and His relation to the Father and the Son, and Hergenroether took occasion in his comments and footnotes to correct many of the false assertions of Photius at the hand of the Fathers and the early Christian writers. He contributed essays on the same work and on the *Amphilochia* to the *Tuebinger Theol. Quartalschrift* (1858). Also in the Migne edition of the works of Photius he took a prominent part and offered many textual emendations.[17] These studies of Hergenroether in the fifties and sixties of the last century happened to coincide with certain aspirations in Germany towards the creation of a National Church in intimate union with the State. We all know how

[14] DOELLINGER, *Hippolytus und Kallistus,* p. 6 sq.
[15] BARDENHEWER, *Geschichte der altchristlichen Literatur,* Vol. 2, p. 510.
[16] Regensburg, Manz, 1857.
[17] *P. G.* Vols. 101–104 (1860); see *Cath. Encyclopedia,* Vol. 7, article *Hergenroether.*

Bismarck, who just at this time was rising to greatness in the Prussian State, only a decade later made the fusion of the Protestant and Catholic Churches into one great national German Church one of the main points of his program in the *Kulturkampf*. Byzantine and Photian ideas were in the air; one heard Catholic writers openly accuse the Papacy of having caused the Greek Schism. This, for instance, was the thesis laid down by PICHLER in his *History of the Separation of Eastern and Western Churches* (1864).[18] Pichler was no mean opponent; he was well versed in the history, doctrine, canon law, and liturgy of the Eastern Churches. But when Hergenroether got through with him in a number of articles in the *Chilianeum*[19] and the *Archiv fuer katholisches Kirchenrecht*,[20] there was little left of Pichler. In fact, if one wishes to get an idea of the vast erudition of Hergenroether in the domain of dogmatic theology, Church history, and canon law, one need not read through any of his larger works; it will be sufficient to page one or the other of his articles against Pichler, hidden away among the book reviews and miscellanies of these periodicals.[21]

---

[18] *Geschichte der kirchlichen Trennung zwischen Orient und Occident* (1864).

[19] *Neue Studien ueber die Trennung der morgenlaendischen und abendlaendischen Kirche*, Separatabdruck aus dem Chilianeum, Bd. V (Wuerzburg, Stehel, 1864). Vide *Chilianeum*, Vol. III, p. 369; VI, p. 246; VII, p. 20. I have not been able to consult these volumes of the *Chilianeum*, a periodical which has long ceased to appear. The citations above are given according to STAMMINGER, *l. c.*, p. 36.

[20] Vol. XII, p. 471 sq.; Vol. XIV, p. 140 sq.

[21] For some interesting particulars on the rôle of Pichler in the movement called " Reformkatholizismus " and on his tragic end see WEISS, *Die religioese Gefahr* (Herder, 1904), VI, 1; VII, 18, 66.

It would seem providential, therefore, that while such ideas were being ventilated in Germany, Hergenroether published his classical work, *Photius, Patriarch of Constantinople, His Life, His Writings, and the Greek Schism,* in three volumes (1861–67),[22] the fruit of twelve years of labor and research. It may be mentioned that, Hergenroether's eyesight failing, he had instructed his sister Theresa in Greek to such an extent that she was able to read and write it, so that he had but to compare her copies with the originals. This work created a sensation not only in Germany, but also in Athens and St. Petersburg. If Hergenroether had never written anything but this great work on Photius, his name would live forever in the history of scholarship. The work may indeed be called a history of the Byzantine Church from the fourth to the thirteenth century. No student of Byzantine Church history can even today, after a lapse of sixty years, approach his subject, without familiarizing himself with this masterpiece. Speaking of Hergenroether's *Photius,* Monsignor Kirsch says: " In this monumental work it is difficult to say whether the palm belongs to the author's extensive knowledge of the manuscript material, to his profound erudition, or to his calm objective attitude." [23] And Krumbacher, an authority on Byzantine literature and a non-Catholic, remarks: " Solidity, great

[22] *Photius, Patriarch von Constantinopel, Sein Leben, Seine Schriften, und das griechische Schisma,* 3 Bde. (Regensburg, Manz, 1867–1869).
[23] *Catholic Encyclopedia,* Vol. 7, article *Hergenroether.*

learning and objectivity are recognized merits of this work which seldom betrays the religious viewpoint of its author." [24]

Of the qualities of *Photius* noted by the two writers quoted, we have been most impressed by the objectivity, impartiality, and fairness of this great biography. Hergenroether set out to prove that not Rome, but Photius was the cause of the sad schism which rent the Church in two, and of all the unfortunate consequences which followed. He proved his case on overwhelming evidence. But this result of his research did not blind him to the greatness of the man whose life he was writing; it did not hinder him from paying homage to his marvelous knowledge, his great merits in theology, philosophy, history, philology, and science in general. In his Foreword to the first volume of *Photius* [25] he tells us of the principles which guided him in the preparation of his great work. He admits that his long occupation with his subject had evoked in him a certain affection for the famous patriarch, which inclined him rather to deal leniently with his faults than to exaggerate them, which kept him from an overseverity of judgment, wherever undeniable facts did not absolutely command an acknowledgment of his moral weaknesses and crimes. " The historian," he says, " will distribute praise and blame according to the uncompromising demands of truth and the commands of conscientious research. He will never cover up

[24] *Geschichte der byzantinischen Literaturgeschichte,* 2te Auflage, p. 78.   [25] *Vorwort*, p. vi.

moral weaknesses out of sympathy for a man of
eminent mind, nor will he permit himself, on account of antipathy for these weaknesses to belittle
or misjudge him. . . . There is one judgment for
the man, another for the scholar." The author,
therefore, willingly grants Photius his merited
place among scholars, but he denies to him the
niche on the altar to which the Greek Orthodox
Church has assigned him. It has been well said that
only a man of genius and universality equal to that
of Photius could have given us this biography. A
fourth volume was later added, bearing the title:
*Monumenta graeca ad Photium eiusque historiam
pertinentia.*[26]

We have considered the stand taken by Hergenroether against political liberalism and its attacks
on the Temporal Power of the Popes. In the meantime the first stirrings of ecclesiastical liberalism
became audible at the Congress of Catholic Scholars held at Munich in 1863. In his opening discourse Doellinger, who had been the main promoter
of the Congress, launched forth into a bitter attack on scholastic theology, past and present. In
Doellinger and many others the sad change which
was to end in apostacy had already made great
progress. Hergenroether was under no illusions as
to the great dangers which were soon to menace the
Church. He was one of the eight men who considered it their duty to lodge a protest on the
floor of the Congress against some of the state-

[26] Regensburg, Manz, 1863.

ments made by Doellinger in his discourse, and in several articles in the *Chilianeum* he took him severely to task for his contemptuous treatment of Italian theological literature.[27] When, in 1864, the *Syllabus* called forth a veritable storm in the liberal camp, Hergenroether did his part to enlighten and quiet timid Catholics by his fine essay: *The Errors of Modern Times Judged by the Holy See.*[28]

But all these were mere skirmishes. The real division of spirits and the main battle were caused by the opening of the Vatican Council (1869–1870), in the preparation of which Hergenroether had been active as a consultor since 1868. The Vatican Council led Hergenroether to the heights of his activity. The noble battle which he waged with all the weapons of his scholarship and with the whole strength of his love for the Church against the opponents of the Vatican Council and of its fundamental definitions on the relation of Faith and Science and the Infallibility of the Roman Pontiff forms the most beautiful page in the book of his life and gives him a high claim to the undying gratitude of posterity. Undoubtedly many others, indeed some of the best men in Germany, France, England, Belgium, Ireland, and Italy took a meritorious part in this great struggle; still one may say, it seems to me, that Hergenroether stands forth among them all. He was " The Great Ultramontane," in the good sense of the word.

<hr/>

[27] Vol. 3, pp. 28, 118; Vol. 4, pp. 114, 152.
[28] *L. c.*, Vol. 6, p. 192 sq.

The controversies of that time, however, as is well known, dealt not merely with the Infallibility of the Pope, but had reference to a great number of dogmatical, historical, and canonistical questions. After having shown in two different experts' opinions,[29] which had been demanded by the Bavarian Government from the University of Wuerzburg, that the fears of that government with regard to the so-called *New Vatican Dogmas* were unfounded, Hergenroether now took up the defense of the Church against the attacks of Doellinger, Friedrich, Huber, von Schulte, and a number of others.

The polemical treatises exchanged between Hergenroether and Doellinger prove, beyond a possibility of doubt, that in keenness of mind and thoroughness of theological knowledge Hergenroether was not only the equal of Doellinger, but his superior. Anyone who will take the time and trouble to make a comparative study of Doellinger's *Janus* and Hergenroether's *Anti-Janus,* will soon find how true this judgment is. In the autumn of 1869 Doellinger together with Huber published a book entitled *The Pope and the Council* by *Janus,*[30] a symposium of all the objections that Doellinger could dig up in the past to discredit the Papacy and its

[29] *Gutachten der theologischen Fakultaet der Julius Maximilians Universitaet Wuerzburg ueber fuenf ihr vorgelegte Fragen in Betreff des kuenftigen oekumenischen Konzils* (Wuerzburg, Woerl, 1869). — *Ueber das vatikanische Konzil. Entwurf einer Beantwortung der elf vom kgl. bayerischen Staatsministerium des Cultus den theologischen und juristischen Fakultaeten vorgelegten Fragen.* (Mainz, Kirchheim, 1871).

[30] JANUS, *Der Papst und das Konzil* (1869).

claims. At the end of the same year Hergenroether opposed to Doellinger's *Janus* his *Anti-Janus*,[31] a booklet of one hundred and eighty-eight pages, in which he subjects the whole tissue of ancient errors and modern sophisms of *Janus* to a searching historico-theological criticism. From a literary point of view it may be admitted that the *Anti-Janus* is not on a par with the larger works of Hergenroether which are remarkable for their lucidity and beauty of diction. The language is sometimes obscure, the style slovenly, but this may be explained by the fact, attested by Hergenroether himself,[32] that the book was hurriedly written, under the stress of many other labors. Abstracting from this, however, no candid reader of the *Anti-Janus* can fail to see how great an asset to Hergenroether was his thorough theological training at the Collegium Romanum, and how sadly Doellinger was handicapped by the lack of a firm grounding in Catholic principles.

It would be impossible to enter into a discussion of the numerous smaller controversial brochures and articles in which Hergenroether illustrated the dogma of Papal Infallibility and defended it against its various opponents. It may suffice to mention here his *Critique of Doellinger's Declarations of 21 January 1870* [33] and *of 28 March 1871*,[34] his articles

---

[31] *Anti-Janus, eine historisch-theologische Kritik der Schrift " Der Papst und das Konzil " von JANUS* (Herder, Freiburg, 1870).

[32] *Anti-Janus*, pp. 9–10.

[33] *Die Irrtuemer von mehr als 400 Bischoefen und ihr theologischer Censor* (Freiburg, Herder, 1870).

[34] *Kritik der v. Doellingerschen Erklaerung vom 28 Maerz, 1870* (Freiburg, Herder, 1871).

against the lay canonist von Schulte and against
the *Letters from the Council* of the *Allgemeine
Zeitung* of Munich. These letters were later on
published in book form under the title *Roman Letters from the Council.*[35] Their author was the notorious Dr. Friedrich. In 1871 Hergenroether published the solid study *The Infallible Magisterium
of the Pope.*[36] It was Hergenroether's intention to
reply to the critics of his various brochures and
especially of his *Anti-Janus* in an *Anti-Janus Vindicatus,* but he soon convinced himself that with a
mere anti-critic nothing would be gained, that there
was need of a larger, more comprehensive work.
The accusations hurled in a babel of voices by Old
Catholic theologians and canonists, by Protestants
and infidels against the Catholic Church and the
Papacy, as the enemies of the state and of civilization, needed a thorough refutation. Rarely have
men of any age brought together such a mass of
objections, of half-truths, falsehoods, malicious insinuations from all the centuries and from all cor-
ners of the Christian world against the Papacy, and
all this under the guise of science and the plea of
Catholic sentiment, as Doellinger, von Schulte, and
their adherents in the years immediately preceding
and succeeding the Vatican Council. To this fortress
of attack Hergenroether decided to oppose a fortress

---

[35] *Roemische Briefe vom Konzil 1869–70* von QUIRINUS
(Johann Friedrich), (Munich, 1870). Vide Hergenroether's reply
in *Historisch-politische Blaetter,* Vol. 65, pp. 707, 737, 865; Vol.
66, pp. 21, 132, 198, 421, 500, 557, 653.
[36] *Das unfehlbare Lehramt des Papstes* (Passau, 1871).

of defense, solidly founded on the bedrock of historic truth. This he did in his great work: *Catholic Church and Christian State in Their Historical Development and in Their Relation to the Questions of the Day. Historico-theological Essays* (1872).[37] Hergenroether's intentions in writing this work were completely fulfilled. The *Janus* literature will be forgotten, when this work will still be a rich source of information, an arsenal for the defense of truth against the attacks and prejudices of centuries, an arsenal for the historian and canonist, for the journalist and the parliamentarian in all questions pertaining to the relations between Church and State.

One cannot peruse the controversial literature published by Hergenroether without being impressed by the objectivity, the calm, dispassionate, dignified tone which characterizes all this writing, although he suffered almost constant provocation. More than once, he himself assures us, as for instance in his controversy with Pichler, his patience was strained to the breaking-point, and he felt indignation welling up in his heart at the glaring bad faith and prevarications of his opponents.[38] But he

[37] *Katholische Kirche und christlicher Staat in ihrer geschichtlichen Entwickelung und in Beziehung auf die Fragen der Gegenwart. Historisch-theologische Essays und zugleich ein Anti-Janus Vindicatus* (Freiburg, Herder, 1872). Literaturbelege und Nachtraege (ib. 1876). The work was translated into Italian (3 vols. Parma, 1877–1878). An English translation was published in London under the title *Catholic Church and Christian State* in 1876 (Burns and Oates); another in Baltimore in 1889.

[38] *Archiv fuer katholisches Kirchenrecht* (1865), Vol. 14, p. 142 sq.

mastered himself; he refused to employ the poisonous weapons of abuse and to indulge in personalities. The Anti-infallibilist pamphleteers, on the contrary, were remarkable for their vindictiveness, for
the scorn, abuse, and insults which they heaped
upon the defenders of the Holy See. The tone which
characterizes most of their writings might be compared to that prevalent on the fishmarket in Paris.
Even some Catholic writers, for instance Louis
Veuillot in France and one or the other clerical and
lay theologian in England did not always withstand
the temptation of helping along the good cause by
abusing their opponents. In the Introduction to his
Catholic Church and Christian State [39] Hergenroether complains of the insults showered upon him,
of the insinuations against his intellectual integrity,
of the dishonest methods of controversy of those
who attacked him, of the numerous abusive, yes,
threatening letters which he was receiving daily,
and asks: " When have I ever in one single line
permitted myself to indulge in similar invectives? "
No one acquainted with his books will fail to give
an immediate verdict in his favor. Noble in polemics, he was moderate and just in his judgments.
And if he was compelled to pass a severe verdict
on some person or institution, he was not satisfied
with one reason, he looked for ten. For his great
opponent Doellinger he always had the greatest

[39] *Katholische Kirche und christlicher Staat,* Einleitung, p.
III sq. Hergenroether admits, however, that Doellinger, Friedrich,
and Huber generally kept within the limits of those decencies
which one has a right to demand in controversy.

veneration, even after his apostasy, and he frequently spoke of his deep grief at being compelled by his love for the Church and for truth to use his pen against his old teacher. As late as in his Introduction to his *Manual of Universal Church History* he says of Doellinger, "Ubi bene, nemo melius."

Hergenroether's *Catholic Church and Christian State* closes what one might call the polemical period of his literary activities. He had not sought all this strife and controversy; he had been forced into it by his realization of the dangers confronting the Church and by his love for his faith. The years that follow are years of calm and peaceful labor. The first work of importance in this second period of Hergenroether's literary life is his *Manual of Universal Church History* [40] in three volumes (1876–1880). It is a synthesis of all of Hergenroether's preceding studies, and makes a strong appeal to the reader by the lucidity with which the vast material is disposed and by its nobility of diction. The author was prevailed upon to compose this *Manual* by the repeated pleas of his friends and students. It permits one, more than any other of his works, to cast a glance into his workshop. One is at a loss what to admire most, the vast amount of literature, upon which the work is founded, or the complete mastery which the author displays in handling his material. Whosoever is

[40] *Handbuch der allgemeinen Kirchengeschichte*, 3 Bde., 1876–1880; sixth revised edition by J. P. KIRSCH in 4 volumes (Freiburg, Herder, 1925).

called upon to pursue studies of detail and to use
Hergenroether's scientific apparatus, as found in
the footnotes, will be inclined to rank the work
very highly.

For years one of Hergenroether's favorite plans
had been to write a comprehensive history of the
Catholic Church in the eighteenth century. This
plan was never to see fruition; but among the
essays preparatory for this work may be mentioned his sketch of *Cardinal Maury* [41] and his
studies on *Piedmont's Negotiations with the Holy
See in the Eighteenth Century* [42] and on *Spain's
Negotiations with the Papal See.* [43] The main reason
why the large work was never written is to be found
in the fact that in 1877 he was prevailed upon by
his friend Benjamin Herder to take charge of the
second edition of the *Katholisches Kirchenlexikon.* [44]
Hergenroether at the head of an undertaking of
that kind was a pledge of success. With great industry he mastered the preliminary labors, always
of great importance, assigned the articles to the
various authors and completed the first installments
of the work, so that, when he was called to Rome,
his successor, Franz Kaulen, whom he himself had

[41] *Katholische Studien,* vol. IV, n. 3 and 4, Wuerzburg, 1878.
[42] *L. c.,* Vol. II, n. 3, ib. 1876. The *Katholische Studien* have
not been accessible to the writer.
[43] *Archiv fuer kath. Kirchenrecht,* Vol. 10, pp. 1, 185; Vol.
11, pp. 252, 367; Vol. 12, pp. 46, 385; Vol. 13, pp. 91, 393; Vol.
14, p. 211; Vol. 15, p. 169.
[44] *Wetzer und Welte's Kirchenlexikon oder Encyclopaedie der
katholischen Theologie und ihrer Huelfswissenschaften,* Zweite
Auflage begonnen von JOSEPH CARDINAL HERGENROETHER, fortgesetzt von FRANZ KAULEN (Freiburg, Herder, 1880 ff.).

chosen, found the main difficulties removed and a smooth path before him.

As early as May 18, 1877, Pius IX had made Hergenroether a member of his household. But greater honors were in store for him. On the 12th of May, 1879, Leo XIII, in the same consistory with Monsignor Pie of Poitiers, Joseph Pecci, John Henry Newman, and Thomas Zigliara, elevated him to the Cardinalate. Stamminger is right when he numbers Hergenroether among the learned Cardinals, and when he says that the continuator of EGG's *Purpura Docta* will necessarily assign Hergenroether, if for no other reason than for his accomplishments as a Cardinal, a place side by side with such men as Pallavicini, Baronius, Angelo Mai, and others.[45] At Rome a number of difficult duties devolved upon Hergenroether. He was a member of four Congregations and Protector of several religious communities. But although these offices absorbed a great deal of his time, they were after all only secondary. It was as Prefect of the Vatican Archives that he has rendered services to science which cannot be overestimated.

It is well known that the Papal Archives at that time were not in the best of order, and men whom one will not accuse of animosity against the Apostolic See had complained bitterly of this state of affairs. Thus the Protestant Boehmer writes during the Pontificate of Pius IX: " If some one would only call the attention of the Holy Father to the

[45] *L. c.*, p. 22.

fact that everything needs to be improved here,
and that a man must be placed at the head who is
qualified by knowledge and character to represent
Rome before the forum of European scholarship,
and who has the ability and the will to serve science
without selfishness. Would to God that the next
Pope, preannounced by the prophet, as ' lumen de
coelis ' will see in the truthloving science of history the light from heaven in the darkness and
errors of this age, so devoid of all principles." In
Leo XIII the right Pope had appeared for this work
and in Hergenroether a scholar qualified for this
task had been found. It is hardly doubtful, that if
Boehmer had lived till 1879, and if his advice had
been sought, he himself would have suggested Hergenroether or his own scholar Janssen for the
position.[46]

Convinced of the truth of the adage that the best
justification of the Papacy is its history, Leo XIII
determined to make the treasures of the Vatican
Archives accessible to the scholars of all lands. In
order to realize this plan most effectively, he appointed Hergenroether, on the 10th of June, 1879,
Prefect of the Apostolic Archives. In a memorable
brief (August 18, 1883), directed to Cardinals
De Luca, Pitra, and Hergenroether, Leo correctly
characterized the anti-Christian historiography of
our times as " a conspiracy of men against truth,"
proclaimed as the supreme law of history, " ne
quid falsi dicat, ne quid veri taceat," and opened

[46] *Hist.-politische Blaetter,* Vol. 106 (1890), p. 725.

up, for this very purpose of truth, the Papal collections to the scrutiny of the world.[47] Leo's letter found in Hergenroether a most intelligent interpreter and a most conscientious executor.

Restlessly he devoted himself to this honorable task, notably assisted by Father Denifle, O. P., and Father Franz Ehrle, S. J., now Cardinal Ehrle. The first fruits from this new field were garnered by Hergenroether himself. Faithful to a promise, made by him years before to his dearest friend, the venerable Hefele, to continue his *History of the Councils*,[48] he made an extensive use of the rich treasures of the Vatican Archives in the composition of the eighth and ninth volumes of that monumental work. Both these volumes are characterized by Hergenroether's usual carefulness of research, by vividness and beauty of language. Unfortunately, ill health and his manifold other duties hindered him from completing the work.[49]

But he also was one of the first to edit and make accessible to scholars the manuscript treasures of the Vatican. His *Regesta of the Pontificate of Leo X*,[50] which place that Pope in a more favorable

[47] Leonis Pp. XIII *Epistolae* ad S. R. E. Cardinales Ant. de *Luca* vice-cancellarium S. R. E., Jo. Bapt. *Pitra* bibliothecarium S. R. E., *Joseph Hergenroether* tabulariis Vaticanis praefectum. For the text of the letter see *Archiv fuer kath. Kirchenrecht*, Vol. 50, p. 428 sqq.

[48] *Conciliengeschichte*. Nach den Quellen bearbeitet von KARL JOSEPH VON HEFELE, fortgesetzt von JOSEPH CARDINAL HERGEN-ROETHER. Bd. VIII und IX (Freiburg, Herder, 1887–1890).

[49] See his *Introduction* to the eighth volume for the difficulties with which he had to contend.

[50] Leonis *X P. M. Regesta*. Fasc. I–VIII (Friburgi, Herder 1884–1891).

light than that in which he had hitherto appeared,
were edited by him conjointly with his brother, Monsignor Franz Hergenroether, and take us to the
year 1515. Of equal value were the care and labor
which he gave to the interior arrangement and to
the administration of the Archives, thus putting
them into such a condition that they could be used
by others. The merits of Hergenroether as admin-
istrator and organizer of the Vatican Archives are
so well known the world over, that no scholar will
apply the sickle to this immense harvest without
remembering the great Cardinal.

In the midst of all these duties the Cardinal was
ever ready to give his precious time not only to the
many scholars and persons of prominence who
called upon him, but also to the lowliest, and to
help financially wherever there was need. But for
all that, his means were very limited. At Wuerzburg the income from his professorship and from
his writings had given him a comfortable living;
at Rome, where he had to live in conformity with
his station, he was a poor Cardinal and often sorely
worried by financial cares. He was wont to refer
jokingly to the fact that from a highly salaried
professor he had become a poor Cardinal.[51]

Nobody realized how grievously Hergenroether
suffered in body during those last years which he
spent at Rome as Cardinal and Prefect of the Papal
Archives. His eyesight grew weaker, and he was
frequently tortured by severe attacks of nervous-

[51] *Katholik* (1890), II, p. 494.

ness. A number of paralytic strokes, the first of
which he suffered on the 24th of February, 1882,
as he was about to go to the Vatican to assist at
the Lenten sermon, crippled him so seriously that
from now on he was forced to drag himself along
wearily on his cane. But although his body was
broken, his mind was as alert as ever. What worried him now was not so much the loss of his health,
as rather the fact that his hand could no longer
follow his thought with accustomed alacrity. He
grieved also, because at frequent intervals he had to
forego the sacred privilege of saying Mass, or at
least of saying it publicly. He died on the 3d
day of October, 1890, at the Cistercian Abbey of
Mehrerau, while on his way to Rome from his beloved Wuerzburg, whither he had gone in order to
pray at the grave of his brother Philipp, the former
professor of canon law at Eichstaett. In the crypt
of Mehrerau the great Cardinal now rests from his
many labors. In 1897 a monument was erected to
his memory. His best monument is undoubtedly
his works. But it is to be hoped that some day
Catholic Germany, which has given us so many excellent biographies of the great men of the Revival
and the Kulturkampf, will present us with a comprehensive life of Joseph Hergenroether. Doellinger
also died in 1890. Doellinger and Hergenroether!
In the death of the one the Church deplores the
lost son, who in his old days heaped insult upon
insult upon her, who seemed to have forgotten all
the love which he once bore her; in the other she

grieves over one of the noblest, most courageous, and ablest defenders she ever possessed, a son whose love for the Church grew as the years passed,[52] a man who always remained faithful to his watchword: "Alles fuer die Wahrheit, nichts gegen die Wahrheit, alles fuer die Kirche Gottes und mit ihr." [53]

BIBLIOGRAPHY

A. BIOGRAPHY

STAMMINGER, *Zum Gedaechtnisse Cardinal Hergenroethers* (Herder, 1892).

HEINRICH, in the *Katholik* (1890–92).

HOLLWECK, in the *Historische-politische Blaetter* (1890).

STEINER, *Der Episcopat der Gegenwart in Lebensbildern dargesstellt* (Wuerzburg, 1883).

Catholic Encyclopedia, Vol. VII, article, *Hergenroether* by Monsignor Kirsch.

Allgemeine Deutsche Biographie, Vol. 50, pp. 228–231, article by F. Lauchert.

B. GENERAL WORKS ON HERGENROETHER AND HIS WRITINGS

Kirchenlexikon, Vol. VII. *Introduction* by Streber.

ZOBL, *Trauerrede beim Leichenbegaengnisse seiner Eminenz des Cardinals Hergenroether* (Feldkirch, 1890).

NIRSCHL, *Gedachtnissede* (Wuerzburg, 1897).

The more important works of Cardinal Hergenroether will be found touched upon in the article of Mon-

---

[52] *Hist.-politische Blaetter, l. c.,* p. 729.

[53] *Katholische Kirche und christlicher Staat. Einleitung,* p. xxix. "Everything for the truth, nothing against the truth, everything for the Church of God and with her."

signor Kirsch in the *Catholic Encyclopedia*. Many of his interesting and valuable contributions to theological and controversial literature are scattered in German Catholic *Zeitschriften*, too numerous to list here.

JOHANNES JANSSEN (1829–1891)

Rev. Alfred Kaufmann, S.J.
Creighton University, Omaha, Nebraska

AFTER the Congress of Vienna, 1815, Europe settled down to enjoy a prolonged respite from international wars. The horrors of the revolutionary period made thinking minds once again realize the fundamental importance of the Christian traditions of Europe and enkindled everywhere a remarkable revival of religious faith and practice. In France an Ozanam, a Montalembert and Lacordaire and many others proved that not all Frenchmen of the day were " Sons of Voltaire," but that the " Sons of the Crusaders " meant to dispute every inch of ground with advancing rationalism and licentiousness. English Catholics were cheered by the glorious fruits of the Oxford movement, while in Germany the thirties witnessed the beginning of that wide-spread renewal of faith and fervor that were to furnish the troops for the great Catholic leaders in the Kulturkampf. This general revival extended also to the field of Catholic scholarship. While the revolutionary and Napoleonic periods are singularly sterile in this respect, the first half of the nineteenth century contains a number of names that fill every Catholic heart with pardonable pride. These names prove that where

Catholic faith and practice flourish, one of its finest flowers, Catholic scholarship, will not be sought in vain.

Johannes Janssen, the subject of this sketch, was born into this Second Spring. He lived in the midst of it, inhaled its fragrance, was inspired by its most distinguished representatives. In his own country, and during his childhood and early manhood, Moehler, Doellinger, Hefele, Hergenroether, Ritter, and others carried aloft the torch of Catholic learning and even extorted a hearing from their unwilling opponents.

Janssen was born April 10, 1829, in the quaint old town of Xanten on the lower Rhine. The genius loci was decidedly of a historical turn of mind. Xanten, the site of a Roman camp, the birth-camp of Siegfried of the Nibelungen, the Troja of the medieval legend, the proud possessor of the church of St. Victor, one of the finest specimens of medieval architecture on the Rhine, was eminently qualified to contain the cradle of one of Germany's greatest historians. Janssen's parents were simple God-fearing people, blessed, not with wealth, but with a modicum of this world's goods, the result of unwearied labor and strict economy. Father Janssen had seen the "Franzosenzeit," with its lawless liberty and license. Under his eyes the armies of Napoleon had crossed and recrossed the Rhine on their marches to and from their eastern campaigns. His heart had thrilled to the martial songs of the War of Liberation, and down to his old age he loved to tell of those stirring times. John often avowed that these early impressions awakened in his boyish heart the interest and love for the past. Whatever historical books he could lay hands on he eagerly devoured. Mother Janssen was the ideal German Hausfrau. Always active, sincerely and unostentatiously pious, she carefully instilled into the heart of her John that simple faith and devotion, together with habits of unremitting labor, that remained his outstanding characteristics throughout life. Indeed, the best qualities of father and mother were so harmoniously blended in the son that they gave to his nature an irresistible charm that won hearts wherever he went.

If it is true that the poet is born, the study of the childhood and boyhood of many an eminent man seems to show that the axiom holds in the case of intellectual and artistic excellence in general. With young Janssen the historical bent of mind revealed itself unmistakably. He loved to tell the story how he once aroused the impatience of his gentle mother when on the return from a pilgrimage to the far-famed Kevelaer he regaled their fellow passengers with stories from Annegarn's Weltgeschichte which a kind aunt had bought for him, instead of joining in the devotions of the pilgrims. When leaving the elementary school his studious habits were so pronounced that relatives and friends interceded with his father to permit John to continue his studies. For a long time Father Janssen hesitated. Instead, he gave his son as an apprentice to his brother-in-law, who was a copper-smith. Young Janssen tried to do his best, but the historical complex proved too strong. Again and again he was caught with books under the smith's apron, and — what was worse — by his continual narration of stories he interfered with the progress of his fellow apprentices. In the end his employer, with whom the future historian maintained a life-long friendship, became his staunchest advocate with Father Janssen. John was released from the smithy and threw himself on his books with the eagerness of a prisoner freed from long captivity. It is doubtful if Janssen, even if his inclinations had been otherwise, could have succeeded in a trade. His health was never robust. His delicate frame, his want of physical vigor, his passion for books, mani-festly predestined him for a profession.

In the autumn of 1846 he left his home to com-plete his college course at a Gymnasium. Being a conscientious student, he neglected none of the courses taught; yet he found it possible to devote a considerable part of his time to historical reading. To his chagrin, instruction in history was not in competent hands, and — what was worse — it was permeated with the ideas of the " enlightenment " of Josephism. In this atmosphere the Catholic Middle Ages received little consideration and still less appreciation. To compensate himself for the loss, Janssen, during vacation, guided by the monu-ments of his native town, delved into the medieval period of his Rhineland, and in imagination reconstructed the splendors of the communal and social life of those times. His Catholic instinct and sound historical sense prevented him from accepting the contemptuous views of his teachers. He once confided to a fellow student: "Wait till we are in a position to do independent research. Then we shall see if the age that built the cathedrals of Cologne and Xanten has been as dark as our professors paint it."

In the meantime he had resolved to prepare himself for the priesthood, and in the fall of 1849 set out for the theological school at Munster, Westphalia. Soon he earned the reputation of being the most industrious student of his class. But history was not forgotten. Besides the courses prescribed by the theological curriculum, he attended lectures on various phases of history. But his health proved unequal to the strain. In his very first semester he was frequently confined to the sickroom. This, and a conscientiousness sometimes bordering on scrupulosity, made him give up the thought of adopting the life of a pastor of souls. In 1850 he left Munster and decided to go to the University of Louvain. What attracted him to that venerable seat of learning was, besides the wish of perfecting himself in French and English, the thoroughly Catholic atmosphere of the University. He was not disappointed. From the outset he felt at home. The spirit permeating everything in and out of the lecture halls reminded him of the happy times he had spent in the bosom of his family. He is enthusiastic over

the country and its people, " the land where there
is not schism and error, where one does not mock
and ridicule the religious convictions and feelings
of the other, where young and old, rich and poor,
are animated by the same religious spirit " (Letter
to his parents). Often the thought of the religious
divisions of his own country, — divisions which
later were to become the chief subject of his research, — weighed heavily on his mind. During vacation he visited the quaint old towns of Belgium
and studied the artistic monuments of the past.

It was at Louvain, too, that he definitely made
up his mind to devote his life to historical research.
He had the good fortune of coming under the influence of three excellent professors. The historian,
John Moeller, interested him in medieval studies,
while Freije directed his attention to the Reformation, and especially to that phase of it which was
enacted in the Netherlands. P. Gachard had just
begun the voluminous publication of the sources
which made such studies fruitful. Janssen conceived
the profoundest admiration for Laforêt, the philosopher and historian, who later was to be one of the
most distinguished presidents of the University.
Besides pursuing his historical studies Janssen made
use of the cosmopolitan character of the University,
and perfected his knowledge of French, English,
and Italian.

In the summer of 1851 we find our historian back
in his beloved Rhineland and matriculated at the
University of Bonn, where he intended to win his

doctorate. There again he found excellent guides
in his chosen field. Aschbach, the acknowledged
authority on early German history, was his principal mentor. Dahlmann, the noble unselfish patriot
and renowned author of the monumental " Quellenkunde zur deutschen Geschichte," won Janssen's
gratitude for the readiness with which he put his
time and knowledge at the disposal of his students.
Julius Ficker, who later was to win fame by his researches into Italy's legal and imperial history, was
Janssen's fellow student, and was bound to him by
the ties of intimate friendship. The preoccupation
of his teachers and friends with medieval history
induced Janssen to select the subject of his thesis
from that field. He presented for his doctorate a
study of Wibald of Stablo and Corvey, an outstanding figure of the twelfth century, equally distinguished as churchman, head of a large monastic
family, confidante and adviser of three emperors,
and eminent scholar. The work found a very friendly
reception among Catholic and Protestant scholars
alike, and aroused the fondest hopes of even greater
things. The Prussian Department of Education was
so favorably impressed that it offered to our young
doctor, whose means were then very limited, a purse
which enabled him to spend several months in the
libraries and lecture halls of the capital. As usual,
his talents and charming manner won him many
and valuable friends, among them Wattenbach, the
great paleographer, and Ritter, the founder of modern comparative geography.

In August, 1854, Janssen returned to Munster where the position of assistant professor of history at the Akademie was offered to him. In the ordinary course of events this would have been the first step towards a regular professorship and a brilliant university career. But Providence decreed otherwise. His inaugural lecture at Munster proved to be the last he delivered there. From Frankfurt, the city of the coronation of the Holy Roman Emperors, and then still the seat of the Diet of the German Confederation, came the offer of a professorship in history for the Catholic students at the non-Catholic Gymnasium. The prospect of having a position secure for life and, above all, of being near the great Boehmer, with whom he was already in correspondence, induced Janssen to decide quickly. He entered upon his new duties in October, 1854, and for the rest of his life the man who soon was to be a star of the first magnitude in the historical firmament remained a teacher of undergraduates, rejecting many a tempting offer of a more distinguished career.

In the old imperial city on the Main Janssen soon became a member of a circle of highly cultured men and women. Daily intercourse with these high-minded and intensely interested people was to fructify his genius and energize his faculties to bring forth their ripest fruit. Among these Frankfurt friends John Frederic Boehmer easily holds the first place. He was Janssen's senior by more than thirty years, and had won his laurels by his massive publications of sources of medieval imperial history, especially of his *Regesta Imperii*. Yet the two men soon became so much one heart and one soul that one seemed to be indispensable to the other. " I lived in Boehmer," Janssen wrote after the death of his friend, " and his departure means for me the conclusion of one period of my life." In almost daily intercourse the master imbued the pupil with the principles of sound historical research, and, Protestant though he was, he insisted that the Christian and Catholic viewpoint is the only one that sheds light on much historical detail and gives it shape and meaning. Janssen loved to quote the following golden axioms on the task of the historian: " If the efforts of the historian must, above all, be directed towards the acquisition and understanding of truth, they must proceed from the sources. These sources must be critically sifted, arranged, and put in ready form. Then we must visualize them clearly and vividly, without being diverted by unessential detail. One's gaze should remain fixed on the total and the essential, and one should proceed in one's work with a judgment of men and things which has not been warped by the narrow ideas and party spirit of the present time." Such words were carefully treasured by the younger man. But Boehmer, too, was full of praise for his friend " for his eagerness to learn, his zeal and conscientiousness that mark the true scholar, combined with so much modesty and simplicity of heart as are seldom found in a young man." Janssen in turn writes to a friend:

" I have every reason to be contented in my present surroundings. . . . I wish you could have a chance to be with Boehmer just for a few days. A real man, every inch of him, so instructive and inspiring that I have not found his equal during my years at the University."

Unfortunately during the first years at Frankfurt Janssen's weak health frequently checked his ardor and at times showed such alarming symptoms that his devoted friends feared for his life. Despite such obstacles he kept at his work. Under Boehmer's guidance he devoted the first part of his residence at Frankfurt to the period covered by his friend's *Regesta*, the twelfth and thirteenth centuries, but after 1857 his principal interest drifted toward the later Middle Ages and the beginnings of modern history.

His first undertaking was inspired by the duty of friendship. Henry C. Scholten had begun a two-volume life of Louis the Saint, but death prevented him from finishing the task. Janssen then took over the work, and in 1855 completed it with the publication of the second volume. In the same year two series of valuable articles appeared under his name. One, treating certain phases of the Rebellion of the Netherlands, was the fruit of his Louvain studies; the other discussed the sources for the history of Cologne in the Middle Ages. The following year he appeared with a volume of critical editions of the Chronicles of the Munsterland. It formed the third of a series undertaken by his friends, Ficker and

Cornelius. For the next four years nothing of importance appeared from his pen. His health was feebler than ever, and he found himself more than once on the brink of the grave. Still he used every ounce of strength to collect materials for his great *History of the German People,* on which he had set his heart. During the same period he prepared another important contribution to historical science. Boehmer had called his attention to the rich materials for the history of the later Middle Ages that lay hidden in the Frankfurt archives. Other depositories were laid under contribution, and thus he was able to publish, in 1863, the first part of his *Frankfurt Imperial Correspondence,* from 1376 to 1519. Three years later the second volume appeared, and only in 1872 the last one. Experts in the field spoke of the "colossal industry" to which these tomes bear witness. They are simply indispensable to the student of this period. But these labors did not absorb all the energies of the author. The year 1861 saw the publication of a little work on France's Rhine policy. Three years later he produced his *Schiller as Historian.* The great poet had written a history of the Rebellion of the Netherlands against Philip II, and one of the Thirty Years' War. His splendid prose had secured him a place among often-quoted historians. Janssen's critical inquiry does not pass judgment on these works of the poet on the strength of later documentary evidence, but proves that Schiller misjudged events with the evidence then on hand. His handling of facts furnishes abundant proof of how literally Schiller carried out his own principle: " History is the storehouse for my fancy. The facts have to put up with what shape they receive under my hands."

Janssen's letters of these first years at Frankfurt breathe contentment and happiness. His position as teacher provided him with a modest but secure income. The few hours devoted to instruction left him ample time for research. Near at hand he had excellent historical libraries and one of the richest archival repositories of Germany. A circle of warm friends had formed around him, and proved a never-failing source of encouragement and interest. Boehmer gave him the advice of a ripe scholar interested in the same field, and bestowed upon him the affection of a father. And yet he was not wholly satisfied. From childhood on, the altar had been his goal. It was merely on account of weak health that he had suspended the execution of his design when, in 1850, he left the seminary of Munster. A very profound realization of the responsibilities of a pastor of souls made him hesitate for a long time before he took the decisive step. In Munster as well as in Louvain he had attended courses in theology. All who knew him during his early years at Frankfurt agree that as a layman he led a singularly devout life, a life of prayer and of work sanctified by the purest intention. That historical studies alone would never satisfy the longings of his Catholic soul became increasingly evident to him in his daily intercourse with Boehmer. That eminent scholar stood

at the end of a career of unselfish devotion to truth.
He was sincerely religious, had long since severed
all connections with the Protestant communion, and
in his studies had become imbued with an admiration and love for things Catholic. But he was so
engrossed in his work that he never found time
seriously to consider the question of his own allegiance to the Church. Yet Janssen knew that he
was not happy. " For a long time," he later on said
to his biographer, Pastor, " I knew Boehmer's spiritual condition, the void in his soul, his mental anx-
ieties that sometimes bordered on despair. Yes, my
friend, the sight of the interior unhappiness of one
of the most gifted minds of our century more than
anything else drove me into the clerical state." In
1859 Janssen temporarily retired from Frankfurt
and completed his theological studies at Tuebingen.
Then he prepared for the final step under the guidance of the saintly Capuchin, Father Borgia. In
March, 1860, he received Holy Orders from the
bishop of Limburg. All who knew him personally
testify that Janssen was the model of a good priest.
Those who saw him at the altar felt as though they
were in the presence of a Saint. From the daily
Sacrifice he gathered strength courageously to per-
severe in his arduous labors. From now on he looked
upon his work as a real apostolate entrusted to him
by his Divine Master. Not only did he pursue his
studies with renewed fervor, but despite the demands made upon his time he interested himself in
all Catholic endeavors. Thus we find him address-

ing one of the great annual meetings of the German Catholics. For a time he even accepted from the Center party a mandate in the Prussian house of representatives. A journey to Rome in 1863 and an audience with the Holy Father, Pius IX, filled his priestly heart with enthusiastic loyalty to the Holy See. He was gladdened, too, by the appreciation which his labors found with the highest authority in the Church.

Shortly before this journey his beloved Boehmer passed away. In three stately volumes Janssen erected an enduring monument to his master, 1868. As this meant the reading and sifting of a vast amount of correspondence and other papers the labor involved was enormous. But it obtained for its author, almost at once, a place among the best biographers of the country. Catholic and non-Catholic critics were unanimous in their praise. Ranke thought the work important enough to give it an honorable mention in his presidential address to the National Historical Association. Somewhat later Janssen wrote for a larger circle of readers a one-volume life of his hero, which to the present time is recognized as the model of a popular biography. His talent for biography was equally evident in another popular work which he published somewhat later. His friend, August Reichensperger, one of the leaders of the Center during the Kulturkampf, had often urged him to publish in book form various character sketches which Janssen at different times had written for periodicals. The

author finally consented. But nearly all of them —
twelve in number — were rewritten and enlarged.
The work appeared in 1875. Its success was immediate and lasting, as Reichensperger had predicted.
The critics admired the masterly characterization,
the plastic individuality of the different portraits,
the graceful diction, and the phenomenal many-
sided information of the author. Representatives
of the most divergent schools of thought in art,
politics, and religion are introduced to the reader,
almost all of them depicting themselves in words
taken from their own published and unpublished
writings. The book was, however, only a by-product
from the author's literary workshop. Janssen had in
the meantime seriously taken in hand the execution
of the work which had been planned for many years,
and which alone would suffice to secure him a place
among the foremost Catholic historians.

In 1853 Janssen, then a student at the university of Bonn, met for the first time his future intimate friend, Frederic Boehmer. The veteran historian loved to discuss literary plans with his
younger friends. One of his favorite maxims was
that in historical studies the beginner should at once
set himself a great goal, worthy of his best efforts.
In particular, the broad-minded scholar regretted
the fact that Catholics left the field of history too
much to others, especially those periods during
which the influence of the Church was so predominant and far-reaching that it cannot be ignored.
Boehmer, though an outsider, had caught a glimpse

of the grandeur and dignity and charity of that Church. " We live on her inheritance," he said to his young friend. " Would that in our day, as of old, she again exercised that ennobling dominion over the hearts and minds of Europe! " What was needed was, in Boehmer's opinion, Catholic scholars in the field of history who would combine thoroughness of research with good judgment and a mastery of form. " Catholics should give us the true picture of our people. Others have given us a distorted picture." Such words from the lips of the venerable medievalist enkindled a fire of enthusiasm in the heart of the young student, and he resolved then and there to become the historian of his people. But more than twenty years were to elapse after that memorable interview before Janssen's plans reached fruition.

In 1870 Janssen wrote to his friend and publisher, Benjamin Herder: " Since 1853, when at the age of twenty-five I conceived the plan of a German history, I have collected material and made preparations more extensive than I myself realized before I began to revise and rearrange my notes. If God gives me health and strength you will be delighted with the work. It will not be without practical fruit." But the more he delved into the mass of primary sources and special monographs, the more he understood the necessity of limiting the field of investigation. Boehmer had long before spoken of this, and had advised the elimination of social and cultural history. It cost Janssen a considerable mental struggle before he could come to any decision in this matter of concentration on one aspect of his favorite subject. He was a typical son of the Rhineland, being endowed by nature with the proverbial lightness of heart and mental elasticity, with the vivacity and many-sided interest of his countrymen. Boehmer's advice to eleminate the cultural features did not appeal to him. Man's endeavors and man's vicissitudes in every-day life had always interested him intensely. In the end he departed from his original idea of a complete German history, and confined himself to the period of the close of the Middle Ages and the beginnings of modern times. The spirit in which he deliberated is apparent from the following remarks in one of his letters: "On September 8, 1857, as I returned from St. Leonard's Church, I made up my mind to begin the History with the close of the Middle Ages. That day I formed my plans under the patronage of the Blessed Mother of God, whose help and intercession I had invoked."

While composing his History Janssen frequently solicited and obtained advice and information from his many friends. It was partly due to the influence of Reichensperger that the cultural element was not excluded, but on the contrary became the most prominent feature of the work. Janssen drew the whole life of the people into his purview. Such a plan made, of course, much greater demands on a capacity for work than any of his predecessors had undergone. But he was determined not to spare himself in bringing forth something of which his fellow Catholics could be proud.

At last, in March 1876, part of the first volume appeared. His friend Herder had done his best to give the book a worthy typographical garb. Janssen gave the work the sub-title: *Intellectual and Spiritual Condition of the People.* While nearly all his forerunners had confined themselves to political events and the character of the outstanding figures, our author enters into the very heart of the nation. Before our eyes educational and scholarly activities, the art and amusements of the common people, all of them illustrated by numerous citations from contemporary sources, pass in orderly review. In fact, it was Janssen's method to weave his narrative almost entirely in the words of his authorities so that his works have not ineptly been compared to those colorful Roman mosaics. Although composed of countless little stones of divers colors, they reproduce the original with perfect fidelity. There was no lack of recognition. Appearing in the midst of the Kulturkampf, this work cheered the Catholics in the struggle in which they were so often taunted with the reproach of backwardness in scholarship. The evidence of the relatively prosperous and happy condition of the people previous to the great Lutheran upheaval furnished a very effective argument against the endless tirades on the blessings of the Reformation.

But the success of the book among non-Catholics was even greater. For once the old saying,

"Catholica non leguntur," proved untrue. It would take too much space to quote the encomiums bestowed upon our author by very competent non-Catholic critics. One must suffice. George Waitz, the famous editor of the *Monumenta Germaniae Historica,* simply declared: "Janssen is now the first among living German historians." And Ranke was still among the living!

Janssen was not the man to rest on his laurels. While he devoted the greater part of his time to the continuation of his History, he undertook as a labor of love and as a recreation for mind and heart the biography of Count Leopold von Stolberg (1750–1819). As a student he had imbibed enthusiasm for the greatness of the Church and love for historical studies from the works of the noble convert, and when his grandson put the letters and literary legacy at the disposal of our historian he set to work with his usual energy. The life, narrated in two stately volumes, is made up almost entirely of the writings of his hero so that it might be called an autobiography (1876–1877).

The following year the second half of the first volume of his History appeared. It completed his description of the conditions of the people on the eve of the great upheaval. The picture becomes less attractive. Agriculture, trade, and commerce are flourishing, but we perceive how excessive wealth and luxury begin to loosen the bonds of morality. The evils of capitalism, greed and usury, are only too apparent. Even less cheering is the decay of the old native law and the introduction of a foreign code, the Roman law with the consequent growth of absolutism. The chapters on the Holy Roman Empire exhibit the well-known features of weakness abroad and disunion at home. Again the reception of the book was all that could be desired. Especial praise was accorded to the chapters on the economic history of the time.

The next four years are perhaps the most laborious in Janssen's career. In the spring of 1879 his second volume was ready for the printer. " Delving into the sad period which it treats," says the author, " has moved me deeply, more than any previous research. I felt as if I were writing the history of our immediate future." Prophetic words! The sub-title tells us what to expect: " From the Beginning of the Political-Ecclesiastical Revolution to the Social Revolution of 1525." We see the rise of the radical revolutionary party, the semi-pagan younger humanists, with their leader, the sceptical, mocking Erasmus. We divine the character of the coming catastrophe in their ugly controversy with Reuchlin, in their deadly hatred against Rome and papal authority. Into this atmosphere steps Luther. The most fateful event was the association of the fiery demagogue with the revolutionary humanists, occasioned by the preaching of the Indulgence. We then hear of the rapid progress of the religious decline down to 1525. The picture of the downward course of the religious and intellectual life of the nation is followed by that of the great social upheaval, the

Peasants' War of 1525, not caused, indeed, but fostered by the religious revolution. The movement was crushed in an orgy of bloodshed and destruction. It marks the turning point in the history of the Lutheran revolt. From now on territorial princes and aristocratically governed imperial cities become its standard bearers. This second phase, reaching a temporary stop in the Augsburg settlement of 1555, forms the subject of the third volume. The indefatigable Janssen, though almost exhausted by the herculean labors of the second volume, permitted himself no rest, and as early as October, 1881, the last sheets of the manuscript went to the printer. Janssen's peculiar gift not only to press into service an enormous mass of material, but also to dispose of it in such a manner that the arrangement is clear and lucid and seems perfectly natural, is perhaps nowhere more evident than in this third volume. Chronological sequence and causal connection are so skilfully blended that the work might well excite the envy and despair of less gifted workers. Hundreds of printed and unprinted sources have each made their contribution to the great tableau of which every line is drawn with the consummate ease and sureness of touch of the master. One never loses one's way in that forest of varied testimony. Decisive events and impelling causes stand out clearly and unmistakably.

With the appearance of the second and third volumes the wave of praise from non-Catholic sources gradually subsided. Instead, such a storm of denun-

ciation and passionate protest broke loose that the
name of the humble college professor divided almost all Germany into two camps. Every obscure
scribbler in the Protestant camp felt called upon to
denounce him. Even Gregorovius, the hostile historian of the medieval popes, remarked in disgust:
" On Janssen every Lutheran preacher and semi-
narian vents his rage; to them he is an outlaw. The
scolding and abuse is becoming unbearable." But
when men of standing in the world of scholarship
joined in the attack, Janssen's friends thought an
answer imperative. Decisive for him was the letter
of a Protestant friend, asking him: " Are you willing to let all this pass over you in silence? If you
do not answer, you arouse the suspicion that you
cannot, that you consider yourself beaten." His answer: *To my Critics,* was a masterpiece of dignified,
gentlemanly, yet crushing refutation. In many cases
the opponent merely has his quotations or his references corrected, and the matter is settled. Here and
there he takes the opportunity to explain more fully
points of Catholic dogma and practice, where he
shows himself a competent theologian. Some of his
more honorable opponents declared themselves satisfied. Letters of congratulation poured in from all
sides, even from the Lutheran camp. Nevertheless
the storm increased in fury. A number of Protestant
writers formed a Society for the History of the
Reformation, with the avowed purpose of crushing
Janssen. A wealthy German-American offered a
prize of $5000 for the best refutation, but no one

earned it. All hopes to destroy the influence of
Janssen's work proved vain. Its sale only increased,
and among the purchasers there were more Protestants than Catholics. Janssen himself answered
some of his later antagonists in a *Second Word to
My Critics.* Gradually the storm subsided and
made room for discussion more worthy of scholars.
It is remarkable that during this campaign not
one of the non-Catholic friends of Janssen — and
he had many, among them men eminent in
the world of art and scholarship — abandoned
him.

It was feared in some quarters that our historian
might be drawn into endless controversy, and thus
endanger the continuation of his History. But immediately after the completion of his *Second Word
to My Critics,* in 1883, he returned to his customary labors. Soon, however, another danger loomed
up. Leo XIII, the great promoter of historical
scholarship, had conceived the plan of calling Janssen to Rome and putting him in charge of the
Vatican archives. There were other rumors of ecclesiastical dignities. Janssen was thunderstruck. Dignities of any kind held no charms for our humble
college professor, and the prospect of being taken
away from the study of his history filled him with
horror. Luckily, influential friends made representa-
tions in Rome, and Leo XIII gave up the plan.
When Hergenroether, the first Cardinal-Archivist,
died in 1890, the project of bestowing the sacred
purple on Janssen once more frightened our his-

torian, but owing to the intercession of Archbishop Roos of Freiburg the cloud passed away.

His fourth volume appeared in May, 1885. It treated the conditions of the German people from 1555 to 1580, that is, from the religious peace of Augsburg to the futile attempt at union by the Protestant princes in the so-called Formula of Concord. The story becomes less dramatic. It is the period of endless bickerings within the camp of the Reformers, abounding in bitter personalities and disgustingly vulgar treatment of the most sacred things. Faithful to his purpose of writing a history of the people, Janssen dwells on these theological battles only long enough to show the influence of the disedifying spectacle on the masses. Of these Bucer's statement holds true, that " the people consider themselves perfect Christians as soon as they know how to attack their adversaries." Meanwhile the Empire's decline of prestige continues. We are made acquainted with the influence of the Huguenot wars and of the rebellion of the Netherlands on German affairs, with the selfish attitude of the Lutheran princes in face of the Turkish danger, of those princes who could not declaim enough against the tyranny of Rome, yet often were in the pay of foreign potentates against their own people. Janssen then diverts our attention to more inspiring scenes. We see the beginnings of real reform, the reawakening of Catholic life after the Council of Trent, the apostolate of St. Peter Canisius and his companions. The chapters on this Second Spring prove once again

that the Church may at times exhibit all the symptoms of decay of a merely human society, but that
in her unexpected recovery she shows the divine
element that is within her. — This time adverse
criticism was remarkably reticent. A non-Catholic
reviewer observed: " Many a man has tried his luck
with the previous volumes, but without much success. It is not likely that anybody will feel the impulse of breaking his teeth with the present one."

Despite failing health and an almost ruined nervous system Janssen kept at his task, and the next
year, 1886, brought out his fifth volume. According
to the author's confession, it cost him more labor
and more mental depression than any of its predecessors. Throughout the narrative we hear the first
rumblings of the terrible storm of the Thirty Years'
War. In the first part Janssen shows that the
Lutheran and especially the Calvinist party aimed
at nothing less than the overthrow of the house of
Habsburg and the total destruction of the Catholic
faith. We are next introduced to a survey of the
effects of the religious polemics on the people. So
constant and so rancorous had been the contest that
it had eaten into the very vitals of the nation. All
consciousness of a common brotherhood seemed to
have been destroyed. No one has ever shown with
such wealth of detail the poisonous effects of the
religious revolution. The last part depicts the formation of the battle fronts for the oncoming struggle,
the alliances formed on one side and the other, and
the disgraceful weakness and shortsightedness of

the imperial house of Habsburg. No one who reads these pages can speak of the purely defensive character of the Lutheran and Calvinist preparations for war.

With the year 1618 Janssen interrupts the political history and returns to the study of the intellectual and cultural conditions of the people with which he had begun his first volume. The sixth, and as it proved, the last volume of his History, appeared in 1888, bearing the sub-title, *Civilization and Culture of the German People from the End of the Middle Ages to the Beginning of the Thirty Years' War*. Janssen had, however, accumulated such a mass of material that on the advice of friends he resolved to devote a seventh volume to the same subject. Death overtook him before he could complete this project; but as his pupil and intimate friend, Dr. Pastor, undertook the task, we are the fortunate possessors of the entire work. The whole of the sixth volume is devoted to the art and literature of this period. It begins with a survey of artistic activity of the later Middle Ages and proves conclusively that German art had received a mortal wound through the religious revolt and its practical consequences. It ceased to be a popular art and became the servile handmaid of princely courts, where through foreign influences it lost all originality and spontaneity. The new teaching deprived it of the sources of inspiration, the glorification of the Eucharistic Presence, the veneration of the Blessed Virgin and the Saints. Art was now frequently degraded in the service of religious polemics. We are then given a picture of popular literature, more detailed than was usually found in the histories of literature. Popular song had ceased to be an expression of the simple joy and humor of a happy people. Books and pamphlets full of satire and defamation have flooded the market. Dramatic literature has become the mirror of moral decay and vitiated taste. The epic and the story delights in the treatment of the most unsavory subjects. The lowest depth of depravity is reached in the widely spread literature on magic, occult arts, and devil manifestations. On reading through these chapters one ceases to wonder at the hold on the popular mind of witches and witchcraft trials.

By this time criticism of the furiously hostile kind had become rarer. It was realized that our historian could not be silenced nor his influence be neutralized by charges of falsification or superficial information. His stupendous labors had amassed such an amount of evidence that in the main his thesis seemed proved. Several eminent historians, among them L. Freytag and F. Paulsen, admitted this. The Reformers were not actuated by the pure motives hitherto ascribed to them. The Reformation was not that blessing of the people that a certain tradition has represented it to have been. If among non-Catholic historians the attitude towards the Reformers and their work has become more circumspect, Janssen must be given a large share of the credit.

The man who had performed the herculean task was soon to be the victim of his zeal. The manuscript of the sixth volume was scarcely in the hands of the printer when the author began to sift the material he had collected for the story of economic and educational conditions of the period 1517 to 1618. These were to form the contents of his next volume. At the same time he was constantly engaged in revising his former works, especially the earlier parts of his History, of which the publisher called for edition after edition. So great was its popularity that Janssen was forced to prepare the fifteenth edition of the first volume while he was busy writing the first edition of his seventh volume. Stronger constitutions than his could not have kept up such a pace. From 1889 on there appear in his letters complaints that mental exertion is becoming increasingly harder. Although he had not yet given up his original plan of continuing his History to the end of the Empire (1806), he sometimes expressed misgivings about finishing even the seventh volume. His physicians, too, became alarmed, and insisted on a complete rest. " After the seventh volume," was his only answer. Sometimes, too, the nature of his studies added to his depression. " It is not easy for a Catholic priest," he says in his diary, " to renounce almost entirely all priestly occupation and to devote the best part of his energies to such profane things and at the same time to have the feeling that one is in bad company. . . . Of the period I am engaged in the saying of the poèt is only too true: 'Man's history is man's disgrace.'" He was not to enjoy the happiness of reaching even his immediate goal. A cold contracted on a visit to the graves of his dear friends in the Frankfurt cemetery developed into pneumonia. His overworked and always delicate constitution offered but little resistance. On the Vigil of Christmas, 1891, he passed away, in the arms of his priestly friend, Alexander Baumgartner, S. J. His death was the image of his life; the bystanders were deeply moved by his childlike faith, the peace and serenity with which he surrendered his soul to his Creator. He was grieved to leave his "magnum opus" incomplete, but consoled by the promise of his great pupil, Ludwig von Pastor, to bring it to a conclusion.

Long before the end the storm of abuse against the great Catholic historian had given way to a juster estimate of his merits. It is generally admitted by friend and foe that whatever are one's individual convictions, Janssen cannot be ignored. The mass of evidence he accumulated forbids this. Has he achieved the ideal of objectivity which must always be before the mind of the historian? It would be rash to assert this of any historical writer. Janssen, too, has paid tribute to human weakness that always makes us fall short of the ideal. At times in depicting the life of the people, especially in his first volume, subsequent studies have taught us to distribute the lights and shadows more exactly. Later research, to no small degree inspired by his labors, to some extent has changed the picture of German lands as they were on the eve of the revolt. Pastor, himself the continuator of Janssen's work, admits that prior to the Lutheran movement there existed a rather wide-spread anti-Roman spirit, due in part to the abuses in the papal administration. One would wish, too, a comprehensive description of the clergy and of religious life in general as they were during the declining Middle Ages. Remissness, worldliness, and " externalism " in religious practice had their full share in nation-wide apostasy. Perhaps Janssen, in common with other Catholic historians, has at times stressed too much the evil effects and minimized the causes of the great catastrophe. — One would hesitate, too, to subscribe to every statement of our historian on the high standard of national art before the Reformation and its consequent decay. The Renaissance was certainly a break with national traditions, but its influence had set in north of the Alps some time before the Lutheran movement. That many carping critics found among the innumerable citations of the six volumes a few misreadings of the sources and other minor inaccuracies is not surprising. To speak of conscious falsification is unjust to the author, and betrays a lack of insight into the difficulties that beset a work of such magnitude.

During part of his career Janssen had been the object of violent abuse. Yet our historian was the last man to arouse personal antagonism. Indeed, his ability to disarm opposition by personal contact, and to make loyal and steadfast friends wherever

he went, must be counted as one of his most striking characteristics. What the anti-Catholic *Frank-
furter Zeitung* said at his death is true: " Janssen
never had an enemy among those who knew him
personally." He possessed the irresistible charm of
unselfish modesty that made him a welcome member of any circle. His sunny humor and childlike
candor won the heart of even the most determined
antagonist. It is astonishing to learn from his correspondence with how many men eminent in Church
and State he was on terms of intimate friendship.
The great Catholic leaders, Windthorst and August
Reichensperger, in the midst of the parliamentary
battles of the Kulturkampf, find time for numerous
encouraging letters. Among his friends and correspondents one finds the names of the Cardinals
Reisach, Franchi, and Manning, of scholars like
de Rossi and Hettinger, of the well known Jesuits
Kleutgen, Perrone, and Baumgartner, of the diplo-
mats Huebner and Bach, and numerous others.
Many distinguished non-Catholics considered it an
honor to be counted among his friends, as, for instance, the Prussian ambassador von Sydow, the
diplomat Ludwig von Gerlach, the painter Karl von
Passavant. The man who could win and hold so
many friends of widely divergent views and states
of life cannot have been the narrow, bigoted fanatic
that some have represented him to be. To those who
knew him best, his sincerity, his warm affection for
the real welfare of the people, his loyalty to God
and His Church, his truly heroic devotion to his

labors, made him a model of historians, and as such he remains an inspiration to the humblest worker in his own chosen field.

BIBLIOGRAPHY

A. BIOGRAPHY

LUDWIG VON PASTOR, *Johannes Janssen, 1829–1891, Ein Lebensbild* (Freiburg, 1892).

LUDWIG VON PASTOR, *Johannes Janssens Briefe,* 2 vols. (Freiburg, 1895).

The *Stimmen aus Maria-Laach* (since 1915 *Stimmen der Zeit*) brought detailed reviews as the single volumes of the *History* appeared, mostly from the pen of Alexander Baumgartner, S.J. See Vols. 10, 11, 17, 22, 29, 31, 36, 46, 48. The *Dublin Review* (July, 1881, and January, 1882) under the title *Recent Works on Germany in the 15th Century* has a valuable study of Janssen's position in the historical world by the well known Dutch historian, Paul Alberdingk Thijm. *The Month,* the periodical of the English Jesuits (March, 1893), contains a brief sketch of Janssen's life and work by F. Galton, S.J.

B. GENERAL WORKS ON JANSSEN
AND HIS WRITINGS

FUETER (*Historiographie Moderne,* pp. 498, 578, 715–719, 749) discusses Janssen's place in modern historical literature with his customary depreciation of the Catholic aspect of the *History of the German People.*

DELBRÜCK, *Historische Methode des Ultramontanismus,* in the *Historische und politische Aufsätze* (1887, p. 5).

LENZ, *Kleine historische Schriften* (Mainz, 1910).

SCHWANN, *J. Janssen und die Geschichte der deutschen Reformation* (Berlin, 1893).

Articles on Janssen's *History* will be found in the following periodicals: *American Catholic Quarterly Review*, 1889; *American Historical Review*, 1895, 1906, 1907, 1921; *Berliner Nationalzeitung*, 1887; *Catholic Historical Review*, 1921, 1925; *Civiltà Cattolica*, 1890, 1909, 1915, 1922; *English Historical Review*, 1887, 1889, 1897, 1910; *Goettinger Gelehrten-Anzeigen*, 1887; *Historische-Politische Blaetter*, 99, 118, 132, 159, 161; *Historisches Jahrbuch*, 1880-1925; *Hochland*, 1904; *Katholik*, 1876, 1893, 1895, 1900; *Zeitschrift fuer katholische Theologie*, 1907; *Zeitschrift fuer oeffentliche Angelegenheiten*, 1886.

DENIFLE (1844–1905)

Rev. Boniface Stratemeier, O. P, S. T. Lr., Ph.D.
River Forest, Ill.

AMONG the historians of the Order of Preachers who contributed very remarkably to the science of history such as Bartholomew De Lucca, Saint Antoninus of Florence, Vincent of Beauvais, Abraham Bzovius, Natalis Alexander and Cardinal Orsi, the name of Henry Denifle holds a prominent place.

The beautiful Tyrol was the native land and Imst the city where, on January 16, 1844, Joseph Denifle was born. His father, who was a school master, early imparted to him the rudiments of learning, and, as he gave signs of great promise as a student, he was sent to the seminary at Brixen. At the age of seventeen, the young Denifle sought and obtained admission to the Order of Preachers at Graz, in Austria, and was clothed in the habit of the Friars on September 22, 1861, receiving the name of Henry Suso. He had now set out on the way which he was to follow for all his years, a life of assiduous study, of successful teaching and of writing, during which he was to leave to posterity the monuments of his erudition and piety.

During the years devoted to philosophical and theological study, the young friar was especially

354

given to the mastering of Aristotle and St. Thomas Aquinas. He was elevated to the priesthood in 1866. Three years later Denifle went to Rome in order to follow the lectures on the *Summa* of the Angelic Doctor in the College of St. Thomas, at the Minerva, where he had as professor Father Thomas, later Cardinal Zigliara. Later he went to Saint Maximin near Marseilles and there he obtained the Lectorate in Theology. He then occupied posts as professor in the Houses of Study of Hungary and Austria for ten years. On September 2, 1877, he passed the examination " ad gradus " before the Dominican General as a partial requirement for the degree of Master in Sacred Theology.

In applying himself to the works of St. Thomas, Denifle was convinced of the necessity of a historical consideration of the works of the Angel of the Schools. He found that in the study of the *Summa* and his other works as well, it was of great importance to understand the sources of these great theological works and for a long time he planned a commentary especially on the *Summa* from a literary and historical standpoint.

In 1873, Denifle wrote a series of articles in the *Grazer Volksblatt* on " Tetzel and Luther," an indication that even then his mind was occupied with a subject about which his last and perhaps his greatest work was destined to be written. From 1873 onward, though he preached occasionally and with great success, the biography of Denifle is a narration of his literary and historical achievements. His life accordingly might be divided into periods characterized by works on Theology and Mysticism, the Medieval Universities, the Hundred Years' War between France and England with its consequences to the Church and Luther and Lutherdom.

Denifle's first work in the field of German Medieval Mysticism appeared in 1873 under the title: *Das Geistliche Leben — Eine Blumenlese aus den deutschen Mystikern*. To get an idea of the work entailed in the field of mystical research, suffice it to state that this book comprises twenty-five hundred passages gathered from the Mystics grouped and embodied to illustrate the three stages of perfection. In 1875 an article appeared in the *Historisch-politischen Blaetter* under the caption " Eine Geschichte der deutschen Mystik." Another article published in 1875 in the same review was entitled " Der Gottesfreund im Oberland und Nikolaus von Basel." In the *Zeitschrift fur deutsches Altertum und deutsche Literatur* of 1881 appeared the article " Die Dichtungen des Gottesfreundes im Oberland." The result of Denifle's combined studies concerning the *Gottesfreund* was the discovery that the *Gottesfreund* was a myth.

In November, 1880, Denifle was made an associate to the Dominican Master General at Rome where a new field of research awaited him. Leo XIII had ordered a critical edition of the works of St. Thomas and Denifle was commissioned to search for the best manuscripts. Within three years he had visited many libraries in Germany, England,

France, Spain, Portugal, Austria, Holland and Italy. On the recommendation of Cardinal Hergenroether, Prefect of the Vatican Archives, Denifle was named on December 1, 1883, by Leo XIII as Sub-Archivist of the Vatican. He was also appointed a consultor of the *Commissione Cardinalizia per gli Studi Storici.* The advantages of his new position and the experience derived from his researches in the archives of Europe enabled Denifle, after a study on Abbot Joachim of Fiori, the *Evangelium Aeternum,* and the University of Paris in the middle of the thirteenth century, to prepare an extensive work on the Universities of the Middle Ages. Denifle wished to accomplish this work in five large volumes. The first volume was to treat of the origin of the Universities until 1400; the second, the development of their organization; the third, the origin of the University of Paris; the fourth, the development of the organization of this University until the end of the thirteenth century, and the last volume was to deal with the strife between the University of Paris and the Mendicant Orders. The only volume that appeared was the first: *Die Entstehung der Universitäten des Mittelalters bis 1400,* published in Berlin (1885) and consisted of over 850 pages. In a lengthy introduction Denifle gives reasons for undertaking this work and therein he speaks on the literature that existed on the Medieval Universities which, according to his own admission, offered no particularly pleasant picture. Then, accordingly, he unfolds his own plan for the work and the reasons for using the method which he intended. He decided, according to his natural inclination, to begin at the bottom and to base his study entirely on the documents that were in part printed and in part first had to be searched for in the libraries and the archives. Although with regard to the University of Paris, the libraries and the archives at Paris would be of most avail, nevertheless with regard to the sum total of the history of the Medieval Universities, the Vatican Archives would preponderate. Despite this, Denifle affirms that he was the first to have used the Papal Archives for this purpose. Aside from the manuscript material, Denifle employed in the field of his research the vast and often out of the way printed literature.

The large volume referred to is divided into five parts. The first division treats of the nomenclature of the medieval university and the concept of the same, such as *studium, studium generale, universitas,* etc. And Denifle remarks that of all the designations of the medieval university as an institution of learning, *Studium Generale* or *Studium* are alone in proper usage and official.

The second division treats of the origin and development of the two oldest and most renowned universities, Paris and Bologna. As the factors that were effective toward the origin of the higher institutes of learning Denifle designates the following: 1. The cultivation of new methods in teaching. 2. The conferring and extension of high privileges. 3. The formation and expansion of academic corporations.

The third section treats of the origin and development of the other universities of Europe until 1400. Of these superior institutions of learning, nine existed without letters of foundation from any ruling power, sixteen were founded by Papal briefs, nine came into being by imperial or sovereign together with Papal letters; nine projected schools never came into existence.

The fourth section treats of the universities in their relation to earlier schools. Denifle here cleared up the error of assigning the origin of the universities to cathedral or cloister schools. This can be assigned as the origin of the University of Paris which was an evolution of the cathedral school of Notre Dame. This also holds true of Cologne and Erfurt. Otherwise the universities are new creations or, as is the case with Italy, they are evolutions of the town schools. Only with a small amount of these higher institutes of learning and especially Paris University was the theological faculty the basis of their evolution. With the greater half, theology was not taught in the early days.

The fifth division deals with the reasons for the origin of the medieval universities. It is a comprehensive treatise on the results of his researches in the work. Here he openly admits the relation between secular and ecclesiastical power working for the foundations.

The medieval universities are fundamentally creations of the Christian spirit, which permeated their whole structure, in which Pope and Prince, the clergy and the laity, all had their befitting and authorized place. The monumental work, without any effort on the part of the author, becomes an apology for the universities of the Middle Ages. Whether they were the same as our concept or not, yet they met the needs of the Middle Ages perfectly and furnished the upper educational institutes with their modern requirements and aspect and therefore the foundations for the modern university.

One of the greatest testimonies to the work of Fr. Denifle on the medieval universities was the fact that the French Government entrusted to him the editing of the *Chartularium Universitatis Parisiensis,* a documentary work on the Paris University. The *Conseil général des Facultés de Paris* had on December 28, 1885, decided upon the publication of this work. On March 27, 1887, on the suggestion of the President of the *Conseil* Denifle undertook the task and he was given the assistance of the Librarian of the Sorbonne, Emil Chatelain, as co-editor.

Denifle immediately began work on the *Chartularium.* In the following year he spent much time in Paris in various archival depots and in the different libraries of the city. He resided with the Dominicans at Chatillon-sous-Bagneux. Here he also celebrated, on July 22, 1891, the silver jubilee of his priesthood.

Denifle justified the confidence placed in him by the French Government in full measure. With the assistance of his able co-worker, Chatelain, he gave to the historian four large folio volumes of the

Chartularium and two folio volumes of the *Auctarium Chartularii* in a little less than ten years. This standard work will ever remain the source for the history of the greatest university of the Middle Ages and will be a great aid to the student of medieval culture and educational achievement.

The purpose of Denifle was above all to find the original documents and to edit them. When these were no longer to be had, he edited the oldest transcripts with notes on the discrepancies between the different ones. With the original documents he indicated no different readings except with Papal documents for which the Vatican " Registri " offered material to vary the reading. Another care was to date the documents. And in case the sources were printed elsewhere, he always indicated this.

The manuscript documents for his work were collected by Denifle in the archives and libraries of France, Germany, Italy, Spain and England. The National Archives and the archives of the University of Paris, the Vatican Archives, the archives of Dijon, Troyes, Marseilles, Avignon, Rouen, Barcelona, Luzerne, the archives of various religious orders, the National, Arsenal, Mazarin and Genevieve Libraries at Paris, the Vatican and other Roman Libraries, the libraries of Munich, Vienna, Auxerre, Chartres, Toulouse, Rouen, Oxford, Cambridge, Erfurt, Leipzig, etc., all these furnished the stones of his monumental work.

The first volume of the *Chartularium* appeared

in 1889 at Paris. In the Introduction, Denifle gives a criticism of the works of Du Bouleys and Jourdains. Then he gives an account of the earliest histories of the Paris University and then he dilates on the office of the chancellor and the rector of the University. In a Pars Introductoria he gives 55 documents from 1163–1200 to the origin of the university proper. For the history of the development of Scholasticism in the second half of the twelfth century, valuable details are given.

The *Chartularium* proper now follows for the period from 1200–1286, the period of the zenith of Scholasticism, and contains 530 documents. This wonderful array begins with the privilege of King Philip Augustus of the year 1200. The relations of the monarchs of France as well as the Popes (notably Gregory IX, Innocent IV, Alexander IV) with the Paris University are clearly set forth in a rich number of interesting documents. Much light is also thrown on the spiritual life at the University, the scientific history, the fostering of the scholastic method, the history of Aristotelianism in the thirteenth century and for the scientific working of the various faculties. Fifty documents deal with the religious Orders, especially the Franciscans and the Dominicans. New light is thrown on the controversy between the Mendicants and the doctors of the University. For the biography, chronology and bibliography of the most famous scholastics this volume contains much valuable source material. Many notices are contained therein relative to the earlier authors of *Summas*. The historian of Scholastic philosophy and theology will find in this as well as in the other volumes of the *Chartularium* material of the utmost importance.

The second volume, published in 1891, offers 661 documents for the period between 1286–1350. In the Introduction, Denifle states that he examined 200,000 letters from the Papal registers and that he used 8,000 in the notes. This second volume deals with the period of decline of the Paris University and of scholasticism. Denifle finds the cause of this decadence to have been the neglect of the study of the sources of theology, the Scriptures and the Fathers. This second volume also gives valuable details regarding the history of religious orders, the history of various scholastics and the history of the divers political and ecclesiastical, and theological controversies of the declining thirteenth century and the first half of the fourteenth. An appendix contains the oaths, statutes and calendars of the University.

The third volume, given out in 1894, portrays in 520 documents the further history of the University between 1350–1394, and deals with the period of the Great Schism.

In 1897 appeared the fourth volume, comprising 988 documents regarding the University's history from 1394–1452. Notable among the rich information afforded are the documents relating to the trial of the Maid of Orleans.

Simultaneous with the publication of the third

and fourth volumes of the *Chartularium* appeared the first and second volumes of the *Auctarium Chartularii*. These volumes contained the documents which in Denifle's estimation were too lengthy for the *Chartularium*.

The greatest recognition was accorded Fr. Denifle for this work. He received from the French Government a reward of 25,000 francs; in 1897 he was named, in the place of the deceased Wattenbach, a member of the *Académie des Inscriptions et Belles-Lettres* and also *Correspondant de l'Institut de France*. He also was made a Knight of the Legion of Honor. His achievement was also acclaimed by the greatest historians. By his history of the universities and his *Chartularium,* Denifle merited the encomium of "generalium studiorum historiae splendidissimus Auctor."

Aside from these works on medieval universities, Denifle wrote a number of works on different periods and phases of medieval culture and Church history. For the diffusion of medieval texts and studies Denifle, together with Ehrle, founded the *Archiv für Literatur- und Kirchengeschichte des Mittelalters,* the first six volumes of which, appearing from 1885–1890, contains a series of erudite contributions by Denifle.

Denifle's vast knowledge of the Middle Ages, his solution of numerous historical problems as well as discoveries of new sources are explainable by his great accomplishments in the field of medieval paleography and diplomatics. In fact his knowledge in these auxiliary sciences to history, both practical and theoretical, was extraordinary. He published a remarkable paleographical work entitled: *Specimina Palaeographica Regestorum Pontificum ab Innocentio III ad Urbanum V*, published at Rome, 1888, and was presented by the personnel of the Vatican Archives as a tribute to Leo XIII, on the occasion of the golden jubilee of his priesthood. The learned introduction and the splendid paleographical annotations to each of the specimens are all the work of Denifle. The facsimiles are carefully chosen to illustrate the development and the history of the script of the Papal chancery. Denifle also published other studies on the Papal registers in different publications notably in the *Archiv*.

Besides Denifle's history of the universities of the Middle Ages and his *Chartularium Universitatis Parisiensis*, he published kindred studies notably in the *Archiv für Literatur- und Kirchengeschichte* referred to above. In the same work he also wrote and gave texts valuable for the history of the scholastic method. In the *Archiv*, he also throws much light on the history of different religious orders, especially the Mendicant institutes.

The research work of Denifle for his *Chartularium* in many archives led him to the publication of a work that is of great importance for French history of the fourteenth and fifteenth centuries. In 1897 appeared at Macon a stately volume of 600 pages under the caption: *La désolation des églises, monastères, hôpitaux en France vers le milieu du*

XVe siècle. Two years later at Paris was published the continuation of the same work under the title: *La guerre de cent ans et la désolation des églises, monastères et hôpitaux: tom. I. Jusqu'à la mort de Charles V (1380)*.

The author tells us in a Foreword to the first volume the genesis of this exceedingly interesting work. He had scrutinized page for page 300 volumes of registers of petitions in the Vatican Archives searching for documents and notes for his *Chartularium*. During the course of this research the thought occurred to him what a work he could have composed on the desolation of the churches of France toward the end of the Hundred Years' War. And so he decided to peruse again the 300 volumes referred to though he had at the same time to examine several hundred more registers for the *Chartularium*.

The title " desolation " is clearly explained through the sources the author gives. Under this heading he places all the material and spiritual misery brought upon the erstwhile flourishing ecclesiastical institutes through the Hundred Years' War. In the Preface to the work the author explains his purpose, method and the character of the history. The principal sources he employed were the registers of petitions from Martin V to Nicholas V, as well as other material gathered in the Archives of the Vatican. The printed French literature regarding churches and monasteries was also utilized to the utmost.

In the first volume of the work Denifle published 1063 hitherto unedited and unknown documents.

They are carefully dated, the source indicated and explained by learned remarks. The documents are arranged according to the 123 dioceses into which France was divided in the fifteenth century. The documents graphically describe the ruin of the French churches during the Fifteenth Century, the demolition of churches, monasteries and hospitals, the decrease and abolition of church revenues, the scattering of monks and nuns, the damage done to religious worship, the weakening of ecclesiastical discipline — all these things present themselves to us most forcibly in the original documents. And in many other respects, these sources have their value and interest, especially for the historian of art, for the liturgist, the monastic historian and the canonist.

It is characteristic of Denifle that whenever he undertook a scientific work he always saw the possibilities of enlargement of his subject and of broadening his plan. In fact he seems to have had a mania for exhausting his subject and of never being content to narrow it down to certain limits. Originally the second volume of the work under consideration was to give an elaboration of the source material printed in the first volume, but the friar was soon convinced that he would have to undertake the study also for the fourteenth century since the calamity reached back to the preceding century. The destruction of the churches and monasteries led him to the investigation of the various military engagements and successes that caused this desolation. So the second volume developed into a history of the Hundred Years' War itself, always, however, with a certain regard for the principal theme of the whole history.

Denifle in this work undertook a very involved task and in the two volumes into which the second is divided, he describes the battles of that war to the death of Charles V, in 1380. Then he narrates the ruin in the various dioceses. The unpublished sources from which the author drew are the volumes of petitions from Pope Clement VI to the fourth year of the pontificate of Urban V, and many other documents of the Papal archives. Nor was he content here for he searched all the printed materials as well.

This work on the Hundred Years' War received general recognition from historians. Battifol, Haller, Schrörs — all are full of praise for this scientific work of the Subarchivist of the Vatican. In the year 1897, appeared the fourth volume of the *Chartularium*, the second volume of the *Auctarium* and the first volume of the *Désolation des églises*.

It is worthy of note that Denifle's great French work on the Hundred Years' War became the guide for the composition of his last work, his study on *Luther and Lutherdom*. His work on the Paris University and the work just considered gave the tireless historian the inducement to further research for material dealing with the decline of the secular and the regular clergy in the fifteenth century. He pursued the various phases of the development of this decadence and at the beginning gave not the least thought about writing a work on Luther and Lutherdom. He prosecuted his studies on this decay into the six- teenth century and found when he had reached the third decade of the century that Luther was in the midst of the debasement. Henceforth he could not put Luther aside and accordingly resolved to study the life of Luther back to the first years of his stu- dent life and his first years of teaching. To control the result of his researches, he reversed the process and followed Luther year by year in his downfall. His main object was to fix the precise thing that slowly drew Luther into the stream of the decay and finally made him the creator and mouthpiece of the group that represented the height of the decline.

The chief sources for Denifle's *Luther und Lutherthum* were, above all, Luther's writings. Only after he had carefully studied these did he investi- gate the expositions of Luther's life and teachings. One of the principal depots for this research was the *Biblioteca Palatina* of the Vatican Library. The newer literature on his subject was sent to him at Rome though he made several visits to Germany to visit the libraries personally.

In the autumn of 1903 the first volume of this work was published in Mainz, a tome of 860 pages. A numerous edition was exhausted within four weeks. The storm of discussion and agitation pro- voked by the book will be passed over to consider the work as a scientific accomplishment. The sig- nificance of Denifle's work on Luther for the scien- tific investigator rests on the following points:

1. Denifle secured a reputation as an expert in Lutheran research and as a textual critic of Luther's works by his handling of the Weimar edition, the *Kritischen Gesamtausgabe* of the works of Luther. From the viewpoint of historical criticism, he showed that the edition gave signs of much haste and contained a series of errors that he was able to indicate from a rigorous examination of the originals.

2. The author made a careful study of Luther's inner life and threw remarkable light on the psychological problem of Luther's apostasy. He showed that Luther's later statement with regard to his soul history, the process of his change, did not agree with his earlier statement and was untrustworthy.

3. Denifle undertook a critical analysis of the teaching and writing of Luther viewed from the standpoint of the history of dogma and showed the deficiency and superfluity of Luther's theological training. Luther's knowledge of the scholastics was negligible. Nevertheless he gave profuse pronouncements on them.

4. Denifle took the Protestant study of Luther and the history of dogma to task summarily. He makes the statement that no one comprehended Luther less than the Protestant theologians and the biographers of Luther.

It was to be expected that the energetic language of Denifle in his *Luther* was not to go unanswered by the Protestant theologians. A number of them, Harnack, Seeberg, Kohler, Kolde, Baumann, Walther, Fester, Sodeur, appeared against him in replies. None of these silenced the friar. He promptly responded in a work that appeared in March, 1904, under the title: *Luther in rationalistischer und christlicher Beleuchtung. Prinzipielle Auseinandersetzung mit A. Harnack und R. Seeberg.* In May, 1904, appeared the second edition of the first part of the first volume, in which Denifle did not retreat one step from his former position. The second part was brought out in 1905 and the third in 1906 by Father Albert Weiss, O. P. He also got out the Second Volume for which the author left material in 1908.

Father Denifle died on June 10, 1905, at Munich, while on his way to Cambridge where he and his friend Father now Cardinal Ehrle, S. J., were to be made Honorary Doctors of that University. He was laid to rest in the crypt of the Basilica of St. Boniface, Munich.

Denifle's achievements are excellently summed up in the encomium of the University which was to be pronounced on the occasion of his reception of the Doctorate:

Raetiae inter montes, fluminis Aeni prope ripas, olim natus est Sanctae sedis Romanae tabularius doctissimus, qui Praedicatorum Ordini insigni adscriptus, historiae praesertim studiis sese dedicavit. Non modo Pontificum Romanorum res gestas celebravit, sed etiam Medii aevi Universitates plurimas penitus exploravit: Universitatis Bononiensis Statuta antiqua, Universitatis Parisiensis Chartularium, opus laboris immensi, erudite et diligenter edidit; calamitates denique ab ecclesia Gallicana in saeculo decimo quinto toleratas luculenter explicavit. Ut ad Germanos transeamus, non hodie prolixius prosequemur neque Martinum Luther, ab eodem ad fidem monumentorum nuper depictum, neque scriptores illos mysticos, in litterarum Archivis ab ipso et a collega ejus magno conditis, olim accurate examinatos. Italiam potius petamus, Romam ipsam et Palatium Vaticanum invisamus, et Pontificem illum venerabilem, poetam illum Latinum, animo grato recordemur, qui virum doctrinae tam variae dotibus instructum Sanctae sedis tabularium merito nominavit.

Duco ad vos virum doctissimum reverendum patrem HENRICUM DENIFLE.

BIBLIOGRAPHY

" De Vita et scriptis Magistri Henrici Denifle, Commenta Varia " and " Necrologium Fratrum Sacri Ordinis Praedicatorum " in *Analecta Sacri Ordinis Fratrum Praedicatorum*, Vol. VII (series secunda), Rome, 1905. *Acta Capituli Generalis Diffinitorum S. O. P. Viterbii*, 1907, Rome, 1907. D. Dr. Martin Grabmann, *P. Heinrich Denifle, O. P. Eine Wurdigung feiner Forschungsarbeit*. Mainz, 1905. Dr. Hermann Grauert, *P. Heinrich Denifle, O. Pr., Ein Wort zum Gedächtnis und zum Frieden. Ein Beitrag auch zum Luther-Streit*. Freiburg im Breisgau, 1906.

LUDWIG VON PASTOR (1854–   )

VERY REV. FELIX FELLNER, O.S.B.
St. Vincent Archabbey, Beatty, Pa.

HISTORICAL science has been developed to a remarkable degree during the last generation. It contributed in many ways not only to a better understanding of past events but also to a more amiable relation with men of the present times. One of the most prominent promoters of this science in the realm of Church History is Dr. Ludwig von Pastor.

In 1914 Dr. Lucian Pfleger wrote in the *Historisch-Politischen Blaetter:* "Ludwig von Pastor's renown as an historian is international and unquestionable." Since that time many changes have taken place in the world, but our historian not only continued his studies for the benefit of all mankind, he extended and deepened them, and today we can say without fear of contradiction that he has no rival as "the Historian of the Popes."

Ludwig von Pastor was born at Aachen, on the 31 January 1854. His father, a prominent merchant of that city and a deeply religious Lutheran, persuaded the mother, a Catholic, to have their oldest son baptized by the local minister. Without doubt Herr Pastor, whose ancestors had long been associated with this Protestant congregation, showed thereby that he intended to raise the child in accordance with the principles of his own religious belief. There was, however, no contract made as to this point. In 1860 business affairs induced the family to transfer the domicile to Frankfort a. M. Four years later Herr Pastor died.

Both these events were of great consequence for young Ludwig. The most important was the change in his religious education; for Frau Pastor determined to remain in Frankfort and to bring up her children as Catholics. Among his teachers Father Siering, the tutor, Father Tyssen, the pastor, and Dr. Johannes Janssen, a friend of the family, exercised the greatest influence on our future historian. Naturally the early death of the father led the mother to the thought of educating her oldest son for a business career to enable him later to manage the extensive mercantile affairs of the family. Ludwig himself showed a predilection for the study of Natural Sciences and Geography. But Professor Janssen convinced mother and son that he had extraordinary talents for History. It is related that he came to this conclusion through an essay on the value of the colonies of England to their mother-country, in which his pupil, at such an early age, showed remarkable talents by distinguishing well between the important and non-important points of the subject. Thus as Leopold von Ranke diverted George Waitz from Law to History, and molded him into his most prominent disciple, Janssen, we may say, "discovered" the talents of Pastor, who became his great successor.

At that time two events contributed largely to direct our student's attention to Rome and to the popes. He read with great enthusiasm J. Fichard's *Italia* which had been published half a century before in Frankfort. Later he acknowledged that this book made a lasting impression on him. But above all a copy of Ranke's *History of the Popes*, the gift of his professor Janssen, must be mentioned as decisive in his development to historical fame. As he studied and admired this classic in history he frequently said to himself: " If Ranke, a Protestant who had no access to the Vatican Archives, could give us such a grand picture of this great subject, how much more perfect must not be a description by a Catholic who has a true concept of the papacy and who would have access to this first depositary of historical sources! " Thus our young historian of not yet twenty years of age already made plans for a work that required a lifetime of constant research. And with living faith, great talents, extraordinary opportunities, tireless energy and a long life all in his favor, he became the rival and finally the superior of Ranke.

It may be interesting to hear what his professor of history thought of him at that time.

In 1875 Pastor graduated at the local gymnasium and by Janssen's advice went to the University of Louvain, to specialize in History. On this occasion his teacher wrote to Professor Paul Alberdingk Tjim the following lines: " The student Pastor who is going to Louvain will please you. As long as I am teaching I had no pupil that was more talented. In him every good seed will fall on good ground. He is above everything else a sincere Catholic and a painstaking student. Every favor shown him I will consider a personal favor and I will be grateful for such tokens of friendship."

At Louvain Pastor wrote his first historical essay for publication, entitled *Eine Kritik der Quellenkunde zur deutschen Geschichte von Waitz.* He intended to have it printed in the *Historisch-Politische Blaetter* and sent it to his former professor to censor and to recommend it. But he must have been surprised when he received the following answer: " The theme is well worked out; the style must be improved before it can be published; the penmanship is so bad that the proper nouns are illegible; during the next vacation months we will revise it, you will rewrite it and after these changes are made Mr. Binder may accept it." (The article was later published in a different form in the *Katholik.*)

In 1876 Pastor matriculated at the University of Bonn and attended the lectures of Karl Menzel, Morel Ritter and Henry Floss. His stay in this town, although short, became important from the associations that he formed there and which contributed much to his success. Here he was introduced into the Kaufmann family and later, in 1882, chose the only daughter of that staunch *Oberbuergermeister* as his life's companion. She became not only his wife and the mother of his children, but also an assistant in his literary work. Here also he formed a friendship with three men who, as long as they lived, aided him by counsel and patronage: August Reichensperger, sometimes called the German Montalembert, George von Hertling, later Chancellor of the Empire, and Hermann Cardauns, the well-known literary critic and for many years chief-editor of the *Koelnische Volkszeitung*. At one time his talents were already recognized by the celebrated circle of churchmen and artists of Mainz founded and directed by Emmanuel von Ketteler. From this association he learned to appreciate the value of monuments of art in the study of a given period of history, particularly that of the Renaissance.

Pastor's next aim was to attend the lectures of some of the famous professors of history at the University of Berlin. Here he studied under George Waitz and Karl Nitsch and was introduced to Leopold von Ranke. But while always admiring the eminently scientific work of these men, the academic atmosphere of Berlin never appealed to him. On the contrary he felt at home at once at the University of Vienna, where he matriculated in 1877, and Onno Klopp, the author of the standard work on the Thirty Years' War, received him into his house with open arms. Without doubt this fearless champion of historic truth exercised, next to Janssen, the greatest influence upon young Pastor. In many ways Klopp's ideals to present the truth without caring either for praise or contradiction became a guiding star in the literary activity of our historian.

Finally at the invitation of J. B. Weiss, the well-known author of the *Weltgeschichte,* Pastor entered the University of Graz to apply for the doctorate in philosophy. His thesis *Die Reunionsbestrebungen waehrend der Regierung Karls V* showed originality. He received the coveted title and he decided to go to Rome to continue his researches in the historical field which he had chosen long ago and for which he had already gathered much material: " The History of the Papacy during the Reformation."

At that time one question was preëminently in his mind: the access to the Vatican Archives. In his studies on the attempts made by Charles V and others to reëstablish union after the outbreak of the Reformation the work of Cardinal Contarini in Germany in 1541 presented a number of difficulties. Various circumstances led him to believe that these could only be solved by an examination of the original documents and he surmised that these were in the secret Papal Archives. In his zeal for obtaining this information he determined to apply for this most extraordinary permission. His endeavors and his success must forever elicit the thanks of all honest historians of the civilized world.

There exist various accounts of this *coup d'état* in modern historical research. The following facts are taken from his own address of welcome to Cardinal Francis Ehrle, S. J., at the Anima in Rome, 17 December 1922. He said he knew that the papal secret archives had never been opened to any one except to a limited degree and for very special purposes. Moreover he was well aware that in 1870 on account of the indiscretion of an official of this department, Pope Pius IX had ordered them closed altogether to all persons except the Pope, the Cardinal Secretary of State and the Prefect of the Archives. Nevertheless he determined to get access to this much coveted historical treasure. As he believed that patronage of ecclesiastical dignitaries would be the surest means for obtaining this privilege he wrote a petition and applied to a number of churchmen for recommendation. Among these Msgr. Jacobini, the Apostolic Nuncio at Vienna, later Papal Secretary of State, Msgr. de Montel and Msgr. de Waal, a literary friend of Dr. Janssen cheerfully endorsed his efforts. When he presented his petition to Cardinal Nina, then papal Secretary of State, he became more than ever aware of the difficulties that had to be overcome. How can I, said the kind churchman, grant you this privilege of entering the papal archives, when not even Cardinals are allowed to enter under pain of excommunication? To this Dr. Pastor replied: " Your Eminence, I do not ask that I be allowed to enter, I will be glad if the tomes are brought out for inspection." This answer pleased the Cardinal so well that he promised his assistance. But in spite of such help and the encouragement from Cardinals Hergenroether, Franzelin and Pitra the majority in the Sacred College was opposed to such radical

changes in the policy of this Department. Undoubtedly most petitioners would have considered the
decision final. Pastor thought otherwise. He wrote
a new petition describing the exact scope of his
work and asked for an audience with the Holy
Father himself. This finally brought the desired result. First he received the personal privilege of the
use of the Archives and he could examine the desired volumes in the scriptorium of the Library.
Later Cardinal Hergenroether, a special patron of
the historian, was appointed Prefect of the Department and he granted him greater liberty in the examination of the documents. Finally, 13 August
1883, by a special Brief *Saepenumero considerantes*
Pope Leo XIII threw the whole Archives open to
all the historians of the world. Up to that time no
such offer had been made by any ruler, civil or
ecclesiastic. The results of this generous measure
are well known today. Neither Burckhardt, Voigt,
Gregorovius, Ranke nor Creighton had access to
these treasures, even Reumont's privilege in this
respect having been limited.

Naturally students from all nations flocked to
Rome, to profit by this papal bounty, but none
made better use of these treasures than our historian and later, in 1888, he was granted some special favors for his research work. What the generous pope himself thought of this permission is
evident from the following: On the 24 of February
1884 he granted an audience to a number of historians, among them Cardinal Hergenroether, Msgr.

de Waal, Father Denifle, Dr. Ehses and Professor Pastor. After Dr. Pastor in the name of all had thanked the Pontiff for his generosity towards historical science the Holy Father answered: " Owing to this decree you have good advantages over Ranke. Indeed the joy of historians must be great, because they are able to get new material from this depositary of documents. The fact that many of these writings have never been used and some not even been known, must increase the value of your work considerab!y. Naturally it will also spread your fame as an historian. However, our highest aim in this grant was the honor of God and the glory of His Church." Then addressing all the historians present he said: " True history must be written from the original sources. Therefore we opened the Vatican Archives to the historians for investigation. We have nothing to fear from the publication of these documents. (*Non abbiamo paura della pubblicità dei documenti.*) Every pope, more or less, worked, some even under the greatest difficulties, for the propagation of the kingdom of God on earth and among all nations, for the Church is the mother of all. . . . Work courageously and perseveringly, not only for earthly reward and worldly honor, but for the glory of Him that He may crown these labors with heavenly bliss."

Pastor showed his gratitude to the pope by dedicating the first volume of his *History of the Popes* to Leo XIII, the *Eroeffner des Vatikanischen Archivs.*

But before this came from the press our historian passed through the most critical period of his life.

In 1880 he determined definitely to devote himself to the teaching and the writing of history. The most difficult question, however, was the selection of a prominent University, where a sincere Catholic professor would be received and later promoted as he deserved. Owing to the Kulturkampf he saw no such opening in Germany. This induced him to apply to the Ministry of Education at Vienna to be admitted as Associate Professor at the University of Innsbruck. But even in Catholic Austria the opposition to such men, whom they called ultramontane, was so strong that he had to wait more than a year before this was granted. Dr. Janssen wrote, 8 January 1881, about this to Johanna Pastor: "Ludwig who is suffering from sore eyes is still here. Eleven months have passed since he applied for this position which is usually granted within a month. It is indeed very deplorable that the liberal Ministry of Education at Vienna does not admit a Catholic into the faculty of the University of Catholic Tyrol although, as Professor Stumpf writes, all his testimonials and his trial lecture were very satisfactory." Even after he was admitted several of his academic colleagues put everything in his way to forestall any promotion to an ordinary professorship. In 1886, however, he became "extraordinary" professor, in 1887 ordinary lecturer of modern history at that same seat of learning and from that time his rise in the academic world was rapid. Numerous universities granted him honorary degrees, the Austrian emperor raised him to the rank of hereditary nobility and in 1901 his country of adoption entrusted him with the directorship of the Austrian Historical Institute in Rome. The entrance of Italy into the World War forced him to leave the Eternal City, but in 1920 he returned to Alma Roma, this his second home, as ambassador of the Austrian Republic at the Vatican. The Holy See has repeatedly expressed its admiration for him by decorations and documents. Our present Holy Father, Pope Pius XI, wrote in 1922: " Dilecto Filio in Christo eidemque Exmo Viro Ludovico de Pastor Romanorum Pontificum Historiographo celeberrimo in signum singularis benevolentiae cum Apostolica Benedictione. Pius, PP XI."

Ludwig von Pastor is of small stature, but of robust appearance. His almost constant work with old documents brought about a very annoying shortsightedness. This cannot but increase our admiration for his tireless energy. Several times extraordinary tasks caused a nervous breakdown which forced him to discontinue his labors for a time. Invariably, however, as soon as his health permitted, he resumed his researches with renewed zeal. Early in life he chose as his motto " Vitam impendere Vero " and he follows this guide with unflinching ardor, his opponents may say with too passionate devotion to the Church. He is subject to the proverbial professorial absentmindedness and frequently amuses his friends by relating some episode connected with this weakness. Very devoted to his family and to his students he shrinks from no sacrifice if he sees any of them wronged. To give only one example: In 1901 Dr. Kempf of the University of Munich wrote a severe criticism on the first volume of the *Geschichte des deutschen Volkes* of Father Emil Michael, a young Jesuit scholar and a student of our Professor at Innsbruck. As Dr. Pastor was a member of the editorial staff of the *Historisches Jahrbuch* in which this criticism was to be published, he sent a letter of protest to Dr. Joseph Weiss, the editor-in-chief. When this proved futile, he appealed to his friend, Dr. von Hertling, then President of the Goerres Society (under whose auspices the above named Journal was published). It seems, however, that the printing of the article had already advanced to such a stage, that the editor-in-chief deemed it advisable to publish it together with Dr. Pastor's protest. Still this was unsatisfactory to our historian. He telegraphed at once his resignation from the editorial staff to Dr. Weiss. The latter could do nothing else than put into the next issue the whole correspondence and express his regret of losing such a prominent contributor. Today Dr. Pastor's standpoint in this controversy is quite generally approved by historians. Michael's history of the cultural conditions of Germany during the later Middle Ages (in six volumes) is the most important work on this subject. It has been compared to Janssen's *History of the German People* and might be called its first part. Similar controversies with Drs. Bachmann, von Druffel and Schnitzer prove that in matters of faith and historic truth, whenever the latter is once firmly established by authentic documents, he knows no compromise or palliation. This attitude, however, implies by no means that he is obstinate in his views. The very fact that he is ever ready to amend his literary productions and that he has recast so many of his earlier editions is sufficient proof of this statement.

During the last fifty years Pastor's coöperation has been sought in almost all works on the Fifteenth and Sixteenth Centuries. At present no good history of the Church of that period can be published without quoting from his *History of the Popes*. His association with historical publications of Europe has been very extensive. He was a contributor to Herder's *Staatslexikon;* he succeeded Cardinal Hergenroether on the editorial staff of the *Kirchenlexikon;* he wrote the "History of the Papacy from the Fourteenth to the Seventeenth Century" for the *Encyclopedia Britannica*. At the same time he was one of the co-editors of the *Historisches Jahrbuch,* of the *Historische-Politische Blaetter,* contributed articles to the *Hochland* and to the other prominent Catholic periodicals of Germany and Austria, to the *Törtenelemi Tar* of Hungary, the *Revue des Questions historiques* of France and to several Italian magazines.

His principal works are:

Die kirchlichen Reunionsbestrebungen waehrend der Regierung Karls V. (1879).
Johannes Janssen, ein Lebensbild. (1892).
August Reichensperger. (1899).
Allgemeine Dekrete der Roemischen Inquisition. 1555–1597. (1912).
Janssen-Pastor: Geschichte des deutschen Volkes seit dem Ausgang des Mittelalters. 8 Vol.
Geschichte der Paepste.

These last two are by far the most important and established his fame as an historian.

In regard to the first only a few words. In 1891 at Msgr. Janssen's death only six volumes of his epochal work *The History of the German People at the End of the Middle Ages* had been published. By his last will Dr. Janssen entrusted all the manuscripts to his former pupil and late associate, Dr. Pastor. Without doubt no scholar at that time was better equipped and more able to continue this great work of presenting to the world the first cultural history of the Reformation of Germany. He had already assisted this " Pathfinder in Reformation History " in the publication of previous volumes. Dr. Janssen wrote, 29 November, 1888, to Fr. A. Baumgartner, S. J.: " Pastor is here and read the first ten sheets of the sixth volume. He found great pleasure in this work, he says, because I avoided extreme statements especially in the description of the Renaissance." A comparison of the first volumes of this history edited by Janssen and the subsequent

editions published by our historian will at once reveal the work of the latter. The plan is Janssen's
own, the execution shows Pastor's tireless activity.
Without changing the spirit of the work he emended
and improved it in matter and form, until it is now
as much Pastorian as it began Janssenian. To give
only one example: The first edition of the first
volume comprised 615 pages, the ninth (Janssen's
last) contained 628 and the present, the twentieth
has 838. Moreover, the same first volume had nine
pages of " Literature " and eight pages of " Index,"
the last contains twenty-seven of the former and
thirty-eight of the latter. But what is more important, Janssen's literary heir not only added much
material and incorporated into these new editions
the result of modern historical research on the subjects in question, but as he himself improved in objective presentation and literary form he gradually
perfected also Janssen's whole work. In the first editions the vivid style of the author seemed to many
opponents the expression of a gigantic propaganda
against Protestantism. Today this objection is
hardly ever made by scholars. All this brought it
about that the work is now quoted as *Janssen-Pastor: the History of the German People*. Finally our
historian, it seems, felt the necessity of supplying
new material that was not or could not be incorporated into the original work. Therefore he began in
1898 a Commentary on the same, the *Erlaeuter-
ungen und Ergaenzungen zu Janssen's Geschichte
des deutschen Volkes.*

In many ways Pastor's continuation of Janssen's history was a work of love and gratitude towards him who had guided him in the beginning of his historical career as a teacher and friend. This is especially evident in his biography and the publication of the letters of this his master. Every student of them will agree with Dr. Fr. Dittrich who called Janssen's *Lebensbild* by Pastor a literary monument for a great historian, a testimony of reverence of a grateful disciple and an inspiration for a thoughtful reader.

The work, however, by which our historian is best known is his *History of the Popes from the Close of the Middle Ages*. It is his *Opus magnum*, considering the time which he spent on it or the importance of the subject which he treated in it or the talents which he showed by it. The first edition of the first volume was published in 1886, the tenth volume is now ready for publication. A number of them have two sections and many of them have been rewritten. At times the translators cannot keep pace with these new editions. At present Pastor's history is being translated into English, French, Italian and Spanish. The English version comprises fourteen volumes, corresponding to six of the original German edition, and therefore the complete translation of what has been published so far will have at least twenty octavo volumes of four hundred to five hundred pages each.

Pastor's aim in this history differed from that of every other Church-Historian.

In 1829, G. H. Pertz, the well-known first editor of the modern classic in documentary collections, the *Monumenta Germaniae Historica,* wrote: "Die beste Verteidigung der Paepste ist die Enthuellung ihres Seins." These words which our author chose as the motto of his first volume indicate in the fewest words the aim of Pastor in writing this history of the Popes of modern times. No better defense of the Popes of the Fifteenth and Sixteenth Centuries has been written. Very naturally as a true and trained historian he scrupulously avoided everything that savored of apologetical tendencies. For example: A comparison between the second (German) edition of the third volume (1895) (which corresponds to the fifth and sixth English volumes) and the seventh edition (1924) will prove that the statement in the *Catholic Historical Review* (October, 1925) about Pastor's aim in writing history is not correct. The author of this article says: "Pastor in seeking the justification of the papacy was compelled according to his conclusions to deal harshly with the friar (Savonarola)." In the *latest* edition (1924) our historian not only quotes twenty-five of the thirty-five authorities mentioned in the treatise above, but in his "Notes" he has many more sources favoring his views in this perplexing question and in a special "Nachtraege" (III, 2, page 1143) he answers the *very latest* defense of the friar by Dr. Schnitzer (1923). Evidently the writer of the article in this *Review* had not the latest edition of the third volume of the German edition at hand.

In a similar manner Pastor answered already in 1891 the objection that he is plagiarizing. The first critic who asserted this was Dr. Bachmann of the University of Prague (*Literaturzeitung*, 18 October, 1890). Our historian replied in an article in the *Historisches Jahrbuch* (XVI, 455–471) in which he disproved these assertions with so many and so weighty arguments, that his literary opponent was completely silenced. For the student of Pastor's *History* this article is also interesting because he finds therein another objection solved: that he omits parts that may be against such an " *a priori* history of the popes." He says: " What would this history be if I wished to write a detailed history of every country? With the same plea that Dr. Bachmann demands such a history of the empire, a French critic might want one of France, an English writer a description of the religious condition of Great Britain, an Italian a minute account of the dealings of every town with the Holy See."

In a second defense against Dr. von Druffel of the University of Munich and others (Vol. II, 745–782) he quotes from the criticism of *Merkur* " that he was most exact in his references, giving in every case the sources," and he adds, " I do not belong to those who want to say better something that has already been well said. In such an extensive work as this I must rely on the verdicts of specialists in a particular field, as I have indicated in the preface of the first volume."

We may safely say that *he has already written* a

defense of his verdict about the moral failings of Alexander VI even after the latest attempt of Msgr. de Roo to rehabilitate this Borgia Pope. In the Introduction of the first edition of this third volume (1895) he said: "It *may be safely* stated that in future attempts to rehabilitate Alexander will prove futile." In the introduction to the seventh edition (1924) he declared: "The literature on the subjects of this volume grew to such an extent that nearly every page had to be altered. Also the 'Appendix' was increased considerably. I had the good fortune of finding a remnant of the correspondence of Alexander VI of the years 1493 and 1494 in the papal secret archives. The most important forty-four documents are printed in the Appendix No. 56. They do not change the picture drawn, they only bring out the lines better. These documents *will make apologies* of the Borgia pope as they have lately been attempted again in Italy and Spain as *impossible* as the picture which a Milanese writer drew became a caricature."

Some writers have compared this history to a mosaic put together with modern tools, others with a musical composition of an old master played by a modern virtuoso on an organ fitted out with the best appliances which are only possible through the use of electricity. The documents, many of them printed for the first time, are his spokesmen, the standard verdicts of *Fachmaenner* no matter to what religious tendency they belong, serve as his guides in the printed material and his own genius breathes

life into these dry facts. Thus the reader becomes
not only acquainted with the development of the
stirring events of those times, but he lives, as it
were, in the very atmosphere of the period. This is
the characteristic mark of Pastor's *History of the
Popes*. It distinguishes it from every other that deals
with the same subject. It is a " Kulturgeschichte "
of the Fifteenth and the Sixteenth Century with the
papacy as the foremost power in shaping these times
for better or for worse.

Various factors contributed to make it such a
unique history of the Church of these centuries.

It is true no other modern historian had as many
advantages for such a history as Pastor. As a sincere
Catholic the very purpose of the Church was constantly before his eyes. In theological questions he
consulted theologians of renown, Catholic or non-
Catholic. Thus in the formula of faith of Cardinal
Contarini (1541) Dr. John Heinrich of Mainz declared in favor of its orthodoxy. In medical difficulties he asked the opinions of eminent doctors, even
the best specialists, as may be seen in the dispute
on the death of Pope Alexander VI (Vol. III, 1st
part, 588–595). He received a thorough scientific
training from men who are recognized as masters
in their branch of history and who acknowledged
his abilities by various documents. He found friends
that communicated, like F. X. Kraus, the art critic,
in an unselfish manner the result of their painstaking investigations in a particular field of their avo-
cation. He was granted greater liberty than any

other man in the use of documents and papers. He
has lived a long life — may God spare him many
more years! — and he could work with an energy
which may be called " Pastorian." He has such a
sure historic sense that Msgr. Dr. Ehses, the renowned co-editor of the monumental *Concilium
Tridentinum,* declared in the *Historisches Jahrbuch,*
1920: " As the author had to rely on the Acts of the
Council as edited by Aug. Theiner, so far the best,
but in many ways incomplete and incorrect, the
Volumes VIII and IX of the *Concilium Tridentinum*
will be of great help for future editions. Nevertheless independently of these Pastor gave in the last
section of the sixth chapter a verdict about the result and the consequences of the Council which for
its brevity, its directness and its delicacy in expression can hardly be surpassed." But above everything else Pastor is honest in every fibre of his heart
and even the most exacting critics never denied
this.

Thus under such favorable conditions and with
such magnanimous coöperation he could constantly
improve and even recast entire editions — each one
contains the latest discoveries in documentary evidences, brings the most recent literature on the
questions involved and shows constant improvement of style which is now nearly epic in the description of those times.

The beginning of the *History of the Popes* can be
traced back to the year 1876 when he wrote for the
Katholik, then one of the leading Catholic Reviews

of Germany, the monograph, *Neue Quellenberichte ueber den Reformator Albrecht von Brandenburg.*

In 1874 the famous *Scriptores Rerum Prussicarum* in five volumes were published and naturally attracted the attention of the historians. Our author gave his verdict in the above mentioned article. First he examined the documents critically and found them genuine. Then he expressed his satisfaction at the impartiality of the editors, especially Dr. Toepper. Thirdly he declared that some of these documents, notably the description of the times by Gregor Spiess and the *Relatio* of Philip Creutz, were of extraordinary value for that critical period of the history of Prussia. Finally he made use of them in a truly scientific manner. It is evident from Dr. Janssen's letters, that his teacher stood sponsor to this first literary effort of Pastor. Even without these letters the very style of the article shows the influence of the master. But there is something in the work that reveals already the future expert in historical research. It is his fearless determination to let the documents alone speak, no matter whether they oppose his own views that he had so far, or whether they contradict the theories of other historians or the opinions of the people in general. Thus with all reverence to Ranke the " Altmeister " of history in Germany at that time, he declared that the latter had omitted facts to idealize Albrecht von Brandenburg. Likewise he probably shocked some pious souls by stating that the bishops of that territory, Erhart Queis of Pomesenia and George Polenz of Samland, were even more responsible for the religious change of that territory than Albrecht, the grand master. He became so convinced of the force of these documents that he ended the article with the words: "We can see what the consequences of the bad example of these Bishops were. It proves that the Reformation succeeded, where the Bishops apostatized and it failed, where they remained firm, for the bishops are the columns of the Church."

This courageous standpoint of Pastor is still more evident in his first book: *Die Reunionsbestrebungen waehrend der Regierung Karls V.*

In 1878 he had written his doctor-thesis on this same subject. In 1879 he revised and deepened it for publication in book form. The literary critic of the *Literarische Handweiser* of that year called it the best and, with the exception of one rather mediocre work on the same subject, the first book which treats of this phase of Reformation in Germany. According to this same writer Dr. Pastor proved by documentary evidence that Charles V, the Roman prelates and Melanchthon made honest efforts, to reëstablish (after the Diet of Worms (1521)) religious unity, but that the selfish aims of the Protestant princes, the intrigues of Francis I of France, the cowardice of several bishops and the petty policy of the dukes of Bavaria stood in the way of reconciliation of the two parties. Our critic also agrees with him that the success of the German Reformation was *not* due to any change of faith or morals in the country *but* to the change of jurisdiction. *Both* say that many churchmen preferred submission to secular princes to obedience towards the Pope and consequently these princes who had usurped the papal power in this respect became the main obstacles of reunion. Even writers who disagreed with Pastor on several of these points were unanimous that the book was a very valuable contribution to the history of the Reformation on account of its scholarly criticism, its excellent style and its wealth of original documents. Without doubt many of the readers felt what the critic in the *Katholik* wrote: " We expect that Pastor will accomplish much in the historical field in the near future. He has the talents and the zeal, may God give him the necessary strength."

When the *Unionsbestrebungen* came from the press Pastor was working feverishly in Rome to gather the material for his *History of the Popes*. How his heart must have ached when he saw that after he had been granted the personal privilege of exploiting the secret papal archives even his sheer inexhaustive energy or the abilities of any individual historian were utterly insufficient for the task of transcribing all this vast material for historical inquiry. It was during that time that he suffered a nervous breakdown. In this state of mind, even before others were granted similar privileges, he appealed to the historians of the world at large to come to Rome and help to gather those historical treasures. He expressed this in a criticism of the *Spicilegium Ossoriense* of Bishop, later Cardinal, Patrick

Moran, in the following words: " The historical material stored up in the archives and the libraries of
Rome is so vast that its complete publication and
proper use is impossible for any individual person.
Only by a division of this work anything of importance can be achieved. Let therefore every nation
collect its own documents from this source. This will
be a sure means of advancing historical science.
English scholars have already started by a good example. By this I do not refer to the great collection
of documents which the English government made
here and to which the Vatican archives contributed
much valuable material. On the contrary I have in
mind the private research work which individual historians of that nation undertook and these individual
efforts deserve indeed the praise of all their colleagues."

Finally, after such long and painstaking preparations, the first volume of the *History of the Popes
at the Close of the Middle Ages (Die Geschichte
der Paepste seit dem Ausgang des Mittelalters)* was
published (1886). The author had planned to write
the history of the Church from the Fifteenth Century to the present day in six volumes. But the very
first volume showed that, considering the vast material on hand, this was impossible. In this book he
described the Renaissance in the Introduction, the
Avignon period and the Great Western Schism in
the first chapter and the pontificates of Martin V,
Eugene IV, Nicholas V and Callistus III in three
other chapters.

In his preface he gave the main reasons for the publication of such a work. He declared that scientific histories of the oldest and still vigorous dynasty were scarce, that lately many new treatises had been written, which change the verdicts of older authors, finally that the discovery of important documents in the secret papal archives which had been made accessible through the generosity of Pope Leo XIII made such a work imperative.

It is only too true that up to the time of Pastor no Catholic had written a standard work on this great subject. Thus the lack of such a history of the Popes and the manner in which he fulfilled this task made him famous at once. Especially his friends in Germany were jubilant when, with very few exceptions, all historians hailed his *Papstgeschichte* as a most valuable contribution to historical science.

His former teacher, Msgr. Dr. Janssen, expressed this in a criticism in the *Historisches Jahrbuch:* " Pastor's *History of the Popes* has been received very favorably by Catholic and Protestant scholars. Its merits are particularly the large number of original documents which the author gathered from more than a hundred archives of Italy, France, Belgium, Austria, Germany and Switzerland. He also made use of all the printed sources now available and of the latest monographs on the subjects treated in this work. The wealth of the historical material, so far unequalled in any other history, has enabled him to throw new light on a number of disputed questions and to correct statements made by Burckhardt, Droysen, Haas, Gregorovius, Muentz, Voigt and others."

Purely literary reviews and Protestant theological journals were not far behind this verdict in their praises. The critic in the *Zarnecksche Literarische Zentralblatt* wrote almost at the same time: " The author of the *Papstgeschichte* is a Catholic and he never hides his religious tendency. But this belief in no wise clouds his historic views. Honestly he is always seeking to be just to phenomena and to persons, though he cannot approve the act itself or the intention of the actor. Indeed this religious conviction enables him in many ways to give a truer picture of those conditions than would have been possible for a non-Catholic scholar." In a similar manner Pflugk-Harttung said in the *Illustrierte Rundschau:* " Never before has material of such abundance been brought together and made use of in such a way that the unbiased Protestant can fully rely on its deductions." Dr. Paul Ewald in the *Deutsche Literaturzeitung* called it " a monumental work that far surpasses all other treatises on the history of the Church between 1447 and 1458."

In France M. Ulysse Chevalier, in the *Revue Critique,* described it as " the result of immense investigations, destined to obliterate (*effacer*) similar works of the French authors André and Christophe "; and when the translation of this first volume into French appeared, the *Polybiblion* announced: " L'histoire des Papes, par M. le docteur Louis Pastor, a été accueillie dans le monde savant avec le plus grand faveur."

In Italy, the *Archivio storico Italiano* pronounced it " as objective as possible, a most valuable contribution to documentary collections and conservative in its criticism."

Considering all these favorable comments from such diverse sources the silence of the representative English journals of that period is very ominous. Nor was this only by chance or oversight. The first criticism appeared only after the second volume of the history came from the press. This was written by Dr. B. Garnett. We marvel today how it was possible that a critic of a journal to which J. Gairdner and Lord Acton contributed could say in 1889: " Pastor made no remarkable additions to our previous knowledge. He endeavours to steer a middle course and flatters himself that he is impartial while he is only cautious. Of direct misrepresentation or even disingenuous suppression he is indeed incapable, but he cannot resist the temptation, even more subtly destructive of truth, to minimize the picturesqueness and the moral teaching of history. . . . Professor Pastor never falsifies history; but he leaves the significance of its more pregnant passages unrecognized as the Alpine traveller hastens in silence by the suspended avalanche which might be loosened by his breath. . . . The higher we estimate P. Pastor's superiority to the Audins and Artauds — and it is indeed difficult to overrate it — the more evident it becomes that philosophical history is not to be expected from devout Roman Catholics."

Even after the third volume was published (1895) and when the renown of our historian had spread especially on account of the now famous chapters on the pontificate of Alexander VI, the same writer still declared (XII, 1897): "Either he has braced himself by a special effort to discharge a specially difficult obligation or working as he has been for some years with the eyes of historical criticism upon him, he has insensibly imbibed more liberal sympathy. Indeed, setting aside the peculiar attitude of mind which absolutely is impossible for a sincere believer in the claims of the Roman Church to discard, his volume wants little essential to the character of a really scientific and impartial history"; and again: "It is the work of an advocate — a courageous advocate, no doubt, so convinced of the soundness of his cause that he does not mind making damaging admissions — but still an advocate. The scroll is waved in the hand, but the brief peeps out of the pocket." But even such an adverse critic could not deny "his diligence in investigating every available source of information from the Archives of the Vatican to the latest studies in modern Reviews, his perfect fairness in citation and the highly intelligent use made of his materials." Without doubt these two criticisms of Dr. Garnett contributed in no small measure to the fact that Pastor's history was for a long time little appreciated in the English world of letters. It came only in 1910 that J. P. Whitney, in the same *Review*, Vol. XXV, accorded Pastor the recognition which he deserves. He first called attention to qualities which are now expected of an historian: " fulness of detail always under perfect control, command of the literature down to the latest discussions and skilful use of much unprinted material," and he grants to the work in question all of them in a high degree. Then he wrote: " But if the history is to be coherent, a point of view of the whole area must be found and the papal court has peculiar advantages for such a choice. . . . As regards the representation of the inner workings of the papal court, the work stands alone. The conclaves are described in detail, and of course with use of the best material; likewise the creations of Cardinals for the first time is fully and fairly pictured. What has been often brought before us in the shape of general statements or of detailed sketches of single situations is given here in a continuous history, based on full use of all existing material. . . The spiritual importance of the papal position is always insisted upon. We cannot judge a pope even mainly as politicians or statesmen of their day. Critics and admirers of Creighton's *Papacy* have rightly found in him a lack of this needed moral judgment. The same lack is not found in Pastor's popes. Leo X, Paul III, etc., are all tried by the highest conception of what a pope should be. Creighton was writing when, for an English public at any rate, a fairer judgment of bygone popes was to be sought; he was conscientiously seeking after this and therefore laid stress on the political needs of the papacy and the moral tone as a palliative of much that was bad. Dr. Pastor, on the other hand, starts with the full conception of what the highest responsibilities of the popes were: their religious ideals and endeavours, their political success, their social influence, all are judged as parts of a whole: they themselves are estimated by the ideal of their office and not by the lower conception of the day. This seems the truer method and it certainly gives us the more complete picture. It is possible to lay down Creighton and say about any given pope of whom we have been reading ' that is all true, but after all what was he as pope? ' We do not think that any reader of Dr. Pastor's would need ask the question, for he would find it answered as he read."

Such a comparison of Creighton and Pastor was quite natural for English writers for both wrote almost at the same time on the same subject. But almost invariably the greater talents and more thorough researches of Pastor are conceded. Dr. George L. Burr refers to them in the first volume of the *American Historical Review* in the following words: " Side by side with the Catholic historian an eminent Anglican scholar has grappled with the same theme and the volumes of Creighton have a few years the start. Those dealing with this period devote to it somewhat less than half the space of the German volume. For grasp and lucidity, for insight and fairness, the English scholar has nothing to fear from this comparison; and it should be to him a matter of pride that the German, with all his fresh sources, has found so little to correct or to add. It is clear on the other hand, how much he constantly owes to the English writer's suggestions. But if Bishop Creighton's is the more statesmanly eye, the more picturesque pencil, the more terse and virile exposition, the more luminous consciousness of the general politics of Europe, Dr. Pastor's is yet the surer, the warmer, the subtler touch. And though the Englishman draws more largely on the gossip of Infessura, of Burckhardt, of Paris de Grassis, while the more cautious German ignores many a good story which he cannot prove, the latter is often the more conservative of the two." Then our critic calls attention to the results of both scholars as regards Pope Alexander and Friar Savonarola and ends with the following words: " That in the search of truth, two scholars so severed by religious environment should have reached such agreement, in such a field, is one of the encouraging things of modern historical research; and the generous policy of pope Leo XIII could hardly ask a better proof that the defenders of the Church have nothing to fear."

This may seem a fair estimate of our historian to the average reader. But what are the facts in the case measured from the standpoint of history itself and interpreted by the best critic which the English world had at the time when the works of these two writers appeared side by side? History is above everything else an exact science and as regards this how do the two historians compare?

Creighton says in his Introduction: " The circumstances of my life have not allowed me to make much research for new authorities which in so large a field would have been impossible. What I have found in manuscripts was not of much importance. My work has been done under difficulties which necessarily attend one who lives far from great libraries and to whom study is the occupation of leisure hours and not the main objective in life."

Pastor tells us, in the Introduction to his first volume, that he examined all the archives that were accessible. His tireless work and fearless disposition in this research can be seen in a special way from his dealings with the Holy Office of the Inquisition. He describes this in his introduction to the *Allgemeine Dekrete der Roemischen Inquisition.* In 1901, he says, when he was preparing his work on Paul III he made the first efforts to get access to the archives of this Congregation. After several appeals extending over a period of fourteen months and asking only for the court records in the trials for heresy during that pontificate he received the answer that these records were lost and that only the decrees of the Congregation for this same period were extant. As this reply put restrictions on his description of the pontificate of Paul III he wrote in the fifth volume of his *History:* " If the present Congregation of the Holy Office still persists in maintaining a system of absolute secrecy which has almost universally been abandoned elsewhere, with regard to historical documents now three hundred years old, it inflicts an injury not only on the work of the historian, but still more on itself, since it thus perpetuates belief in all and in the worst of all the innumerable charges levelled at the Inquisition." (Transl. Engl. Ed. 1914.) A European correspondent in the *Fortnightly Review* defended this policy and the editor of the *Review* approved the policy and determination of Pastor with the following words, January, 1910: "We do not deny that there is some weight in the considerations (viz.: that the archives contain much of a private nature) but to our mind they fail to justify such a strict adhesion to the policy of secrecy as that from which Dr. Pastor has been made to suffer."

When this complaint brought no change in the attitude of the officials the author tried to supply this want of material from other sources. At first he believed that the papal secret archives would have the material which he sought. He found in the Armarium X a number of volumes which contained Acts of the Inquisition, but the ones he needed were missing. He made inquiries in the Roman State Archives and discovered four codices which had sources for his purpose. In 1902 at an auction sale he bought another codex which contained a few decrees of the Inquisition which had so far not been published. He examined the private archives of Roman families whose members were now and then officials of

vided the faults are not taken from the context as
several writers hostile to the Church have done."
The author himself indicates this in a number of
his mottoes, especially that of the third volume:
'Petri dignitas etiam in indigno herede non defi-
cit.' In this way his character descriptions of popes
have been compared to those of the Bible.

To make a just comparison between Ranke and
Pastor we must inquire into the aims and the means
of each one in the writing of their history of the
popes. There is no doubt that both showed extraordinary talents for historical research. Considering
purely the resources Ranke was perhaps the more
gifted owing to a special " historic sense " which
led him to surmise facts and causes which he could
not deduce from the documents at his disposal. In
this way Pastor was often the first to prove with
documents the statements of his great predecessor.
This accounts for the opinions of some critics that
Pastor added nothing to our knowledge of those
facts, while we should rather say that he proved the
surmises of other historians by his evidences and
thus really added the most essential in historical
investigations, the surety of the facts. Therefore
Dr. George L. Burr well says: "Where Ranke
could but divine, touching only high points of his
sweep, Pastor establishes the solid proofs or dis-
credits their absence. The reader has the rare satisfaction of feeling that he has in his hand a definite
study. . . . His volumes are of inestimable worth
to men of every faith."

When Ranke published his history (1834–1836), says J. A. Mooney in the *American Catholic Quarterly Review* (1889), "it was a rarely good book, a surprise to all Protestants of all denominations who had been brought up on a literature of fables and abuse, and a greater surprise to Catholics who patiently had reached the conclusion that Luther and the princes had knifed truth beyond the hope of recovery." This book (as mentioned above) given by Janssen to his favorite disciple had been an inspiration for Pastor and he frequently referred to its author as the greatest of Protestant historians. But Ranke had no access to the secret archives of the Popes. Pastor enjoyed in this respect more privileges than any other man. And what is a history of the popes without these documents?

Ranke gives the proof of this statement himself in his Introduction in the following words: " It will be obvious that Rome alone could supply those materials. But was it to be expected that a foreigner and one professing a different faith would there be permitted to have free access to collections for the purpose of revealing the secrets of the papacy? This would not perhaps have been so ill-advised, as it may appear, since no search can bring to light anything worse than what is already assumed by conjecture and received by the world as established truth. But I cannot boast of having had such permission. I was enabled to take cognizance of the treasures contained in the Vatican and to use a number of volumes suited to my purpose; but the freedom of access which I could have wished was by no means accorded."

On the contrary Pastor, in his Introduction, shows that the main, although by no means the only sources of his history are these very documents. He refers to them on many pages giving the exact references in his "Notes." His now famous "Appendices" have become veritable archival depositaries for students and in 1912 he began a special publication of such documents which he could not conveniently incorporate into his history.

How his critics watched for every flaw in these "Appendices" may be seen from the twelfth volume of the *English Historical Review* (1897).

In the Appendix to the third volume (1895) Pastor published a circular letter of pope Julius II to king Henry VII of England calling for contributions to the building of St. Peter's. The Latin document (90a) contained the names of a number of bishops and noblemen of England and were written by an Italian scribe. Our historian in a number of "Notes" suggested several translations of these Latin titles. As he was not quite certain he prefixed each one with the German phrase "vielleicht." The first critic of this interpretation was Dr. Garnett, who corrected a number of them on page 562. The next critic, Dr. J. Gairdner, corrected a number of the corrections of Dr. Garnett on page 762. Finally Dr. Pastor in his next edition (1924) referred to both critics without comment and accepted their interpretations, giving as usual the exact references.

(The English translation of 1914 has still the Pastorian interpretation of 1895.)

Thus, while Ranke never changed his text even after fifty years had intervened between his first edition and his seventh, Pastor not only kept all his editions abreast with the latest investigations, but also as a true scientist he opened new paths for investigation. This may be seen in his remarks on the biographies of Pope Pius V (Vol. VIII, App.). After enumerating the twenty-six principal biographies of this last canonized saint on the throne of St. Peter he concludes: " Thus there is no want of biographies, but there was still a rich harvest of original sources in the archives to present a strictly historical-critical picture in which the personality of Pius V appears more marked than in the usual eulogies." And in a " Note " to this statement he added: " In this question I can only remind the reader that years ago I wrote: It is high time that the Roccoco period of ' Lives of the Saints ' be ended. They do not need pious inventions; they can bear the sunlight of historical inquiry, they only gain thereby." To prove this statement he wrote in 1924 " Character Sketches of Catholic Reformers of the Sixteenth Century." This up-to-date literature is one of the most prominent exterior qualities of Pastor's *History of the Popes* and it has created a school of historians. The spirit of these followers can be seen in a criticism written by one of them for the *Historische-Politische Blaetter* in 1903: " Many historians have been accused of neglecting the practical side of historical composition. They believe themselves free from the laws of historical methods, especially by disregarding the improvement of their works by new editions. The best book can in this way become useless. This was one of Ranke's faults. His new editions were merely reprints of the old. His history of the popes has on this account lost its importance. Today some parts have value only from a literary-historical standpoint. No matter how perfect a work, how gifted an author may be, whosoever believes in a progress of historical science can never be satisfied with the relative perfection of a work, he must give a certain elasticity to such literary productions that lay claim to more than ordinary value. If those who seek real information must constantly ask themselves whether a certain statement has not perhaps been changed by special studies they will follow such an author only with a certain distrust. Nobody can demand that a reader examine and correct these changes. This is the duty of the author and his successors. Indeed, this is a very onerous task. Pastor has not only created such an *opus magnum et perenne* but he is also constantly perfecting it. He is the last to be satisfied with it. He knows that the field of history is so vast that not the most talented historian nor even a generation can exhaust it."

BIBLIOGRAPHY

A. BIOGRAPHY

Katholische Reformatoren. Gedenkwort von Dr. Max
   Scherman.
*Ludwig von Pastor, der geschichtschreiber der Paepste,
   denkschrift zum 40. Jahrestag des erstmaligen Er-
   scheinens der Geschichte der Paepste* (1926).
Pastor, Ludwig von, in the *Historische-Politische Blaetter*
   (1914).
Pastor, Ludwig von, in the *Herders Konversations Lexi-
   kon.*

B. GENERAL WORKS ON PASTOR
AND HIS WRITINGS

Apart from the works listed above the main sources
for a critical estimate of Pastor's historical writings must
be sought in the current reviews. The following list of
Pastor's major works will orientate the reader in his
search for critical evaluation of the great historian's
career:

*Die kirchlichen Reunionsbestrebungen waehrend der Re-
   gierung Karls V.* (1879).
*Die korrespondenz des Kardinals Contarini waehrend
   seiner deutschen Legation 1541* (1880).
*Geschichte der Paepste seit dem Ausgange des Mittelal-
   ters.* (10 Vol. 1886–1926.)
Johannes Janssen, ein Lebensbild. (1892).
*Janssen-Pastors Geschichte des deutschen Volkes seit
   dem Ausgang des Mittelalters.* (8 Vol. 1893–1926.)
Johannes Janssen, ein zweites Wort an meine Kritiker.
   (1895). *Zur Beurteilung Savonarolas.* (1898).
August Reichensperger. 2 Vol. (1899).

Ungedruckte Akten zur Geschichte der Paepste. (1904).
Die Reise des Kardinals Luige d'Aragona 1517. (1904).
Le biblioteche private e specialmente quelle delle familie principesche di Roma. (1906).
Johannes Janssen, Friedrich Graf von Stolberg. (4th ed.) 1910.
Allgemeine Dekrete der Roemischen Inquisition aus den Jahren 1555–1597. (1912).
Leben des Freiherrn Max von Gagern. (1912).
Eine ungedruckte Beschreibung der Reichsstadt Aachen aus dem Jahre 1561. (1914).
Die Stadt Rom zu Ende der Renaissance. (1916).
Conrad von Hoetzendorf. (1916).
Generaloberst Viktor Dankl. (1916).
Johannes Janssens Briefe. 2 Vol. (1920).
Stiftspropst Dr. Franz Kaufmann. (1921).
Katholische Reformatoren. (1924).
Die Fresken in der Sixtinischen Kapelle. (1925).

FINIS

INDEX

ABGAR, King, 179.

Acta Sanctorum, 193, 195, 199, 206, 209; sources of, 197; and modern historiography, 204.

Acta SS. O.S.B. (Mabillon), 221.

Acton, Lord, on Creighton, 407.

Acts of the Marytrs, 17.

Ad Orosium (St. Augustine), 38.

Africanus, 13.

Agapius, Bishop of Caesarea, 4.

Alaric, 59.

Albinus, Abbot, 85.

Albrecht of Brandenburg, 394.

Alcuin, 92.

Alexander, Bishop of Alexandria, 6.

Alexander VI, Pastor on, 389, 401.

Alexandria, School of, 4.

Ambrosian Library (Milan), 213.

American Catholic Historical Association, iii, vi.

American Catholic Quarterly Review, 353, 410.

American Historical Review, 353.

American Revolution, political philosophy of, 132.

Analecta Bollandiana, 196, 203.

Anastasius (Moehler), 242.

Anecdota Graeca (Muratori), 216.

Anecdota Latina (Muratori), 213.

Anglo-Saxons, conversion of, 71; and Britons, 80.

Ann Arbor, meeting (1925), iii.

Annales Ecclesiastici (Baronius), 153.

Annali d'Italia (Muratori), 232.

Annals (Baronius), 159, 164, 166, 167; critical value of, 175; Fueter on, 176; errors in, 177; and the *Centuries,* 180, 192.

Annual Meetings, Amer. Cath. Hist. Assoc., iii.

Anselm of Canterbury (Moehler), 270.

Ante-Nicene Church, 10.

Anti-infallibilists, 311.

Anti-Janus (Hergenroether), 307.

Antioch, synod (324), 6.

Antichità Estensi (Muratori), 217.

Antiphonary, of Bangor, 214.

Antiquities (Lingard), 282.

Apologética Historia (Las Casas), 145.

Apology for Origen (Eusebius), 5.

Apostle of the Indies (Las Casas), 130.

Archiv fuer Literatur und Kirchengeschichte, 364, 365.

Archives, Vatican, 380; of Inquisition, 405.

Archivio Muratoriano, 229.

417

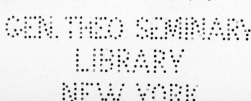

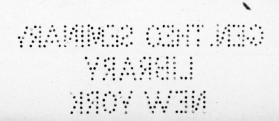